THE THAMES AND HUDSON MANUALS

GENERAL EDITOR: W. S. TAYLOR

Bookbinding

Arthur W. Johnson

The Thames and Hudson
Manual of Bookbinding

with 270 illustrations, in color and black and white

Thames and Hudson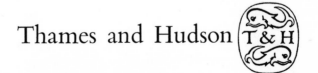

© 1978 Thames and Hudson Ltd, London
Reprinted 1981

First published in paperback in the
United States of America in 1981
by Thames and Hudson, Inc.,
500 Fifth Avenue, New York,
New York 10110

Library of Congress Catalog Card
Number 81-50759

Printed in Hong Kong

Contents

Introduction   7

1 A history of English bookbinding decoration   13

2 Equipment   21

HEAVY EQUIPMENT 21
SMALL TOOLS 23

3 Bookbinder's materials   30

PAPER 30
BOARD 37
pH VALUES 37
CLOTH 38
LEATHERS 39
THREAD, TAPE AND CORD 41
ADHESIVES 41

4 Introduction to a book   45

5 Working procedures   48

SPECIFICATIONS 48
PREPARATION OF THE BOOK FOR BINDING 49
ENDPAPERS 57
SEWING 61
THE PLOUGH AND GUILLOTINE 69
ROUNDING AND BACKING 75
EDGE GILDING 79
HEADBANDS 85
LEATHER PARING 89

6 Binding styles   93

THE CASE BINDING 93
THE LIBRARY STYLE 103
THE LIBRARY STYLE IN BUCKRAM 115
THE FLEXIBLE STYLE 118
THE SUNK CORD STYLE 134
VELLUM BINDINGS 144
LIMP BINDINGS 149
LOOSE-LEAF AND GUARD BOOKS 153

7 Finishing   159

     TOOLS, EQUIPMENT AND MATERIALS   159
     WORKING METHODS   166

8 Boxes   179

9 Changes in bookbinding construction   194

     THE HARRISON GROOVE   194
     STUB BINDING   195
     FLUSH JOINT SEWN ON TAPES   197
     LARGE BINDINGS   197
     ADHESIVE BINDING   201
     THE AMERICAN GROOVE   203

10 Design   204

     EXAMPLES   206

Glossary   211

Further reading   219

Index   220

Introduction

The craft of bookbinding can be taught by demonstration, with a commentary on each operation, but the practised hand of the demonstrator is often too deft for the student to appreciate what is involved. That is why a teaching manual is needed, so that students may work at their own rate and within their capabilities. This book includes the underlying theory, omitted in simpler instruction books, and the detailed practical work is supported by photographs and diagrams.

Books are bound in many different styles, varying according to their age and value, and the use to which they are to be put. Each book is a different problem and may require modification of the working method, but if he absorbs the general principles of construction and the common variations the student will acquire the knowledge and skill to bind to his own satisfaction.

A text which covers all aspects of binding would require several volumes, and so elementary bookcrafts are excluded from this manual. Account bookbinding is outside the field of craft binding and so is book restoration. No one should attempt restoration without skill and experience: much damage is done to valuable books by untrained people, not conversant with binding styles and the history of construction, decoration and materials. Students are advised to practise skills by elementary exercises, to gain control of tools and equipment, before attempting advanced work. In this way they will come to understand the limitations of methods and materials.

The production of a binding is in two parts, forwarding and finishing. 'Forwarding' covers the operations required to complete the binding, and 'finishing' is embellishing it with a title and decoration. The latter is regarded as the more difficult but forwarding is the more important; both, however, require skilful hands, a true eye and some artistic ability. Whereas the title and decoration contribute nothing to the life of the binding they identify the book and make it pleasing to look at and handle. Apart from the utility value of a good binding, pleasure may be given by the forwarding, in the compactness of the book, the way in which it opens and the preciseness of the execution, while finishing delights the eye by the brilliance of gold, the harmony of colours and the form of the decoration. It is not always possible to ascertain how much work has gone into the forwarding as the technique is hidden within the cover. The layman may look first at the title and, if it is bright, legible and accurate, he assumes that the binding is sound, but trade binders have sometimes had to work to close profit margins so in the general run of their work dubious practices have been the rule rather than the exception. However, the high standards required for expensive fine binding are as good today as at any period in binding history.

Bookbinding flourishes because of the enthusiasm of some professionals, teachers and amateurs who, after studying the traditional aspects of the craft, have pursued their own ideas to make their work contemporary and individual. The procedure in binding operations is open to many variations, and few craftsmen work in the same way. Whatever theories are aired, house styles followed or unorthodox methods put forward, the student should be adaptable and use them with an open mind. They can be accepted only if they contribute to the durability and function of the book. The passing of old craftsmen may be lamented but others are emerging with fresh ideas, new skills and a scientific interest in the craft. Traditional methods are a foundation for learning but when the basic skills have been achieved the student should experiment with other forms of construction, and new techniques and materials, so that a personal approach is acquired.

Experience and skills can be gained only by long and repeated practice. To bind one book at a time is impracticable; about six bindings in one style should be carried through at a time. It is the repetition of the same operation on books of different quality and size which will make a craftsman of the student.

Binding books is immensely satisfying but hand skills are insufficient by themselves for a complete appreciation of the craft. Serious students are urged to make a broader study of the art of book production. The history of decoration and the constructional development of books is important, and so is the study of paper manufacture. A further study of printing processes, typography and of the men and women who contributed to the arts is essential. The student should become familiar with the latest trends in book design and the scientific advances in the preservation of books and documents in which the future of the craft lies.

I wish to thank Ray Wright of the Camberwell School of Arts and Crafts, London, who examined the technical information with patience and experience; my wife for her fortitude in reading the text; and all the teachers, colleagues and students from whom I have learned the craft of bookbinding.

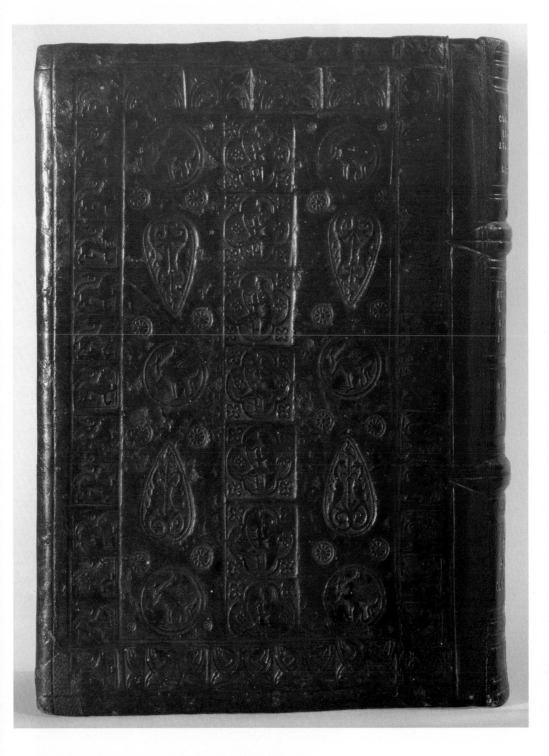

Historia Evangelica (225 × 155 mm). British Library. Probably
bound in London early in the thirteenth century. A beautiful
example of blind stamping on brown goatskin.

The Image of Governance (203 × 150 mm). British Library. Bound in London by Berthelet in 1541 for Henry VIII. An early example of gold tooling on white leather.

Atalanta in Calydon by Swinburne (213 × 165 mm). British Library. Bound in London in 1888 by Cobden Sanderson. The green morocco is gold-tooled and titled on the upper cover.

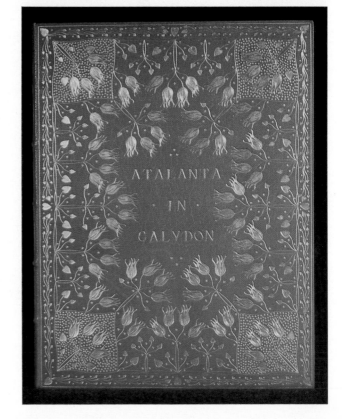

(*Opposite*) *Book of Common Prayer* (370 × 245 mm). British Library. A London binding supplied by Samuel Mearne to Charles II in 1669. The book is bound in red goatskin, tooled in gold to a cottage roof design with the cypher of the King.

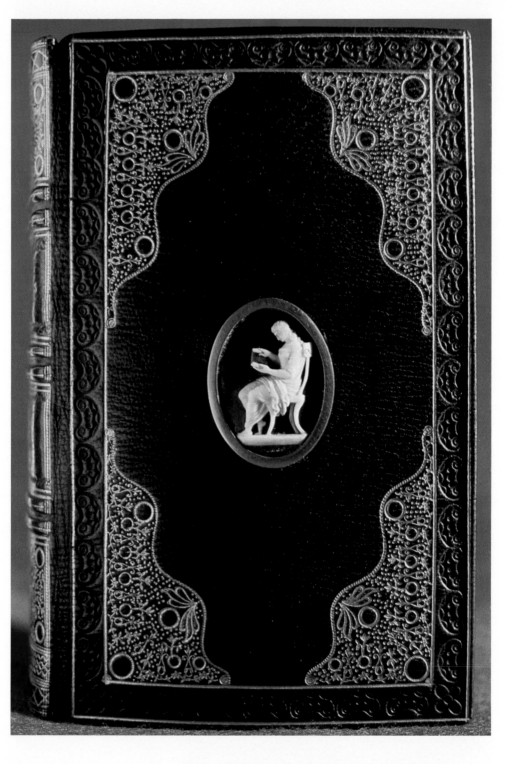

Virgil: Opera (154 × 100 mm). British Library. Printed by
Aldus Manutius in 1505 and bound by Roger Payne in a
blue straight-grain morocco, tooled in gold and blind
with a cameo inserted in both covers.

1 A history of English book-binding decoration

Until this century very little had been written on the construction of bindings, but much on their decoration. It is probable that bibliophiles had no knowledge of how a book was made but could write learnedly on its appearance, while the craftsman had not the ability to write. Therefore we are indebted to the literature on the decoration of books of earlier periods and to the museums and collections which have preserved the bindings. These tooled and coloured bindings have unique charm and beauty; the work was done by professional finishers with a natural flair for originality in the placing of the decoration.

Although other factors – political, economical and social – were involved, definite periods and recognizable styles of decoration have emerged. Old tools for this work are still available and there is great temptation to imitate early bindings. The student should keep in mind that little is gained by copying and the craft can only be kept vigorous by original work. A brief history of English bookbinding decoration, however, is interesting and informative as a background to the craft. A complete history has no place in a manual on the technique of binding but this chapter, it is hoped, will stimulate the reader to make further studies of historic examples from other sources.

In the fourth century AD the form of written communication changed from rolls to flat folded sheets. These 'volumes' were more easily stored and conveyed, but had to be protected. This is where the craft of bookbinding began. The first bindings were simple folded sheets sewn together and wrapped in leather. The preservation of books became a craft, and great skills were lavished on the contents and covers. Literature was dominated by the Christian faith; books became objects of veneration to be carried in processions, and their richly ornamented covers graced and embellished the altars. Precious stones, carved ivory and beaten gold were used on the wooden covers of treasured manuscripts, and these Byzantine 'coatings' predominated in bindings from the fifth to the eleventh century. Books were extremely rare as vellum, the only durable writing material, was scarce and valuable. In the Dark Ages monasteries and similar institutions practised the trades and skills of artists, scribes, goldsmiths, carpenters and leather workers to produce books. The reproduction of literature by hand was a combination of faith, love and great labour.

The earliest known English decorated leather binding is the seventh-century Gospel of St John, discovered with other precious relics in the tomb of St Cuthbert. This delightful binding, measuring 133 × 95 mm (5¼ × 3¾ in.), had wooden boards covered in crimson leather. The decoration is of a stylized plant form of interlaced branches, placed centrally, with narrow panels above and below having an interlaced cable design in intaglio. A cable pattern borders the covers and there is evidence of yellow colouring used to heighten the effect. The design is Celtic in origin.

At the beginning of the eighth century the Emperor Charlemagne combined the Celtic and Byzantine cultures to begin an era in art known as Carolingian. Thus a great impetus was given to the established monasteries to practise their art and to co-operate with independent and professional binders and other craftsmen to produce beautiful books and bindings.

In the twelfth century England earned European acclaim for a fresh and vigorous style of binding decoration. From cities such as Winchester, Durham, York, Gloucester and London came books of unique charm and character. They were ornamented with small impressions from stamps of brass cut in intaglio with such spontaneous simplicity that the cameo effect gave the highlights and shadows life and movement. These round, square and lobe-shaped patterns depicting religious subjects, natural forms and mythical beasts were arranged formally as borders enclosing parallelograms or circles. The stamps were struck individually by blows with a hammer on hide or deerskin which, possibly, had been dampened to make sharper impressions.

This simple form of 'blind' stamping influenced the decoration of books into the sixteenth century but, as the centuries passed, the delightfully naïve stamps of the earlier periods deteriorated. They became larger and more crude in conception; the small stamps were no longer struck separately but were cut into the surface of a brass wheel, or roll, and a mechanical and lifeless impression was made by pushing the wheel across the leather. In the fifteenth century a guild of bookbinders was formed and it became the fashion to incorporate a signature or device into the stamping of the covers as a means of identification.

The spread of learning during the Renaissance was hastened by the introduction of printing in Europe. The phenomenal increase in the number of books meant prosperity to the bookbinder, whose work became more refined and sophisticated. In 1476 William Caxton began business as printer and bookbinder in London. His bindings were decorated by the prevalent blind stamping of leather arranged in the German fashion with a border of stamps containing lozenge-shaped compartments. The large dies of the fifteenth and sixteenth centuries became known as panel stamps, and followed the Continental style. They were cut in metal and sometimes in wood; an impression could be made only by the use of the screw press. At the end of the fifteenth century an English binder named Pynson used a stamp of his own design, of a Tudor rose within a border of vine leaves and other foliage. This style of ornament became popular under the name of 'heraldic panel stamps', often depicting the arms and devices of patrons.

In the opening years of the sixteenth century John Reynes, a notable printer and binder to Henry VIII, used a pair of stamps bearing the arms of his patron separated by a roll stamp of a bird, flower, bee and dog as a trademark. Later in the same century, stamps were more pictorial and bore lively pictures drawn from legend, chivalry and religion. The increasing numbers of books produced in the sixteenth century demanded a speedy method of decoration, and so the use of rolls for blind stamping became prevalent. Early rolls, about one inch wide and cut in intaglio, bore patterns of the Tudor rose, fleur-de-lis and similar heraldic devices. At the close of the century they became narrower, and in the seventeenth century the patterns of flower garlands and formal repeated shapes were cut in cameo to give an impression in intaglio. Similar tools are in use today for gold tooling, and modern equivalents seem to be copies of these rolls.

The finest work was done abroad, commissioned by English patrons, and thus French and Italian bookbinders had great influence on the craft in England. English binders were quick to copy foreign work, and some European craftsmen settled in England bringing their own methods and styles of decoration. There can be no doubt that the change from blind to gold tooling had more impact than anything else in the history of English bookbinding. In the reign of Henry VIII a Frenchman named Thomas Bethelet settled in London to decorate books in the French style of gold tooling – a method that had already been used on the Continent for more than a hundred years. Books bound by him were embellished with interlaced parallel lines, floriated motifs, royal mottoes and coats of arms in burnished gold. Blind stamping, with its subtle and restrained appearance, soon gave way to the brilliance of gold; this had an immediate appeal, and the facets of the stamps put down separately or impressed as a roll made the leather covers glow with light. From this time decoration was lavished on bindings; edges were coloured, gilded, painted and gauffered, while covers were further ornamented by applied coloured leathers and painted coats of arms.

At the start of the seventeenth century James I had many of his books bound in morocco instead of the popular calf. His covers were decorated with a dull 'all-over' pattern of small impressions of thistle and fleur-de-lis tools bordered by a floral roll with a coat of arms in the centre. Since Bethelet's period it has been the common practice to treat the leather cover as a vehicle for gold and blind tooling by first framing it with a border of a floriated roll. Although some of these rolls, designed and cut by the engraver, added distinction, the general effect became monotonous. The smooth, even surface of calf took gold tooling beautifully and most of the hand tools and rolls were very finely engraved. Designs may have been suggested by the patron or his bookbinder, but mostly they were purchased from the tool-cutter's catalogue and used indiscriminately on a variety of books.

Other materials were used for covering books, no doubt as a relief from brown calf and gold tooling. Some were in velvet and damask; embroidered covers, which began as early as the twelfth century, reached an excellent standard in the sixteenth but then deteriorated in craftsmanship and design. These embroidered covers had simple charm and were brilliant in colour. Coloured silks, gold thread, silver wire, seed pearls and metallic spangles were worked on silk, linen and canvas. Embroidery in the best period was flat, raised or appliqué and the designs fresh and original, usually depicting natural forms of plant life, monograms, ciphers and portraits.

England can claim little originality in book decoration apart from the twelfth-century blind stamping and approaches to decoration in two later periods. At the end of the seventeenth century a style that originated in France was adopted and perfected by Samuel Mearne, stationer to Charles II, who is credited with supplying (not himself binding) three distinct styles to the royal library. The first, the 'rectangular', had decorations of single or double gold lines as a border, the corners filled with flower ornaments. In the centre was placed a crest or his patron's monogram formed by two letters C, one reversed. The second, the 'all-over', consisted of coloured inlays elaborately tooled with delicate floral impressions. The third and most notable was the 'cottage roof' style. Boards were framed with the usual decorated roll containing a geometric arrangement of onlays outlined in gold resembling the eaves of a roof. Scrolls and formal flowers surrounded the lines and within the roof shape were massed similar gold impressions radiating from a centre square.

In the early eighteenth century Robert Harley, Earl of Oxford, commissioned many fine bindings which were decorated in an original way unaffected by the fashion of coloured onlays prevalent in France. These 'Harleian' bindings in red morocco had a heavy gold border of one or two rolls with a large centre lozenge shape built up using floral, scroll and vase-shaped tools radiating from the centre.

About 1750, changes were made in book construction. Many books were sewn on cords let into the backs of sections, to give a smooth back, instead of the usual practice of sewing on raised cords. In consequence a change in book design begins at this period. One unfortunate result was that spines began to be lined with many layers of paper, which gave a firm, rigid surface for tooling but made the book difficult to open.

A fundamental contribution to bookbinding was made in the eighteenth century by an extraordinary craftsman, Roger Payne, who changed the course of English bookbinding. An eccentric, he quarrelled with all his associates and, it is recorded, spent more on drink than on food. His bindings were original as he designed and cut his own tools. A typical binding would be straight-grained red, olive or blue morocco with a decorated roll border and massed floral tooling in each corner. An ivory cameo would grace the centre. Doublures were leather or richly toned paper; often his colours were chosen indiscriminately. His bindings were forwarded conscientiously with raised bands; few were sewn on sunk cords. He is credited with the introduction of paper templates to impress his tooled designs accurately on the cover. This practice continues today instead of the earlier method of tooling direct from guide lines made by a folder. The stimulus given to English binding by Payne was notable, for before his time, decoration had become unimaginative, and with few exceptions the only work of merit was by foreigners.

Charles Lewis, a close imitator of Payne, was a sound forwarder, preferring hollow backs with false bands so that his books would open well. However, he was not such a sensitive designer as his predecessor; his tools were not so delicate and his designs were reminiscent of the Grolier bindings of the sixteenth century. John Whitaker, at the end of the eighteenth century, adapted designs from Etruscan vases, tooled romantic landscapes in gold and placed them within gothic or arabesque shapes. This 'Etruscan' style set a fashion which many imitated. The most successful development in this manner came from a binder in Halifax named Edwards. With the same romantic associations he painted castles, urns and churches on the underside of transparent vellum.

The Industrial Revolution stimulated demands for books and bindings; many families were proud to possess a small collection of leather-bound books and every large house had a library. Binding workshops proliferated in every major city as books were still bound by hand, but much of the labour was unskilled and the materials poor. The construction of bindings deteriorated; deficiencies were disguised by a profusion of gold ornament, lavished on the covers and particularly on the spines of books. Although the standard of finishing was high and old decorative tools were used, there was little opportunity for original work.

In a few decades methods were developed for mass-producing books. Machinery for cutting, blocking, case-making and pressing was invented, with an inevitable decline in hand trade work. Machine binding had nothing to add to the decoration of books until late in the century when thick, cloth-covered boards were embossed, textured and printed by machine in black and coloured enamels, silver and gold inks. The designs were factual illustrations of the contents of the book. These are now collected for their quaintness and as examples of the 'new machine craftsmanship'. Meanwhile trade houses suffered a recession from which there was no recovery. Very few cities now have trade binding workshops and although those that remain are often busy, little work of consequence is continued.

A turning point in English binding came at the end of the nineteenth century with the arts and crafts movement led by William Morris. This versatile man inspired many craftsmen, and new ideas flourished under his direction. In book production his achievement was to interest a lawyer, T. J. Cobden-Sanderson, in the craft of bookbinding. Binding and fine printing became Cobden-Sanderson's obsession and both crafts have been enriched by his work. He gave up an established legal practice and set up the Doves Bindery in 1893 and the Doves Press in 1900. A binding (in the possession of the author) made by Cobden-Sanderson in 1898 and used by him as a teaching aid confirms that he was an able instructor. His published articles showed he was a scholar who thought deeply about the craft and made it a scientific study. Although he took lessons from Zaehnsdorf, the London trade binder, he may be called the first amateur binder – the first of many who were economically independent and could experiment in the construction of the binding and in the decoration of the cover. On his ideas for the decoration of the books he admitted that the subject of the book should suggest decoration but should not aim at illustration. This was a new concept for binding design; Cobden-Sanderson was ahead of his time, but his own designs fell short of his aspiration. He continued the traditional methods of gold and blind tooling, designing his tools of flower, leaf and branch ornaments, which he placed in an orderly fashion, geometric in conception, over the whole cover. His delicate tooling on brightly coloured morocco was extremely attractive and original: his books were bound with genuine raised cords and the spine, front and back covers were designed as a harmonious whole. Cobden-Sanderson's work changed English binding design; his influence with amateur binders was extensive and, although he was much admired, to a lesser degree with the trade workshops.

After the war of 1914–1918 there came new forms of expression in literature and music and more freedom in art and craft ideas. Ways of designing books were explored other than the use of the ready-cut floral tools and dentelle borders. For a time designs were disciplined, humourless and austere, with geometric line work in gold and blind tooling. Soon, however, designers and artists made contributions to book decoration. In 1929 Paul Nash was commissioned to design a cover for a book on a serious subject. No gold was used on this work; the cover of light-red morocco was inlaid with black and ivory leather in rectangular shapes placed asymmetrically and tooled in blind. The effect was curiously sombre and calm and marked a decided change in binding decoration – the spirit of the book had been captured in its decoration. At the same period many amateurs, teachers of bookbinding and a few professionals were producing original and advanced work of great merit. Of these, the most notable was Sybil Pye, who executed a series of bindings curiously decorated with architectural-shaped inlays and symmetrically placed gold ornaments. This tooling is an unusual mixture of natural motifs and solid geometric shapes; some appear to have been placed merely to fill space yet the complete effect is modern and attractive. From this time amateur binders made a worthy contribution to the history of the craft but the declining trade workshops produced little of interest.

In 1860 Zaehnsdorf had issued a catalogue of their work in which an illustration showed an almost facsimile design of a Maioli binding of the sixteenth century with dentelle tooling, arabesque patterning and interlaced strapwork. On Winston Churchill's eightieth birthday he was presented with a book whose design was a close imitation of a Maioli. This consistent link with tradition left English trade binding in a state of lethargy. However, the trade had many fine craftsmen who, with incentives, were still capable of beautiful work. An example from the Gregynog Press was highly esteemed – fifteen specially bound copies of *Erewhon* by Samuel Butler. Designed by Blair Hughes Stanton and gold-tooled by George Fisher, they were bound with raised bands. Each was decorated with massed gold lines made by fillet, pallet and gouge tools. These lines were continued from front to back cover across the spine and the asymmetrical design gave a great sense of balance and unity. The meaning of the book may not have been captured and this may not have been the intention but as an abstract pattern it was typical of its period and a great contribution to English binding.

In the twentieth century Paris became the leading city for book-binding, with patrons all over the world. Fine modern printed books illustrated by leading artists are given exciting and experimental covers. A team of craftsmen, each expert in a particular operation in binding, combine their skills in producing superb work. Some books in an exhibition of French fine binding in the middle of the century were decorated with eggshells, emery cloth and an artist's palette let into the cover, but mainly the work is of free design and unrestrained colour. Radiating gold lines in geometric progressions and sweeping rhythmic curves make the covers alive with light and movement. Amateur work in England at this time hesitated between trade reliance on familiar traditional tooling and the influence of abstract painters such as Miró, Klee, Kandinsky and Arp. In 1950 the formation of a society later to be called Designer Bookbinders was an important contribution to English work. Its endeavours to raise standards among profession-als, amateurs and teachers and to make fine binding an art form have changed the aspect of binding in this century. At first the work of this society was considerably affected by French designs but their standard of craftsmanship could not be compared with their Parisian contemporaries. In England the fine binders, with more than an economic interest in the craft, did the complete work from the designs to the protective box instead of working as a team. As a result there was an inevitable drop in standards.

However, in the last two decades a high level of construction and design has been reached and now their work is of an individual style, unaffected by outside influences and representative of the creative ability and personality of each craftsman. No member is singled out for mention for each contributes his or her style in the interpretation of the book. Sculptured boards, embroidery, free gold lines, blind tooling, onlays, inlays, underlays, textured leathers and transparent vellum are methods used to good effect. It is inevitable that, in the future, bookbinding will change in construction, materials and decoration and will progress with imagination and independence.

2 Equipment

To learn and to teach bookbinding, it is essential to have professional equipment. 'Junior' or makeshift equipment will not withstand the strain of the various processes; it makes the work difficult and the results unsatisfactory. Table-top board cutters are inaccurate and unable to cut thick boards. Small lying presses are incapable of solid pressure and small ploughs cannot cut a good edge; light letter presses have a limited value but are useless for the sustained pressing of sections before sewing. The equipment must be of a standard to meet the requirements of the craft.

Board cutter: a standing type made of iron, with a cut of not less than 1050 mm (42 in.), is required to cope with large work, and blades must be changed frequently. The clamping action must be firm, to hold the board in position for cutting. The brass rules are marked in millimetres and inches. The gauge on the bed must be parallel, and the lay edge at right angles, to the cutting edge. All moving parts are shielded to prevent accidents. A board cutter should be used only to cut one board or a maximum of six sheets of paper at one time, otherwise the board will break and the paper tear.

Glue pots: some are fixed and consist of three containers in one water jacket with the heat thermostatically controlled; water must be added daily. The safest and most convenient is the waterless thermostatically controlled type that is plugged into bench sockets wherever required.

A *guillotine* is very useful and convenient for large, difficult work and for sets where it is essential to match sizes. Cut edges cannot be compared in quality with edges cut in the plough but it is efficient and quick for the cheaper type of work. Wheel- or lever-operated blades are reasonably efficient but electrically powered ones with a 530-mm (21-in.) cut, automatic cut-out and safety guards are the best. Duplicate blades are provided and should be changed frequently, and careful maintenance observed. Only when the blade has been ground to the correct angle should boards be cut in the guillotine. The machine illustrated, the Powermatic 21 made by Goodhale Dornier, is simple and safe to operate. Its width is 1016 mm (3 ft 4 in.), length 1245 mm (4 ft), height 1295 mm (4 ft 3 in.), and the operational space required is 1829 × 1524 mm (6 × 5 ft). The back gauge is power-operated and the clamp is hydraulic and automatic. Precision cutting is controlled by a periscope viewer and the blade will cut a 76-mm (3-in.) pile of paper 537 mm (21 in.) wide from 19 mm ($\frac{3}{4}$ in.) to 533 mm (21 in.).

1 Nipping press

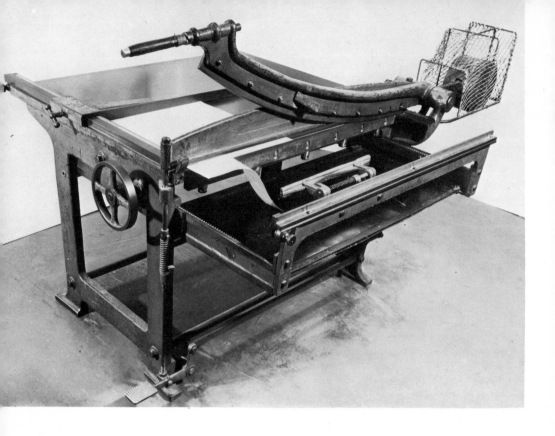

2 Board cutter

3 Glue pots

Lying press or laying press (see Fig. 53, p. 69): those produced today have laminated cheeks instead of solid blocks; the wooden screws are brittle and the threads break unless carefully used. For most work a press with a distance of 600 mm (24 in.) between screws is best; lighter ones of 450 mm (18 in.) are available, but are not really adequate. The stand or tub is extra; it is preferable to fit the press under a work bench with a removable top, to make best use of the space.

Nipping press: of iron construction, it is bolted down to a solid wood or iron bench with a place for pressing boards underneath. A standard size has a platen of 350 × 550 mm (14 × 21½ in.) and a daylight of 375 mm (15 in.). As it is used more than any other piece of equipment it should be positioned close to the work benches.

The *plough* is the part of the lying press used for cutting. Old ploughs were beautifully finished in turned wood; present-day ploughs look clumsy but are just as efficient. The blade, when fixed in the plough, should run flat on to the cheek of the press.

The *press pin* is used to tighten the screws of the lying press, and may be conveniently held by two hooks screwed to the side of the stand.

Sewing frames: tape sewing frames, where tension is unnecessary, can be home-made but screw wooden uprights are essential for all cord work. The professional size has a platform 250 × 650 mm (9¾ × 25½ in.) and measures 375 mm (15 in.) between the screws. Pinning tapes or cords to the platform is deplorable: when keys are not available they should be pinned to a replaceable piece of wood screwed to the underside of the frame (see Fig. 36, p. 63).

Standing press: old wooden French standing presses tightened with a percussion action are beautiful pieces of equipment but are almost unobtainable now. Iron presses are available: the one illustrated has a platen of 525 × 600 mm (20½ × 23½ in.) and a daylight of 775 mm (30½ in.), and can exert the tremendous pressure essential for good work for both preliminary and final pressing. A piece of millboard the same size as, and positioned on, the base plate can be drawn with rectangles to indicate the centre of the press. This will facilitate placing the work to ensure even pressure.

4 Powermatic 21 guillotine

5 Standing press (*above*)

SMALL TOOLS

The smaller tools used in the bindery are readily obtainable or may be home-made. They become very personal to the craftsman, giving great pleasure and pride in use.

Circular files ranging from 1 mm to 6 mm in diameter, are set in handles or frames similar to hacksaws. They can be used instead of a tenon saw to cut grooves in the backs of sections to accommodate cords, and have numerous other uses as they will saw through metal, wood and plastic.

A large *awl* is necessary, preferably with the shaft extending right through the handle. As it is used to make holes in boards to lace in slips, it should be blunt, to erupt a hole rather than pierce one.

Backing boards: these wedge-shaped lengths of beech and oak are oblique at the wide end; pairs must be identical and coded with

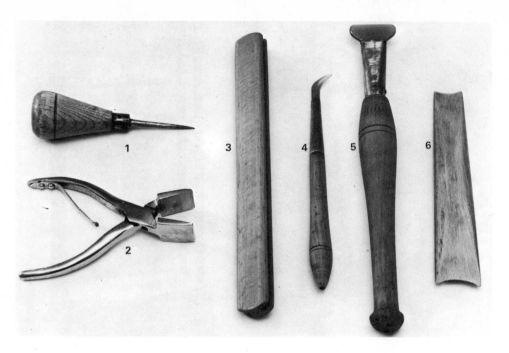

6 Bookbinder's tools: *1* awl,
2 band nippers, *3* band stick,
4 dog-toothed burnisher, *5*
flat burnisher, *6* back scraper

paint for easy recognition. For ease in resurfacing, the direction of
the wood grain should be marked on each board. They are used
for forming the joint; recommended sizes are 200 mm, 300 mm,
450 mm (8, 12 and 18 in.).

A *backing hammer* with a domed and claw-shaped head, approximately 1 lb ($\frac{1}{2}$ kg) in weight, is widely used, principally for knocking out the groove, reducing the swell, rounding, backing and
hammering slips. A jeweller's light planishing hammer with a
square head can be used for light work and for backing books on
raised cords.

Band nippers: this is a pincer-type tool with flat jaws, sometimes
chrome-plated to prevent discolouring leather, which is used for
nipping up bands when covering. (Care should be taken not to
bruise the leather; band sticks are more sympathetic for this work.)

Band sticks are usually home-made from hardwood, well
smoothed and polished. There are two types: one is a simple stick
18 × 225 × 8 mm (0·7 × 8·9 × 0·3 in.), and the other is 300 ×
22 mm (12 × 0·9 in.), curved, with slots cut in the sides. They are
used to mould leather to the bands when covering the spine.

Bone folders are made from ivory, bone, hardwood or plastic.
A very long folder with blunt ends and one thinned side is used for
folding and cutting paper (*1* in figure). The ideal shape for most
work is 160 mm long and 25 mm wide (6 × 1 in.). It should be
smooth and heavy at the bottom, narrowing slightly to a blunt
point at the top (*2*). A heavy folder filed at each end to blunt points
is necessary for box-making (*3*). For finishing and fine work a
folder about 120 mm (4$\frac{3}{4}$ in.) long with a very long and fine point
is used (*4*). A light thin folder with a fine point at one end and a
chisel shape at the other is used for positioning onlays and inlays of
leather (*5*).

A light bookbinding *bodkin* with a fine thin shaft and broad wooden handle is used for piercing holes in paper and board.

Brushes should be of the best possible quality, for inferior and cheap brushes will deteriorate quickly in adhesives. Glue brushes are round with stiff hairs, bound round with wire; paste brushes have long hairs for brushing out evenly, and are usually bound with string. Also required are a large water-colour flood brush, sable 10, for putting on glaire when edge gilding, and a water-colour brush, number 4 (or finer, depending on the work), for painting on the glaire when gold tooling. Various hog's-hair brushes are used for applying dye in restoration work, and shoe brushes with soft hair for polishing blacklead or bole when edge gilding. A small natural-bristle nail brush has many uses, including polishing leather.

Burnishers: agate or bloodstone heads, either flat or dog-toothed, are polished and set in a wooden handle; they are used for burnishing the waxed, coloured or gilded edges of books.

A good *carpenter's square* is essential: an all-metal square is best, with a blade 300 mm (12 in.) long.

Chisels: 6-mm and 12-mm (¼-in. and ½-in.) wood chisels are useful, also a curved carving chisel for rounding corners.

Cheap wooden-handled *cobbler's knives* are used for casual cutting. The blade should be shaped and the curve used as the cutting edge; the point is not used for cutting.

Cutting boards: similar to backing boards, but straight at the wide end, they are used only for cutting books in the plough and for edge gilding. Recommended sizes are 200 mm, 300 mm and 450 mm (8, 12 and 18 in.).

Engineer's spring *dividers*, about 150 mm (6 in.) long, should have the points blunted to avoid scratching the material.

7 Bookbinder's tools: *1–5* bone folders, *6* cobbler's knife, *7* dividers, *8* eyelet tool, *9* hole punch

8 Bookbinder's tools: *1* backing
hammer, *2* light hammer, *3*
knocking-down iron, *4* loaded
stick

Dishes must be large enough for double-page spreads when soaking, washing, bleaching and resizing paper. Stainless steel dishes are best, and easiest to keep clean.

Embroidery scissors: a small pointed pair is necessary for fine work.

Eyelet tool: punch pliers and hole punches are required for making holes, also eyelet closers for using with the punch pliers. The punches should be 3, 6 and 12 mm in diameter.

A selection of flat and shaped metal *files* have various uses, including sharpening scrapers and bevelling boards. For forming and cutting finishing tools, needle files of all shapes are used.

G-clamps: 150-mm and 230-mm (6-in. and 9-in.) sizes are recommended, with swivel heads for clamping down leather while paring and for similar work.

Gilder's tip (see illustration on p. 81): fine hair set between thin card, used for applying gold when edge gilding.

Grindstone: an electric bench-top model with coarse and fine grinding wheels is recommended. While blades are being sharpened they should be dipped in cold water frequently to reduce the temperature, as overheating will soften the metal.

A *hypodermic syringe* is useful for injecting adhesives into the unstuck portions of bindings.

The *knocking-down iron* has innumerable uses in binding and can also be used as a weight. Recommended size, 250 × 100 mm (10 × 4 in.).

Lead blocks are used as a base when piercing holes in boards, also as weights. Recommended size, 180 × 130 × 25 mm (7 × 5 × 1 in.).

Loaded stick: this wooden stick, 300 mm (12 in.) long and 30 mm (1⅛ in.) square, is loaded with lead at the end and covered in leather. It has a shaped handle and is used for beating out swell and firming the sections while sewing.

Needles: these should be large and strong, and the eyes must be large enough to take the thread freely. A curved sail needle, or the

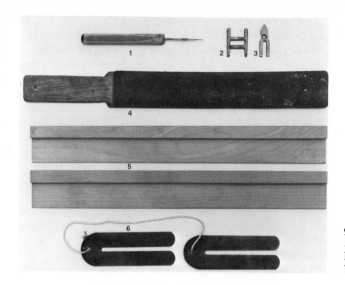

9 Bookbinder's tools: *1* piercer, *2* sewing key for tape, *3* sewing key for cord, *4* strop, *5* tie-up boards, *6* trindles

small curved needle used by surgeons, is sometimes used for repair work.

Oil stones, fine and coarse, should be set in boxes and fixed in one position, for ease in use.

Paring knives and *paring stone*, for paring leather (see p. 90).

Piercer: a strong needle, set in a wooden handle flattened at one side; alternatively, a dentist's probe ground and tapered to a point. It is used to make fine holes when sewing.

Pins: dressmaking pins and drawing pins, for setting up sewing frames.

A small smoothing *plane* is used for resurfacing backing and cutting boards, also for bevelling millboard.

Plates: various types are required – thin tin plates for setting boards after lacing in the slips and for finishing, heavy zinc plates for pressing sections, and chrome-plated or stainless steel plates for polishing books during the final pressing. Recommended sizes are 150 × 225 mm (6 × 9 in.), 225 × 300 mm (9 × 12 in.) and 300 × 450 mm (12 × 18 in.).

Pots, paste (for glue pots, see p. 22): any clean container that stands firm on the bench is suitable for paste. All containers should have a bar of brass or stretched string across the pot to wipe off excess adhesive from the brush. All pots must be cleaned regularly and kept free from rust.

Pressing boards: these are flat boards made of hardwood or laminated hardboard, approximately 15 mm thick. Sizes required are 150 × 225 mm (6 × 9 in.), 225 × 300 mm (9 × 12 in.) and 300 × 450 mm (12 × 18 in.). A few larger boards with Formica surfaces, to fit in the standing press, are used for paper repair and large work.

Press-stud tool: used for fixing studs.

Riveting sets: these are similar to press-stud tools, and are used for riveting on loose-leaf mechanisms.

Rods, stainless steel, wood or plastic, in many thicknesses and lengths, are used in pairs; knitting needles are best.

Sandpaper blocks: various grades of glasspaper or sandpaper are used to abrade or smooth surfaces.

Scalpel, as used in surgery: ideal for precise cutting and paring. Alternatively, a fine craft tool, with interchangeable blades, may be used.

Scrapers: wooden scrapers are used to clean off paste and glue from the spine when setting the back. For metal scrapers, used in edge gilding, see p. 81.

Set squares, both small and large, 45° clear plastic, are used for working out corners and for marking up for cutting. Cheap set squares are usually inaccurate.

Sewing keys: these metal shapes are used to hold cord or tape in place on a sewing frame.

Strong *shears* are essential; they should be blunt-ended and 225 mm (9 in.) in length.

Spokeshave for paring leather (see p. 92).

Sponges: small sponges have many uses.

Steel rulers: 300-mm and 600-mm 12-in. and (24-in.) stainless steel straight-edges; should be graduated in inches and millimetres.

The *steel* normally used for knife sharpening is useful for burring over the edges of scrapers.

Strop: a flat piece of wood, 400 × 60 × 8 mm (16 × 2½ × ⅓ in.), shaped with a handle at one end. On one side is medium emery cloth which is used for coarse sharpening and on the other a thick piece of harness or belting leather. This is prepared by smearing it with tallow and sprinkling fine emery powder over it; when polished with a hot iron the melted tallow carries the abrasive into the leather, making an efficient strop for keen sharpening. As a substitute for tallow and emery, valve-grinding paste may be used.

Tack hammer: the round, flat head is useful for many operations.

Tenon saw: a small tenon saw with finely set teeth is used for sawing for the sunk cord style, and for cutting the cerf. Fine hacksaws are an excellent substitute.

Tie-up boards: these are pairs of long cutting boards with an extra ridge of wood screwed to the wide end. They are used as an aid to firm leather round raised bands of large and difficult books.

Trindles, flat thin bars of metal with a central strip cut away, are always tied in pairs. They are used to flatten the spines of books which are to be cut 'in boards'.

Vise: a small bench-type vise has many uses in binding.

WORKSHOP LAYOUT

Adequate space in which to work is the craftsman's joy. It is also essential to have power, good daylight and artificial light, running water with a large sink, and a separate storage room near by. Adequate heating is, of course, necessary, but the workshop should not be overheated as this can cause warping of materials.

Benches should be a comfortable working height of 1050 mm (42 in.) and at least 1000 mm (40 in.) deep; they should be firm and solid, preferably of wooden construction. Most of the surfaces should be lined with ship's linoleum, and some with Formica for the repair of paper. A little-used corner of the bench should be cut away and fitted with a top of translucent glass over an electric bulb, as a light table. Plan chests for the storage of paper and boards can conveniently fit under benches. Stands for lying presses with the top of the press 1000 mm (40 in.) from the ground can be built as extra benches away from the walls. These should have removable tops and a shelf 200 mm (8 in.) above the floor to store finishing presses. Open ends of benches should be fenced with strips of wood to prevent tools from falling off. It is useful to have power points at regular intervals for stoves and glue pots, and Anglepoise lamps for close work.

Nipping presses and board cutter should be near the work benches to avoid unnecessary walking and carrying, but the standing press and guillotine are better placed away from the general work area. It is wise to reserve a separate place for the paring of leather because of the hazard of moving paring stones, and also to keep the leather dust in one place.

Above the benches glass-fronted, locking wall cabinets contain sets of common tools such as tenon saw, hammer, cobbler's knife, strop, straight-edge, paring knife, dividers, spokeshave, band nippers, shears, awl, carpenter's square and G-clamps. These tools should be coded with coloured paint and their positions sil-houetted on the walls of the cabinet so that they can be checked at a glance. Cupboards for other equipment can be concentrated on one wall and sewing frames stored on top. Drawers are identified by labels with the description of contents, for easy access and replacement. Chemicals, dyes and inflammable liquids should be locked in metal cabinets, with a separate cupboard available for finishing preparations.

Leather must be stored away from direct heat. Pigeonhole racks for cloth and mull can be made from Dexion. Large waste bins are essential, also a storage area for waste paper for gluing. The grindstone and oil stones should be situated in a corner away from materials. Lines can be strung above benches for drying washed and resized sheets. Lockers for students' work are important, as books in the process of binding should not be left out on benches. High stools and a display case should be provided, also a first-aid box, sited in a prominent position.

3 Bookbinder's materials

PAPER

Paper is the basis of the craft of bookbinding. Without a knowledge of the manufacture and properties of the material to be preserved and presented, no binding can be successful.

Paper is cellulose; it has tabular or ribbon-like fibres which felt together into sheets. Some fibres have chemicals added during manufacture to produce papers with infinite differences in quality, use, strength, texture, colour and surface. The binder must appreciate the possibilities and limitations of the paper in order to control and modify his working methods.

Paper was introduced into England in the fourteenth century and paper of that period is still almost as good as ever. Handmade paper production methods have hardly changed during this time although in England mills are fast disappearing and much handmade paper is imported. The technology of paper is an enormous and absorbing subject and can be dealt with only briefly in this book; however, for the serious student a sound study is recommended.

The manufacturer of handmade paper is not concerned with the raw material but uses cotton and linen rags. These are sorted, dusted, washed, bleached, boiled and torn by machine to pulp known as 'half stuff'. After further disintegration has taken place for six to twelve hours in a cogged beating machine, the pulp is strained to remove knotty fibres and foreign matter and pumped into a vat where revolving paddles keep water and pulp constantly moving.

The sheet of paper is made by a worker – the vatman – using a form of sieve containing a frame called a 'deckle'. This determines the thickness of the paper; it is dipped into the pulp and shaken in all directions to felt the fibres together. This web of pulp is turned out by another workman – the coucher – and a post or pile about 450 mm (18 in.) high of alternating paper and felt mats is put under considerable pressure to remove water and compress the surfaces. When it is dry, the paper is called 'waterleaf'. It is passed through a warm bath of animal gelatine; this, which is known as 'tub sizing' or 'surface sizing', combines with the properties of the linen and cotton fibres to give the paper its strength and lasting qualities. The paper is pressed again to remove surplus size and hung to dry and mature in circulating warm air.

Surfaces range from 'very rough' to 'hot-pressed', the texture being imparted by the weave of the mats while under pressure. The surface of the smooth paper is made by subjecting the paper to pressure by hot polished metal plates. The hardness and absence of grain direction make it difficult to use, but it is invaluable for

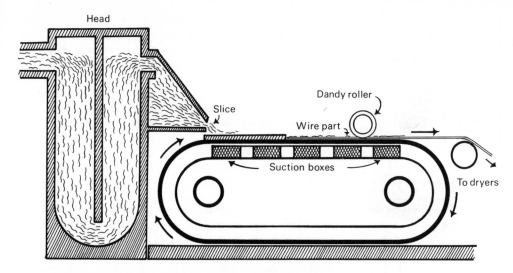

Head
Slice
Dandy roller
Wire part
Suction boxes
To dryers

10 Paper-making machine

fine printing, binding, artists' work, handwritten documents and any work in which preservation, good appearance and permanence are required. It is recognized by its obvious quality and by its deckled (uneven) edges in sheet form. A ream of handmade paper is 480 sheets, whereas machine-made papers have 500 sheets to the ream.

The first successful paper-making machine was developed in Europe and improved in England by Fourdrinier in 1803; by 1830 half the paper made in England was produced by machine. It is now made from a variety of materials, chiefly from wood and to a lesser degree from esparto grass. The best machine-made paper can compare favourably with handmade paper if linen and cotton fibres are used and it is tub-sized. Different fibres are mixed according to the quality, use and price of the paper. Paper for casual literature and newsprint is produced from 'mechanical' wood pulp, the name given to pulp in which the wood fibres are physically crushed and broken down by grinding in water. Better-quality is produced from 'chemical' wood, in which the fibres are separated by the action of heat and alkalis. Coarse fibres are passed through the beating or refining machines, and the pulp is strained and pumped into the 'mixer'. Colour or a loading of china clay is added, depending on its ultimate use, and, if the paper needs sizing, resin is included. The addition of size to the pulp before the paper has been made is called 'engine' sizing.

The pulp is pumped into a tank, known as the 'head', to be made into a continuous web. From the bookbinding aspect, the stage of forming the web of paper is extremely important for it is here that the 'grain' or machine direction of paper is established. Paper pulp containing 99·3 per cent water is passed from the head through the slice, which regulates the thickness of pulp falling on to the wire mesh and determines the substance of the paper. The wire moves away from the slice and shakes from side to side to felt the fibres, most of which lie in the direction in which the wire part is travelling. Handmade paper has its fibres felted in all directions; it has no grain and, when wetted, will stretch both ways. In machine-made

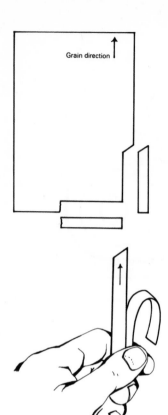

Grain direction

11 Testing for grain direction *1*

paper the fibres tend to lie in one direction and, when wetted, the resulting stretch is eight times more at right angles to the grain than the stretch in the machine direction. As the web of paper is being formed, the water is removed by suction boxes, and the web then passes under a series of rollers. The first, the dandy roller, consolidates the surface and sometimes impresses the laid, wove and watermarks into the web of paper. Further rollers dry, size, finish, coat, wax, polish and emboss according to quality and use. Machine-made paper in a continuous piece has a tear strength weaker one way than the other and is liable to decay more rapidly if poorly sized and dried quickly. Mould-made paper is produced by machine in separate sheets and is of high quality with good fibres, often tub-sized.

The importance of grain direction in paper and board and the direction of the warp thread in cloths and mull cannot be over-emphasized. In every binding the grain and warp of all the man-made materials must run from head to tail. Materials with conflicting grains or warps will cause boards to buckle, endpapers to crease or split, paper to cockle and books to gape; sections will not fold properly. Paper folded with the grain will lie flat and crease without damage, but folded against the grain the fibres will crack and endeavour to straighten. There are many ways of establishing the grain of a piece of paper and four of these are sufficient to test most papers.

1 Cut two strips of paper approximately 80×12 mm $(3 \times \frac{1}{2}$ in.) from adjoining edges of a sheet and identify one of them. Hold them as illustrated above, and lick them. One will collapse into a curve and the other will remain upright. The latter has the grain running along its length, keeping it upright, and the stretch in width is negligible. The other, with the grain running across the width, has the moisture going between the fibres, increasing its length and making it limp.

2 Lay a sheet of paper on the bench and turn over one edge in a curve for 250 mm (10 in.). Repeat this with the other side and it will be observed that the edge that remains curved over or returns more slowly will indicate the grain direction.

3 Hold the sheet the long way and bend the middle. Repeat, holding the paper the short way. Whichever shows the smaller curve or offers less resistance is the grain direction.

4 Run the finger and thumb tightly along the extreme edges of adjoining sides for 250 mm. Against the grain will show as short wavy lines, the fibres having been stretched apart by the rubbing action. The edge with the grain will hardly change.

As most papers are sold in rectangular sheets the grain is described as 'short grain' if lying along the lesser measurement, and 'long grain' if the longer way of the sheet. Boards are tested by bending: the way that offers less resistance is the grain direction (it is important that the same distance is bent on both sides). The warp direction in material is usually parallel to the selvedge. Book cloth will tear straight and more readily down the warp.

Paper can be classified in seven categories. Six of these, including handmade paper, are used in bookbinding; the seventh, known as 'specials', includes cigarette papers, wet-strength toilet tissues and

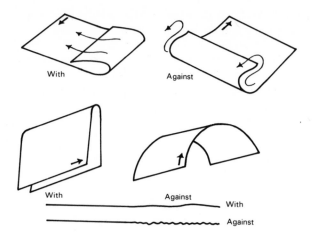

With   Against

With   Against

With

Against

12 Testing for grain direction 2

other industrial papers. 'Printing' papers have the widest variety, from expensive to economical, sized or unsized, the surface finish ranging from rough antique to glossy-coated paper for fine colour printing. The latter, known as 'art paper', is made from chemical wood or esparto grass fibres. Imitation art paper is 'loaded' by adding china clay and casein glue in the pulp stage. Genuine art paper has the body made first and is then coated with clay and glue by brush, spray or blade. Both are calendered to a highly polished finish. This paper, with its glossy surface, is ideal for four-colour printing but is a problem to the binder. It slips on handling and may crack when folded, and the surface dissolves when adhesive is applied. Its pH value is between 9 and 10 because of the addition of clay and glue.

'Wrapping' papers are for the protection of goods and merchandise but of these only wax paper and brown kraft paper are used in bookbinding. Wax papers are made from chemical wood pulp, either surfaced or impregnated with wax as a barrier to moisture. Kraft (from the German word for 'strength') is made from chemical wood fibre well sized with resin. The unbleached fibres are long and strong and some glazed varieties are slightly water-resistant. Brown is the usual colour but others are available. This excellent paper is used extensively for reinforcing endpapers, strengthening spines and making hollow backs.

'Writing' papers are suitable for all stationery requirements; one of these, ledger paper, is manufactured from a rag fibre or a mixture of rag and chemical wood, tub-sized. It is opaque, strong, and almost equal to handmade paper for durability. Its surface is smooth, toned azure or pale green; it is used for fine printing, account and visitors' books and registers. Bank and bond papers are writings of good quality as they are made from well-beaten fibres of chemical wood sized with resin. They are similar but bond has more substance. Strong and durable and almost neutral in pH rating, they are used mainly for strengthening the folds of damaged sections and for counteracting the warp of boards. 'Blotting' papers contain little or no size, and duplicating papers are included in this category. 'Drawing' papers, used by artists and designers, normally have a rough surface; of these, cartridge paper is used for bookwork. It is made from chemical wood well sized with resin. Strong and opaque, its whiteness when used for endpapers often contrasts with the text paper of cheaper books. It is excellent for the common made, or four-page tipped on, endpapers for case bindings. Offset cartridge used for printing by offset lithography is much smoother and of poorer quality.

Decorative papers, used for the sides and endpapers of books and linings of boxes to make them more attractive, come from all categories of papers in an infinite variety of colours, patterns, surfaces, textures and qualities. Making full allowance for personal taste, there still must be discrimination in colour and pattern combination to make a binding harmonious. Italian hand-printed papers are delightful, with their simple motifs in soft colours. Some of these are still obtainable but more recently they have deteriorated in design and colour. The use of marbled paper is less favoured now for fine binding than in previous centuries as there is a trend towards the simplicity of plain and pleasantly coloured paper for sides and endpapers. Any decorated paper used should be strong, and its surface firm, to fulfil its function as part of the construction of the book.

Ingres and similar papers are mould-made papers of excellent quality, made from linen, cotton and a little chemical wood sized with resin. They are made in France, Sweden and Italy in a number of pleasing colours and are used in fine binding for sides, endpapers and box linings.

Japanese papers and tissues are mould-made from rag fibre of good quality and are imported in various substances and tones from white to deep cream. They are used extensively for repairing badly damaged or rotting documents, or mending and replacing torn or missing parts of leaves, as they blend in with the original paper and repairs are almost invisible. They are also used in the making of heat-set tissue for the dry repair of torn leaves. A book with many damaged sections may be guarded with thinner Japanese paper instead of bond paper, thus considerably reducing the swell.

Dover, Roger Powell and similar papers, mould-made papers of high rag content, were originally manufactured in imitation of early handmade paper, specifically for use as endpapers and replacement paper for the restoration of old books.

Chemically pure papers are mould-made papers, mainly of rag fibre, with a neutral pH value, used by archivists for the mounting and repair of documents. The creamy tone is deliberate, so that the difference between it and the original is unmistakable.

Paper sizes

Paper used to be watermarked with various devices to identify the manufacturer and the dimensions. Innumerable variations in sizes for particular uses led to complications in all branches of trade associated with paper and print, and papers of the same name often varied in measurement. Some common sizes for book work, with their commonly accepted names, are:

foolscap	17 × 13½ in.
large post	21 × 16¼ in.
demy	22½ × 17½ in.
medium	23 × 18 in.
royal	25 × 20 in.
crown	20 × 15 in.
imperial	30 × 22 in.
double elephant	40 × 27 in.

In double sizes the smaller measurement is doubled; in quadruple ('quad') size, both dimensions are doubled. A crown sheet folded once, giving two leaves and four pages, is crown folio; folded again (four leaves and eight pages) is crown quarto (4to); folded three times, to make eight leaves and sixteen pages, is crown octavo (8vo). This method is used to specify the size of a book.

It has now been recommended that there should be five standard metric sizes for book production. These are:

metric crown octavo	186 × 123 mm
metric large crown octavo	198 × 129 mm
metric demy octavo	216 × 138 mm
metric royal octavo	234 × 156 mm
A5	210 × 148 mm

The craft binder has to be familiar with the old paper sizes as well as the international ones.

The International Standards Organization (ISO) decided on a standardization of size and shape of paper based on a square metre, subdivisions of which retained the same proportions, to make reductions and enlargements easier. This simplified paper manufacture, printing, binding and the production of associated machinery throughout the world. The ISO measurements are: A size (used for standard printing and stationery), 1189 × 841 mm, B size (charts, posters and maps) 1414 × 1000 mm, C size (envelopes) 1297 × 917 mm. The unfolded size of A paper, 1189 × 841 mm (one square metre), is designated A0. Folded or cut once, this becomes A1 (841 × 594 mm); folded or cut twice is A2 (594 × 420 mm); folded or cut three times, A3 (420 × 297 mm), and so on.

Stock-size papers run larger than the trimmed size of the text and have the prefix R before the size; RA0 is 1220 × 860 mm. Still larger papers, which allow for extra trim and certain production methods, are prefixed with S; SRA0 is 1280 × 900 mm. The term 'pounds weight of paper' was formerly used to specify the weight of a ream of paper. This often led to confusion on the substance of paper of different sizes and now this has been replaced by expressing the weight in grams per square metre of paper (gsm); the 'grammage' would be the same for a sheet as for a reel. The generally accepted division between paper and board is defined at 220 gsm.

'Imposition' is the term used to describe the arrangement of type and blocks set up in a forme and printed on a sheet so that

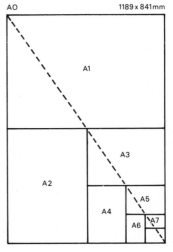

13 ISO paper measurements

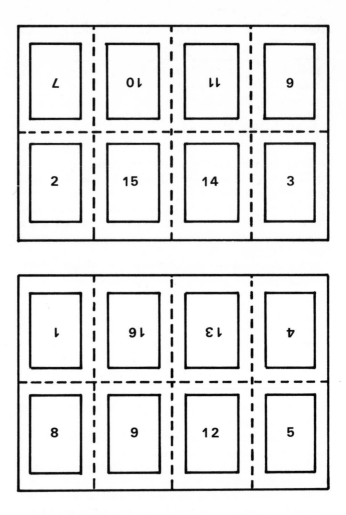

14 Imposition

when folded and trimmed the pages or information will run consecutively. There is a standard method of folding for book work. When the sections are received in sheet form, sixteen pages to a section, the lowest numbered page is placed face down and to the left. In folding the sheet the right-hand edge is brought over to the left, the bottom corner and edges are lined up and the fold is creased with a folder. Place the folder flat halfway up the crease and bring the top edge to the bottom. Remove the folder and crease again. Half turn the section to the right until the short side is nearest and use the folder to slit the long fold or bolt more than halfway and bring what was the left side over to the right. The bolt is slit after the second fold to free trapped air and thus avoid unsightly creases in the centre of the head fold. If the paper is out of true, the sheet is folded by lining up the printed area. If the printer has done his work properly the grain of the last fold should run from head to tail. It is understood that the printer is mainly concerned with the surface of the paper and how it takes his impressions but the binder is more concerned with its quality, grain and limitations.

BOARD

Since the beginning of this century investigations have been made into the manufacture and properties of materials so that their suitability for binding may be assessed and their resistance to the deleterious effect of industrial atmosphere measured. It is better to use materials that are prepared for bookbinding of good quality so that no problems will arise in handling and adhesion. Materials should be avoided if their surfaces are embossed or stamped in imitation of something better, as they look cheap and vulgar on good hand work. However, these may be used when old books are restored or copied. The list of materials is long but the following includes comments on some which are used and are available at this time. The binder should become familiar with their properties as they affect the various operations.

Millboard, a machine-made grey board, is very strong and durable. Manufactured chiefly from printers' waste combined with used rope and coarse cloth, it is capable of bending without cracking and has a satisfactory pH value. It is made in thicknesses of ·065, ·08, ·092 and ·125 in. and these are used for all leather bindings, good-class work and box-making.

Strawboard is manufactured from straw, sand and lime and is imported from Holland. Brown in colour and inclined to be brittle, it resists industrial atmosphere because of its lime content. It is used for case bindings in the cheaper range of books and for boxes. The thinnest used is 500 gsm, and heavier weights are 1000, 1400, 1800 gsm.

Pasteboard is manufactured from chemical wood pulp, esparto grass and other fibres according to quality. Usually it consists of laminated layers of thin white board or it may have a core of poor fibre lined on both sides with good paper. It is used chiefly for mounting.

Manilla card was originally made from manilla fibre, but cheaper imitations are from chemical wood pulp which has been engine-sized and glazed. It is strong, bends and creases without cracking and is obtainable in many colours. Its chief use is in stationery; in craft work it is used for guard books and for filling in the inside of boards.

Pulp card, sugar paper and similar papers, as they are made from pulped printers' waste with very little size, are spongey and weak. They are available in many colours and substances, and are used for scrapbooks and for filling in the inside of boards. Their use is limited in good binding as they can be highly acidic.

pH VALUES

Materials in bookbinding may be acid or alkaline, and either acid or alkali, if present to excess, will cause rapid deterioration not only of these materials themselves but also of any other with which they come into contact. The pH scale, which indicates the acidity or alkalinity of a substance, has a range from 0 to 14. Distilled water has a pH value of 7; values below 7 denote varying degrees of acidity, and above 7 of alkalinity. Excess acidity will discolour papers, ink or bookcloth and may tarnish foils.

Paper and board contain, in addition to cellulose fibres, other chemicals which can be highly acid or alkaline, with pH values ranging from 3·8 to 10·5. Most machine-made uncoated paper has a pH value between 5 and 7 because the aluminium sulphate used in engine sizing reduces the acidity. Cheaper papers, such as newsprint, can have a pH value below 5; therefore the use of newsprint, for lining boards to warp them, is not recommended as this seals into the binding a source of deterioration. Coated papers are alkaline because china clay and casein glue are used in their production.

Papers used for binding should have a minimum pH value of 5·5 for, whatever the quality of the text paper may be, the binding must be sound and durable. The permanence or ageing of papers and other bookbinding materials may be affected by industrial atmosphere; the constant absorption of sulphur dioxide combined with moisture and oxygen results in the formation of sulphuric acid. The stronger the acid content, the more rapid the deterioration, especially in humid conditions.

Adhesives should have a pH value of 6 or 7 as their moisture content may well increase any chemical action, which could result in corrosion, discoloration or fading. Casein glue has a pH value of 9–10 and starch and animal glue of 6–7. Brom Cresol Green (BCG) indicator ink is used to test the acidity of paper, a spot of it being applied to the paper with a brush or a special felt-tipped pen. If the paper is neutral the ink will remain blue-green but if acid is present the colour will change to yellow-green, to yellow and then to orange, depending on the degree of acidity. Books and documents can be de-acidified when dry by cyclohexylamine carbonate (CHC) in the form of a powder, tablets or impregnated sheets of paper; this is known as the 'vapour phase de-acidification' method. For one kilogram of paper, 10 grams of powder or the equivalent in tablets is placed in an airtight container. Bound books are stood up and the leaves fanned out; de-acidification takes about six weeks. If a few sheets of CHC paper are placed between the pages of a book on a shelf, de-acidification takes a few days. The CHC paper is moved through the book gradually until all the pages have been treated; only a few are interleaved at one time as the binding could be strained by additional bulk. Once used, the sheets are discarded. Paper to be washed and resized can be de-acidified by immersion in a bath of chloramine-T for ten minutes (see p. 56).

CLOTH

Mull is an open-weave cotton material stiffened with size. Its quality is indicated by its price, and only the best should be used for craft binding. Alone, it is weak but it reinforces any material to which it is attached by an adhesive. It is used extensively for strengthening the spines of books (first lining), hinging of cheap books and reinforcing maps and documents.

Jaconette, or *Holland cloth*, a closely woven material, is made from bleached or unbleached cotton or linen stiffened with starch. It is used for linings and hinges of books, reinforcing boxes and strengthening the folds of sections, maps and documents.

Bookcloth is the general name given to a range of closely woven cotton fabrics having a pigment filler or tissue lining to prevent the penetration of glue. Some old cloths were embossed with artificial grains and patterns but coloured, natural-surfaced cloths are favoured today and make attractive covers for small and cheaper books. Cloths not prepared for bookbinding and those that scuff and fray should be avoided. All woven cloth used in bookbinding has warp and weft threads and material should be cut so that the warp, or grain direction, will lie from head to tail of the book.

Buckram and similar linen or cotton materials are closely woven and have a pigment filler or tissue lining to prevent the adhesive penetrating to the surface. There is a wide range of qualities and colours and all have a pleasant appearance and 'feel'. Some are glazed to resist finger marks and all are strong and durable. The finest quality is 'law buckram', which is stiff and difficult to work. Most buckrams are softened first by pasting and are glued immediately, or alternatively synthetic glue may be applied. Buckram is used for all good-quality work as covers for large case bindings, covers and sides for the library style, reinforcement for endpapers, boxes and portfolios.

Leather cloth (Rexine) is manufactured by combining cellulose nitrate with camphor oil and alcohol and rolling it on to a woven linen or hemp base. Water- and stain-resistant, very strong, and grained to simulate leather, it sticks well with a synthetic adhesive. It is little used in fine binding, but cannot be entirely dismissed as it is very practical for cookery books, cheap account books, children's books, diaries, albums, boxes and portfolios.

Plastic or plastic-surfaced paper or cloth is manufactured in many colours and is often textured to simulate leather. It is water- and stain-resistant but feels greasy, and some grades can only be applied with a synthetic adhesive or hot welding. It is not used for good binding but is suitable for children's books and school books, and is common in stationery work – for example, loose-leaf covers and pocket diaries.

Paper fabric is a strong paper of chemical wood sized with resin, durable to a certain degree but not resistant to moisture, grease or fingering. It is obtainable in many colours and embossed with a cloth or leather texture. It is not used for good binding but has value as an inexpensive covering material for exercises in simple bookbinding.

LEATHERS

Morocco, the general name given to all goatskins, has superseded calf as the contemporary leather for binding. Ranging in thickness from 0·6 to 1 mm, they are vegetable-tanned by sumach or oak and usually produced with a natural grain but some are grained artificially so that the surface has an even texture. This hardens them, so they do not soften readily when pasted and often present difficulty when covering. Leathers with a cellulose dressing should be avoided as the surface is resistant to moisture, and difficulty is experienced when tooling with gold leaf, though foil presents little trouble.

There is a variety of natural colours, and aniline dyes are also used, but some of these are fugitive to light. Native tanned and dyed leathers from Nigeria have attractive uneven colours and grains, and are sought by fine binders. Levant moroccos, the prepared skins of mountain goats, range in size from 9 to 12 square feet compared to the 4 to 8 square feet of the skins of the domestic herded animals. Levants are beautiful leathers with a pronounced grain; they are very thick and should be used only on large books as paring reduces their strength.

Skins are sold at so much per square foot and the size is marked on the back. For example, a large 5 and a small 1 is five and a quarter square feet. Skins are graded first, second or third according to faults such as scars, tears and dyemarks, but all grades are equally durable and the same quality of leather. Naturally the fine binder prefers an unmarked skin and will take a cover from the best part: thus the figure (backbone) is used to advantage to show the beauty of the skin, and is placed to appear one-third of the distance either across or down the front cover.

All leathers for bookbinding are stamped or labelled with the Printing Industry Research Association's mark (PIRA), which indicates that the leather has been prepared without the use of injurious acids. The PIRA test consists of moistening the leather with sulphuric acid and adding hydrogen peroxide over a short period. In this accelerated decay test, poor-quality leather will blacken and shrivel but durable leather will survive. It is unwise to use any leather not prepared for bookbinding: its durability will be doubtful and difficulty will be experienced in paring, covering and tooling.

Calfskin is a vegetable-tanned, acid-free leather much used in previous centuries and extensively today in restoration work. There is a variety of colours but warm brown is the most popular and the natural skin can be easily dyed to all shades to match old leathers. The smooth, slightly porous surface has a delightful 'feel' and intricate gold and blind tooling has a beautiful effect. It is not so strong and durable as morocco but is used for fine bindings and presentation work. The surface contrasts well with grained moroccos in onlay and inlay work. It must be handled carefully, particularly during paring and covering, as the surface bruises and darkens easily.

Hide is a name for calfskins prepared from more mature animals and soft-tanned for bookbinding. Its strength is reduced by paring, which should be minimal, and the leather should only be used on large books. Hide will take stain evenly and is worked in the same way as calf. Blind tooling is exquisite on this leather.

Seal is a delightful soft leather with a beautiful grain; it has a smooth, oily feel and is very durable. Very little is used today as it is difficult to obtain.

Sheepskin: these vegetable-tanned skins are prepared in a number of colours but the surface is dull and porous and the texture loose, making them difficult to pare and tool in gold. Modern sheep leathers are less durable, have limited use and are not recommended. They are often split, when they are called skivers; these are sometimes embossed to imitate better leathers. Better qualities are used in the restoration of old bindings, and a grade known as 'Basil' for cheap account books.

Pigskin. This is a magnificent and durable leather available in various colours, of which a warm brown is the most common. Alum-dressed or 'tawed' skins are snow-white and these have been used throughout the centuries. Blind tooling creates a beautiful effect and the surface hardens with age, giving it a vellum-like appearance.

Vellum: skins of calf and goat are soaked in lime baths for a week and the hair is removed. After several weeks in lime they are stretched on wooden frames and scraped to the required thickness. This superb material appears to be unaffected by time. It is difficult to handle and reacts greatly to changes in humidity, which may make the vellum cockle and the boards warp unless controlled by the construction. Goat vellum is used for covering large books and calf for smaller bindings and for printed or manuscript pages. Colours are limited but 'natural' ranges from white to deep cream. Skins are translucent and are lined with handmade paper before covering. Transparent skins have great possibilities for design. Vellum bindings are beautiful and the results worth the time and effort.

Parchment made from split sheepskins is prepared in a similar way to vellum. It is not so durable nor so beautiful; it has a greasy surface and scuffing results in a grey appearance.

THREAD, TAPE AND CORD

Linen thread is made of flax fibre, spun, waxed and, for maximum strength, unbleached. Strands are combined to make different thicknesses for the hand sewing of books. Unbleached flax fibres are woven into different widths and stiffened with size to make *linen tape*, which is very durable and used for strengthening and hinging the sections.

Cotton tape is bleached cotton woven in different widths and is not recommended except for temporary case bindings.

Webbing, unbleached linen and hemp fibre woven in various widths and stiffened with size, can only be used for large books and account-book work.

Hemp fibres are spun and combined to make various thicknesses of *cord*. It is used for sewing on sections in the sunk cord and flexible styles. Hemp cord is reasonably durable but jute cord is not recommended as it soon deteriorates.

ADHESIVES

Throughout the forwarding of a book, the choice of the right adhesive for each specific operation or material is important.

Many factors are involved: durability, water content, pH value, action and effect on materials, powers of penetration and adhesive properties. There seems to be no universal adhesive that will satisfy all binding operations although some of the water-based vegetable adhesives can be used as glue or thinned down to act as paste. Organic adhesives produce a substantially permanent union between mutually attracted surfaces but are not water-resistant and they are affected by humidity changes, bacteria, fungi and insects. Paste of root and cereal origin is a stronger adhesive, and is obtained by bursting, with heat and moisture or chemical action, the insoluble film round the water-soluble starch grain. High water content gives paste more penetrating powers. It is clean, flexible and colourless and will dry out without trace. Its adhesion is slow but a longer working time is an asset when, for example, covering in leather. Paper will stretch more when pasted and this is used to advantage in counteracting the warp of boards.

Recipe for paste
   3½ oz. (100 g) plain flour
   1 level teaspoonful alum
   ⅞ pint (½ litre) cold water
   2 drops formaldehyde

Blend the flour, alum and a little water in a double saucepan until smooth, then gradually add the rest of the water. Heat, stirring constantly until the mixture thickens. Remove from the heat, place a piece of polythene over the paste to prevent a skin forming, and allow to cool. Stir in the formaldehyde, which acts as a preservative. The cold paste may be thinned by adding water.

Paste can be obtained in powder form; this is added to cold water gradually, stirring until it is thick. If it is put on one side for a few minutes, it will thicken more, and a little water can be added to facilitate brushing. This paste must be used within twenty-four hours as it reverts and becomes ineffective. Some manufactured pastes are ready mixed and have additives to keep them constant but the pH value of these should be checked.

Organic gelatin (Scotch) glues are prepared from boiled bones, hooves and horns of animals, the grease being removed by solvents. It is manufactured in various forms, of which the most convenient is 'pearl' glue; the granules will dissolve quickly in water in a heated glue pot. 'Flexible' glue, obtained by adding glycerin to prevent hardening, is available in cake form. It is used for gluing the spine of a book, where movement is necessary. Glue should always be clean, and made up frequently as it deteriorates when boiled for a long time. It is used thin; the consistency is ascertained by lifting a loaded brush, when the glue, a rich honey colour, should run off freely.

The introduction of cold glue of starch origin, mainly cassava, has been accepted grudgingly by the trade but with delight by the amateur. It has a number of advantages. It is always ready under adverse working conditions, it does not congeal, nor deteriorate, and the quality is consistent. It mixes readily with water, brushes on smoothly, does not revert nor ruin glue brushes.

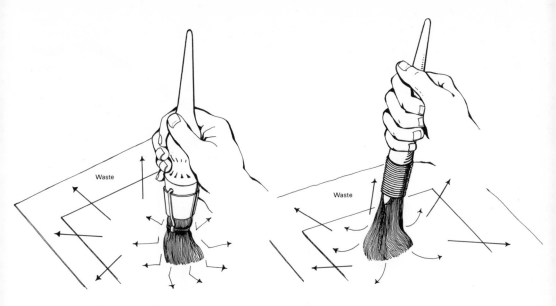

During the last forty years there has been a vast increase in the use of synthetic adhesives, particularly in the polyvinyl acetate (PVA) range for mass-produced work. Thermoplastic or thermo-setting glues are used in machines but the cold-setting glues are more practical for the hand binder. The suspensions of minute particles of solid matter can be diluted with water; on evaporation the particles come together and set and once dry they cannot be divided except by strong solvents. The binder should avoid the use of such adhesives in the binding of fine, old and valuable books and in restoration work because of the difficulty of repair work in the future. It is an ideal adhesive to stick hard buckram when boxmaking. Whereas organic glues tend to be hard, and their setting time is limited by room humidity, the synthetics are highly flexible and their setting time is governed chiefly by the porosity of the material.

15 Applying glue (*left*)

16 Applying paste (*above*)

Application

The beginner may experience some difficulty in applying adhesive. Glue should be applied with short stabbing movements, the brush – which has stubby hairs bound with wire – held almost vertical. Normally, very little glue is required as long as it is evenly distributed. The brush is agitated in the glue, between the palms of the hands, mixing and aerating the glue thoroughly to give a longer working time. After each dip, wipe the brush on the cross bar of the pot to remove excess glue from the outside of the brush, and apply from the middle of the sheet outwards. It is a mistake to use small brushes as larger ones will distribute the glue more evenly. Paste brushes have long, flexible hairs and are used with sweeping strokes from the middle of the sheet outwards. Glue and paste brushes should be washed out thoroughly as soon as the work is completed, and left lying across the pot; this applies particularly to brushes dipped in PVA as they are irrecoverable if allowed to dry hard.

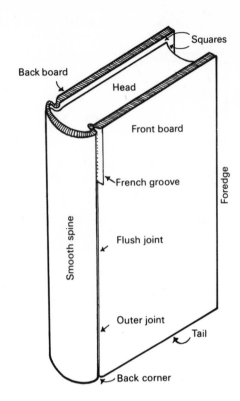

Squares

Back board

Head

Front board

French groove

Foredge

Smooth spine

Flush joint

Outer joint

Tail

Back corner

17 The parts of a book *1*

18 The parts of a book *2*

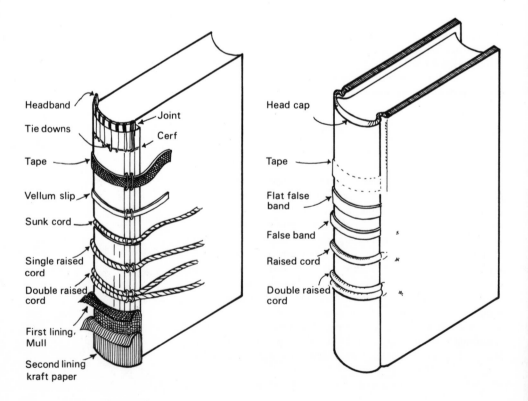

Headband

Joint

Tie downs

Cerf

Tape

Vellum slip

Sunk cord

Single raised cord

Double raised cord

First lining, Mull

Second lining kraft paper

Head cap

Tape

Flat false band

False band

Raised cord

Double raised cord

4 Introduction to a book

Bookbinding terms are simple and the descriptions of operations are in the words of the ordinary men who were the binding craftsmen. The word 'foredge' originates from early books bound in the flexible style where books became concave on opening. For this reason they were titled by painting, writing or burning on the white outside edge which faced outward on the bookstand. The first and last few pages of a book are the endpapers, detailed explanation of which is given on p. 57. At their simplest they consist of a board paper and a fly leaf. Generally the text pages that follow are a blank sheet, a half title, frontispiece, full title, publishers' information, dedication, preface, contents, list of illustrations, author's note and any other information concerning the text. These pages are usually numbered by Roman numerals and called the 'preliminary matter' ('prelims').

Chapter one, page 1, begins on a right or recto page and is often the second section of the book, and signatured B. These signatures occur at the bottom of the first page of each section and assist in the collation of the book. The number of pages in each section is

19 The parts of a book 3

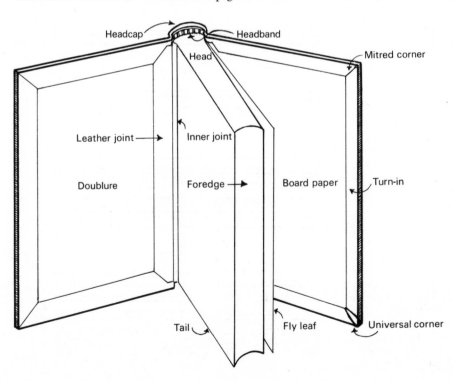

identified by counting the leaves between the signatures. Though the practice varies from printing house to printing house, letters such as J, Q and V are omitted to avoid confusion with I, O and U. Very old books were not signatured and often the first word of the next page was printed at the bottom of the preceding one.

Most sections have sixteen pages, but eight and twelve are fairly common. Cheap productions or books, such as bibles or dictionaries printed on thin paper, can have thirty-two-page sections. Plates, maps and throw-out sheets must be recognized as separate from the printed sections and are not included in the count of leaves to a section, but illustrations printed on the same paper and within the text are part of the section. Single plates are generally printed on art paper for finer reproduction and are tipped into the section wherever the reference occurs. Four-page illustrations are folded round or within a section and are sewn in. Disadvantageously, they are not always near to the text reference. Groups or whole sections of illustrations can be placed throughout the book and provided that they are distributed evenly there is no problem with forwarding. The practice of printing the text as the first part of the book with all the illustrations together at the back makes forwarding difficult. The difference in paper quality and section thickness requires a careful selection of sewing thread so that the resulting swell is evenly distributed throughout the spine. Plates on mounts or multi-folded maps have compensating guards sewn in as a section to make up the extra thickness and the mounts themselves may be hook-guarded with linen or strong paper (see Fig. 27, p. 51).

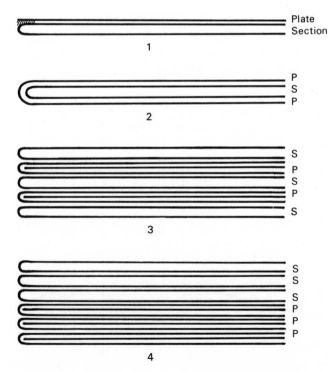

20 Four possible distributions of the illustrations: *1* single plate tipped in; *2* four pages folded round a section of text; *3* sections of plates alternating with sections of text; *4* plates grouped together after the text.

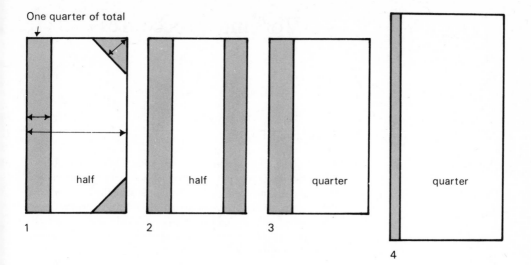

One quarter of total

half   half   quarter   quarter

1   2   3

4

The terms, 'quarter', 'half' and 'whole' bindings refer to covering methods and not constructional styles. A whole or full binding is a book covered entirely in one material, vellum, leather, cloth, paper, silk, velvet, rexine or plastic. A half binding is economical; for the spine and corners, where functional wear occurs, a strong material is used and a cheaper material covers the rest. Another form of half binding has the entire foredge covered by a strip and this may be considered preferable to corners as it is more attractive, functional and lends itself to simple decoration. There is also a trade description of a three-quarter binding, where the leather is extended well on to the board and the corners are huge. The effect is disproportionate and clumsy and may be a method used to make extra charges for very little extra work. A quarter binding is an economic form of covering and on long, upright-format books looks aesthetically pleasing, particularly if the spine material is narrow. A little before 1850, and for some decades later, a popular form was a quarter binding with corners almost invisibly protected with vellum tips. The siding paper or cloth was brought almost up to the corner with the vellum peeping out; these corners were sound and could withstand heavy wear. The first and last sections are the first to break down in a much used book and these are strengthened by overcasting round the fold or through the side in addition to the usual sewing.

21 Half bindings (*1*, *2*) and quarter bindings (*3*, *4*)

22 Overcasting

5 Working procedures

All details of construction and design must be considered before the binding is started; it is useful to make out a written description to outline the intended work. This should state the binding style, the covering style, the construction of endpapers, treatment of edges, edge gilding, number of tapes or cords, sewing method, headbands, leather, board and any relevant points of construction extra to the usual operations. Many factors are involved, based on the text paper, and the value and subsequent use of the binding.

In theory the style of binding is determined by the quality of the production. A cheap book and poor paper should be bound economically, although even a poorly produced book can be protected and preserved by sound binding. The question often arises whether a particular book should be bound at all. For instance, first editions of certain books are more valuable in their original covers, even if dilapidated, and should be preserved in boxes. The covering style and decoration should be consistent with the age of the book, although matching materials to past fashions makes this difficult. The alternatives are binding soundly for posterity or copying a dubiously constructed book; it is preferable to have a durable binding using contemporary methods and materials.

Casual books and textbooks can be bound economically with a degree of strength as case bindings, but similar books, that must withstand constant and heavy use, should be bound in the library style. Books of character and those to be preserved as fine bindings can be bound in the sunk cord style and protected in boxes. Raised cord, or the genuine flexible style, is best suited to books of antiquity or presentation volumes but the deciding factor is the quality of the paper. Weak machine-made paper will not stand up to the strain of this type of sewing and is better sewn on sunk cords or tapes. The edges of antiquarian books of worth should not under any circumstances be cut as cropped edges spoil the appearance of the printed page and reduce the value of the book. Sections folded from the sheets are cut at the head to free the bolts, and the foredge and tail can be left uncut. Bolts occurring at the foredge can be trimmed with a knife.

Reference and text books should have cut edges for ease in turning the leaves, and preferably should be bound in the library style. Uncut edges can be dust traps and a valuable book may have a minimal amount cut off its edges so that they can be gilded for protection. Edges may be coloured, sprinkled, marbled, gauffered or the foredge painted with a picture and protected from dirt, dust and moisture by a surface of burnished beeswax. Strawboard is used for economical bindings and millboard for boxes and books of value. In craft work an extra tape or cord is included as it makes little difference to the time taken for sewing but could add years of life to the binding. Best-quality materials should be used.

PREPARATION OF THE BOOK FOR BINDING

Before binding or rebinding a book, the work must be planned, as already outlined. To avoid errors that might be costly the book must be collated, i.e. checked for completeness, before the old binding is removed. A note is made of maps and missing or torn pages and, if there are enough of them, fox marks, ink, grease and dirt stains are noted for treatment later.

'Pulling' – separating the sections from the original binding – should be done with the least possible damage to the folds of the sections. A publisher's edition binding (a case binding) is cut parallel to and about 30 mm (just over an inch) from the spine so that the endpaper, mull or tapes can be eased off the board. Tear off the single fly leaf and, pulling at the cut flange, ease the back linings off the fold of the first section. If the glue and linings are brittle the pulling presents no difficulty. Count the leaves until the stitching appears, cut these threads and count the same number of leaves to the end of the section. Any illustrations, such as the frontispiece, printed on different paper from the text are not included. The first section, which is the preliminary matter, may not follow the regular imposition. Hold the book firmly with one hand and ease off the first section with a straight pull. Break away the nubs of glue and linings from the second section to free it. The first page of the second section is usually signatured B. Count the leaves to the stitching, cut the thread and count to the end of the section; this should determine the number of pages in each section arranged by the imposition.

Continue to pull the book (this is known as 'dry pulling'). If the spine is lined up well and the glue tenacious, as is expected in a

23 Pulling a case binding

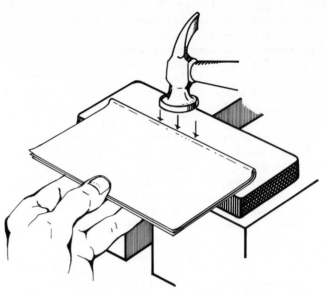

24 Knocking out the old groove

well-bound book, cut away both boards down the joint and remove all loose linings. Place the book between two pieces of strawboard in a finishing press and smear a heavy layer of paste on to the spine. Leave it for ten minutes; the old linings will have been softened by the paste and can be scraped off with the back of a knife. This can be repeated until the back is clean. In this damp state the folds of the sections are weak, and pulling must not be attempted until they are dry; this is known as 'wet pulling'.

As each section is removed, pick off the bits of hard glue from the outside fold and pieces of thread from the inside and lay the sections down in strict order. The outside sections will have the crease from the original backing in their folds; this is known as the 'old groove' and must be removed before repairing and pressing. The knocking-down iron is held in the press and the fold is tapped fairly hard along its length with the backing hammer. Fragile and glossy art papers should be protected by a fold of white waste paper. One, two or three sections can be done at one time, depending on the type of paper. It is easier and safer to tap the hammer in the centre of the knocking-down iron and to move the section.

For the general run of work, sections whose back folds are torn or separated can be repaired or guarded with bond paper. Check the grain direction and cut a strip 9 mm ($\frac{3}{8}$ in.) wide and a little longer than the page. Leaving the end dry, paste it until it lies flat. Pick it up by the dry end and place it on to a piece of thin, strong waste. Line the head of the complete section up to the end so that it covers half the width of the pasted guard. Fold the waste over tightly against the fold of the section so that the bond is turned over on top of the section. Rub it down and trim off any excess at the tail.

Fine work and rare old books need careful and hidden repair. Toned thick Japanese paper is best, as it will blend with old paper. Separate the double pages and place them flat with the outside of the sheets uppermost. Tear the Japanese paper in the grain direction, against the edge of a ruler, just enough to cover the damage.

Paste the guard, lay it on the fold carefully and rub down with a folder. The fibres from the torn edge of the guard marry in well with the paper. Make as few repairs as possible; to reduce swell, tap with a light hammer. When repairing the outsides of sections whose leaves are separated, compensate for the thickness of the remainder of the section or the outside ones will be narrower. Single-plate illustrations, that in the original binding were merely tipped on, should be removed and hook-guarded around or into the section so that they will open more freely. Folded maps and diagrams should be lined up with the head and foredge when folded, and thrown out to the right with as few folds as possible. Allowance is made for cutting the edges. The hinge is linen and compensating guards equal to the thickness of the folded sheets are sewn in. It is preferable to make a separate section of the folds as a bulky text section will affect the balance and shape of the spine. Plates on heavy mounts have a compensating guard sewn into the section to make up the thickness in the spine. The mounts are hook-guarded with linen or strong paper round the compensating guard or the section.

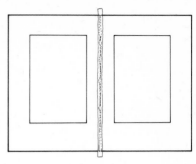

25 Repair with Japanese paper

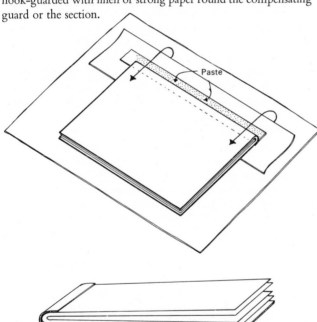

26 Repair of damaged back folds

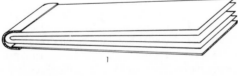

27 Plates and maps: guarding in

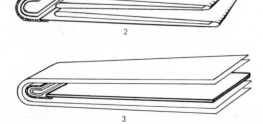

28 Gusseted wallet for loose
plates

Gusseted wallets or pockets containing loose plates are placed at the end of the book and are compensated by wide guards sewn in as for thrown out maps. An alternative is to attach a pocket to the inside of the back board and sew in a compensating section of guards of equal thickness. These guards can be glued solid after rounding and backing. Waste paper takes the place of the missing area to make forwarding simpler; they are cut smaller on completion of the binding. If pages are missing and there is the possibility that these may be obtained later, full-size plain paper guards can be inset; these can be cut away later and the replacement leaves tipped to them. Missing pages may be replaced by photocopies but these should be used only for books of little worth; they are a poor substitute in old and valuable books.

Torn, weak and missing parts of leaves are strengthened and replaced to prevent further damage. A torn leaf is repaired by marrying the overlapping edges and print together with a needle, and pasting the two edges of the tear for 3 mm on either side. Tear thin Japanese tissue of the same grain direction, larger than the tear, and press it on to the pasted area. Rub it down with a folder and repeat the tissue on the other side. Interleave with wax paper and leave it to dry. Later, rub away excess tissue and smooth down.

If there is a risk of paste discolouring or distorting the paper, small tears in leaves can be repaired by a dry method using heat-set tissue. The tissue is prepared as follows. Japanese tissue is laid on a sheet of glass and a strip of 500 gsm strawboard placed under one edge of the tissue to facilitate handling. Brush over the tissue with PVA adhesive (without ammonia), mixed with an equal part of distilled water. When the solution is dry, the tissue will be stuck to the glass. Prepare a solution of methoxymethol nylon by dissolving 2 grams of Calaton C.B. in 100 ml of ethanol at 60°C (140°F). A double saucepan over flameless heat must be used as the mixture is highly inflammable. The hot solution is brushed over the tissue, which within a few seconds will loosen and can be peeled away. (Calaton dissolves the PVA so the tissue can be removed from the glass.) Store the tissue between silicone release paper. The Calaton will gell when cold but it can be reheated and used again. Tear a piece of tissue, larger than the tear on the sheet, and lay it with the shiny side down. Apply a hot polishing iron through a sheet of silicon release paper to fix the repair.

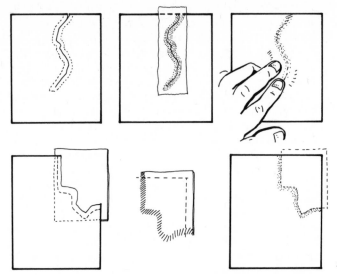

29 Repair of torn pages

Alternatively, instead of Japanese tissue nylon gossamer fabric is used; this tissue is remarkably stronger than tissue and its preparation is simpler. The gossamer is felted, and when set is almost invisible. With a soft, flat, broad brush coat a sheet of glass, very thinly and evenly, with a solution of PVA mixed with an equal amount of distilled water. Lay on this a piece of gossamer and with a dry brush smooth it out very evenly. Peel it off immediately and lay it aside with the glued side uppermost. (Again, a strip of strawboard under one edge will make it easier to remove.) Brush the glass once more with the solution and relay the gossamer on its glued side. This second application is only necessary if too many air bubbles form. Smooth it out with the dry brush and allow it to dry, when it can be removed from the glass. Wash the brushes and glass thoroughly in water. A tear in a leaf is repaired by cutting the heat-set tissue larger by 2 mm all round. It is placed on the tear, shiny side down, with silicon release paper on top. A hot polishing iron is rubbed over to effect the repair, and the process is repeated on the other side.

To replace a missing portion, find a piece of paper of the same weight, colour, texture, grain and if possible age, and position it under the missing part. Mark the profile and tear it 3 mm larger. Pare the edge about 2 mm with a scalpel and, pasting both edges, lay the replacement in position and firm it down. As far as possible the text should not be covered, but some loss is inevitable. A missing portion can be inserted by tearing the replacement paper to the exact shape, positioning it and joining with Japanese tissue on both sides. Old endpapers, odd fly leaves and blank paper taken from books should be dated and carefully stored for repairs. A weak or broken leaf can be sandwiched between sheets of fine Japanese tissue or very thin silk fabric. A piece of smooth terylene fabric is pasted flat on to a piece of glass or Formica. The weak leaf is placed on this and pasted, a sheet of Japanese tissue or silk is laid on and pasted down to remove air bubbles and creases. Peel the repair off immediately, turn it over and paste it; line the other side with the material and brush smooth. When dry the leaf is peeled away from the terylene backing; the terylene prevents it from cockling while drying. Mutilated leaves are mounted on matching paper or chemically pure archivist's repair paper with the aid of a light table. The grain of the original (if any) and the repair paper is ascertained. Paste a piece of terylene on to glass so that it is free from air bubbles and place this on the light table. Paste the surface of the terylene, lay on the original and paste it down. Cut the repair paper larger, dampen one side, paste the other and lay the pasted side down on to the original, brushing it flat with a paste brush or sponge. The light from the table will show the outline of the original. With the point of a needle trace a line 2 mm within the outline. The needle will scratch and separate the wet fibres of the repair paper and the parts not required can be lifted and eased away without further damage to the original. The broken edge is gently boned down with a folder and the repair, including the terylene, is left on the glass to dry. Then it can be peeled off and cut to size.

Some of the type matter may be covered by the repair paper, but this is unavoidable. No attempt should be made to draw in letters or complete an illustration unless one is skilled in the work. Plates or pages smaller than the book may be window-mounted on to larger sheets and cut to size when completed. The original is placed on a matching sheet and the corners marked. A window is cut out 3 mm smaller all round and the edges of the frame pared with a scalpel to this measurement. The original is also pared on the back 3 mm all round and the bevels of both the original and the frame are pasted and one pitched on the other. Bone down the edges gently and allow to dry under a weight. Paste of the finest quality is used for these repairs, made thinner than usual so that the adhesion is perfect and there is no staining.

30 Repair of a mutilated leaf

31 Window-mounting a page
(*opposite*)

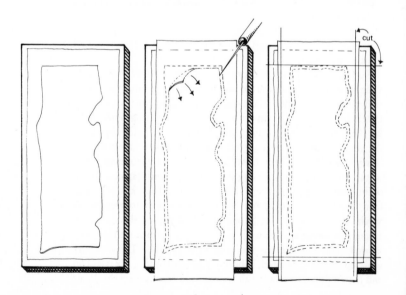

Dog-eared leaves are straightened by dabbing with a damp sponge.

Cleaning paper

Old books will need cleaning before binding; only those of some value are worth the time and energy expended on their renovation. If the paper is strong enough, surface grime is removed; care must be taken to avoid damage and the following methods are recommended. Try them in order, and as each is more abrasive than the preceding one resort to the next only when absolutely necessary. (1) Use a soft-haired brush to remove the dust. (2) Sprinkle granules of powdered rubber on the paper and rub gently with cotton wool. (3) Use, in that order, a soft rubber, a hard rubber and a cuttlefish bone. Lastly, with extreme care, try a flour-grade sandpaper.

Carbon tetrachloride can be used to remove grease and grease stains from paper and vellum. It has no effect on ink or water-colours, and evaporates without trace. A little is poured on to cotton wool and the sheet is wiped over with a little hand pressure on both sides. Too much of this solvent is harmful to the material. Great care must also be taken as it is highly toxic and inflammable; protect the nose with a handkerchief and, if possible, work in the open air.

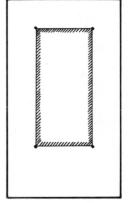

Painting on a 10 per cent solution of citric acid will remove some ink spots, but the paper must be washed for thirty minutes in running water after treatment, and then resized (see below).

A little mild washing-up liquid such as Lissapol, in a deep bath of lukewarm water, can be used for washing 'grubby' paper, but only when dry methods have proved unsuccessful. The water may be agitated, or the paper brushed under water with a soft-haired brush. The paper should then be washed again for thirty minutes in clean water, the surplus blotted off and the paper resized (see below).

Soiled or discoloured paper may also be given a bleaching treatment, but indiscriminate and excessive use of strong bleaching agents should be avoided as they will degrade the cellulose in paper, and fade ink, colour and illustrations. Old books, often subjected to this treatment, would be characterless if all stains were removed and the paper bleached dead white. Any work involving bleach must be done with caution, and none carried out on mechanical wood-pulp paper nor any paper too weak to withstand handling and the prolonged washing necessary. Before resorting to the use of bleach it would be best to soak the leaves in warm water for an hour to reduce water or water-soluble stains. This will dissolve the size in the paper and the leaves must be resized afterwards, as explained below.

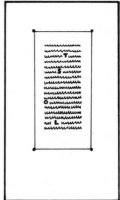

After bleaching, leaves may be whiter than the remainder of the book, but they can be toned to match by immersing them in a bath of dye, or by adding colour to the size bath. Tea, coffee, brown beer or gravy browning can be used; the last seems to give the best results. It is necessary to test the pH value of any of these materials before using them (see p. 37).

For the treatment of paper, boards, cloth and tanned leather against fungi and insects, a solution of 40 per cent formaldehyde in water will give off an effective vapour. Books should be placed in an airtight fumigating chamber with their leaves fanned out, and with the sheets separated, and exposed to the vapour for a week. Thymol is also a useful fungicide for paper. Sheets are immersed for ten minutes in a solution of 20 grams of thymol in 1 litre of industrial methylated spirit, and are washed and resized afterwards. Tests should be carried out on the print with the solution as thymol has a detrimental effect on some ink. A few crystals added to the paste will prevent mould.

Before the leaves are immersed in any liquid the solubility of the ink should be tested. Touch a letter or two with a fine brush dipped in the water or bleach solution and examine them with a magnifying glass after ten minutes for any reaction. If the ink shows signs of spreading it should be fixed with the nylon solution explained below.

Fox marks and stains may be removed by bleaching with one of three solutions, *and no others are recommended*: 1–5 grams per litre of sodium hypochlorite or calcium hypochlorite, or 5–20 grams per litre of Chloramine-T. The last is particularly recommended; it is a slow-working bleach. Badly stained leaves are immersed in a bath until the solution turns yellow, which is a sign that it is exhausted and a new bath must be prepared. It will be necessary to wash the leaves in running water for three hours to remove all traces of bleach. The paper is then resized.

Sizing

Gelatine size, extracted from boiled skins of animals, is available in leaf form or granules. It is used for tub sizing good-quality papers and also as a size bath to add strength to paper after washing and bleaching. A solution is made using 50 grams (1¾ oz) of gelatine size in 4 litres (7 pints) of warm water. After the paper has been washed the surplus water is removed with blotting paper and the sheets are immersed in the bath of warm size for 15 minutes. Excess size is blotted off and the sheets hung up or placed between wax paper under a weight to dry.

Another sizing agent is made by simmering 250 grams (8½ oz) of parchment or vellum pieces in 1½ litres (2½ pints) of water for 1½ hours. It is then strained through muslin and used at 40° C (104° F).

A size can be made of a soluble nylon powder, made into a 5 per cent solution with industrial methylated spirits. This is brushed on to sensitive watercolour paintings, hand-coloured prints and water-soluble inks to fix them before washing and bleaching. It can also be used as a size for weak, soft paper.

Pencil manuscripts and drawings can be fixed by brushing them with a solution of 15 grams of isinglass in 600 cc of distilled water (½ oz in a pint).

Pressing

After cleaning and repairing, the book is collated and is ready for pressing. No sections should be placed in the press until dry. Every book that has been taken apart must be placed under considerable pressure in the standing press for at least twelve hours for common work and a week for fine binding. A binding can only be constructed around a book reduced to its true thickness. Under pressure, air is excluded from between the leaves and a felting action takes place between the paper surfaces. When removed from the press the leaves should be a solid block. Casual work is knocked up at head and spine and placed between pressing boards while quality work is separated into groups of about five sections and placed between thick metal plates.

Work to be pressed is built up in the centre of the press in pyramid form with the spines arranged alternately front and back. The initial pressure is applied, and can be increased after a few hours. Endpapers may be pressed with the book provided that leather and linen joints do not mark the text sections under pressure, though it is better to make endpapers while the book is being pressed. Books with small plates mounted inside must be pressed with the minimum of pressure; alternatively, the illustrations should be framed with waste of equal thickness to prevent marks on adjoining leaves. Great care must be taken that heavy pressure does not damage raised gold or painted decoration in hand-written books, or illustration techniques and type impressions in printed books. As print in new books may offset under pressure, interleaving with tissue paper is recommended. It was necessary in early printing to dampen handmade paper, and the pressure of the forme caused the paper fibres to spread. When the sheets dried the printed area was distorted while the margins were unchanged. These depressions throughout the book are almost impossible to flatten even under considerable pressure.

ENDPAPERS

The endpapers must fulfil two purposes to be effective. The part of the endpaper known as the board paper should counteract or assist in counteracting the outward warp of the board caused by the covering material, and the fly leaves protect the opening and closing pages of the text. Their function is not purely decorative; they can be made not only to strengthen the construction but also to enhance the design of the binding. The method of making endpapers has varied throughout the history of bookbinding, early endpapers being simple and adding little to the strength of the binding. Trade houses and individual craftsmen have contributed their own styles but some have proved impracticable and now are little used.

The paper for endpapers should be of good quality but not necessarily handmade. The binder chooses to avoid the use of handmade paper because some are difficult to stick and the stretch, unlike that of machine-made paper, is in all directions. Generally mould-made paper, such as Ingres, machine-mades such as white cartridge or the antique-finish Abbey Mill is chosen. It is convenient to use few papers and to know their strength, suitability, grain direction and reaction to adhesives.

32 Cross-sections of fourteen endpapers, covering a wide range of work:

KEY

'coloured' paper   ▬▬▬▬

'white' paper   ▬▬▬▬

leather   ▬ ▬ ▬ ▬ ▬

cloth or linen   ▬ ▬ ▬ ▬

waste sheet, if separate from the white   · · · ·

position of sewing thread   ●

adhesive   ////////

waste sheet   **W**

fly leaves   **F**

board paper   **B**

'made' paper or stiff leaf   **M**

first section   **S**

The colour of the endpapers should tone harmoniously with the proposed colour of the edges, headbands and covering materials to make a pleasing whole. The 'coloured' paper or board paper may be an Ingres, or similar type of paper, that has been marbled. The 'whites' should be inferior in colour to the text paper of the book but not inferior in quality, as grey or cream paper will show poorly against dead-white fly leaves.

For endpapers, paste is the better adhesive as it is cleaner, flexible and makes a better bond. All endpapers are made over-size and trimmed later as it is difficult to join two papers together and line them up accurately. When possible it is better to paste the thicker paper to control stretching and to nip them in the press immediately after joining. Once consolidated, they should be placed between boards with a weight on top to dry flat. Endpapers should not be hung up on a line to dry unless they can be taken down at the right moment, i.e. before they begin to cockle. Grain direction must run from head to tail, and any deviation from this rule will cause complications in subsequent operations.

In the diagram, method *1*, the double fold of the handmade paper adds strength to the hinge and the sewing thread is protected under the board paper. It is tipped on the first section for 3–6 mm as well as sewn. Method *2* is not elegant but it is reasonably strong as it is sewn in with the section and reinforced with mull.

The cheapest and weakest, *3*, is not sewn but tipped on the section for 3 mm ($\frac{1}{8}$ in.). All publishers' edition bindings have this endpaper. Method *4* has a jaconette strip 18 mm ($\frac{3}{4}$ in.) wide pasted on to the board paper and guarded round the first section for 3 mm ($\frac{1}{8}$ in.). It is tipped on to the first section after the book is sewn. Method *5* is stiff-leaved on to the first leaf of the section. The waste is later cut down to 25 mm (1 in.) and put down on to the board under the board paper. For a heavier book it is advantageous to use jaconette instead of white waste. In *6* the waste is torn away, the linen is stuck to the board to cover the joint and strengthen the hinge, and the board paper is a separate single sheet put down as a doublure.

1 A strong endpaper: a style with a long past

2 Two sheets folded round a single-section book

3 Four-page, single-fold, tipped-on endpaper

4 A stronger version of *3*

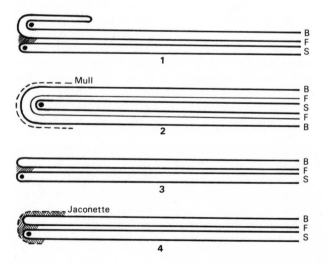

The 'made' endpaper, *7*, is very satisfactory for most work; it is sewn on as a section and tipped on to the first section for 3 mm (⅛ in.). The stiff leaf and two fly leaves give protection to the text opening pages. It is interesting that this endpaper resulted from the use of a type of marbled paper prevalent throughout the nineteenth century. This paper was thin and weak, with the marks of the marbling on the back, so the paper was 'made' on to a white to strengthen it and cover the stains. With coloured paper the habit persists today though it is no longer needed. Care must be taken when sewing to place the needle just under the fold of the outside sheet, to avoid piercing the board paper. Where coloured paper is used to provide an extra fly leaf (*8*), the stiff leaf is not always necessary and is clumsy on a small book.

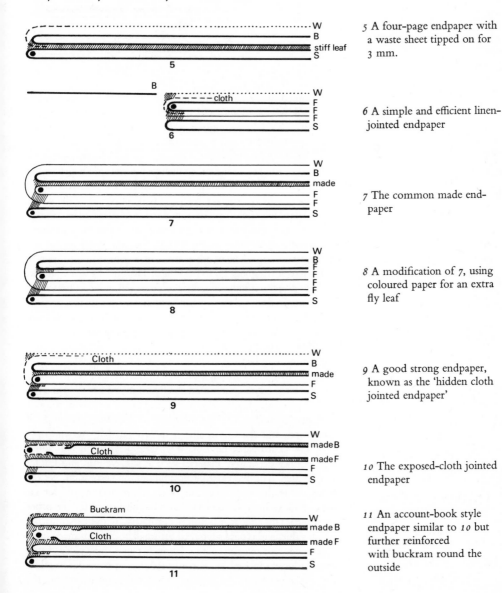

5 A four-page endpaper with a waste sheet tipped on for 3 mm.

6 A simple and efficient linen-jointed endpaper

7 The common made end-paper

8 A modification of *7*, using coloured paper for an extra fly leaf

9 A good strong endpaper, known as the 'hidden cloth jointed endpaper'

10 The exposed-cloth jointed endpaper

11 An account-book style endpaper similar to *10* but further reinforced with buckram round the outside

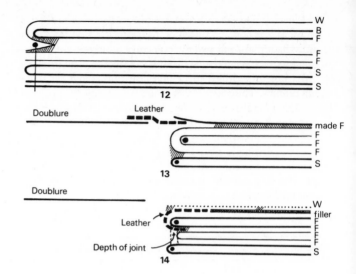

12 An endpaper for use with single sheets or folded sections

13 Leather-jointed endpaper

14 A successful and constructional leather-jointed endpaper, attributed to Bernard Middleton, which can be adapted for leather, vellum, paper or silk doublures

Designed for better-quality library-style work, *9* is effective for any book where strength and appearance are important, and ideal for music binding as it gives additional strength to the hinge. Average width of cloth is 50 mm (2 in.); jaconette is used for small books and book cloth for larger. The cloth joint is not stuck to the board paper, as it may be included in the split board or put down on the board before the board paper. If it is attached, and both are put down together, the paste will not penetrate the whole of the board paper, and crinkles could result. Method *10* is inelegant but extremely efficient in strengthening the join of the sections to the board. Book cloth is the strengthener for small books and buckram for large. The width of the cloth averages 32 mm (1¼ in.), with two-thirds going on to the board. The board paper is 'made' and put down without difficulty if glue is used. It is recommended for all books that will receive hard and indiscriminate use, particularly the library style where strength is paramount and appearance secondary. Method *11* is designed for extreme hard wear and durability. The inner strengthener may be of leather. This endpaper is only to be used on very large and heavy books.

Sewn completely through the side of the book or only the first and last two sections, *12* is used chiefly on guard books. The concertina gives play for the first fly leaf and hides the row of stitches.

A fine binding usually has a leather border round the inside of the boards and the fourth side is incorporated in the endpaper (*13*). The board paper put on as a separate sheet is called a 'doublure'. Other decorative material such as silk, vellum and leather can be used. This has exciting possibilities for decoration, yet the beauty of leather is more pleasing than decoration in gold for the sake of adornment. Leather may also be substituted for the paper fly leaves. This endpaper is purely decorative, with little constructional value, and is only suggested for small books. It is made up as illustrated with an open split in the made paper and a piece of thin manilla loosely placed inside the board during covering to allow for the thickness of the leather. When the book is covered the manilla is removed and a finely pared leather strip is pasted into the split and modelled in the joint and on to the boards. The split is pasted and closed down.

For the leather-jointed endpaper in *14*, make an approximate template of the covering leather needed and position this on the skin. When the main piece has been decided, cut the leather joints out as near to the centre of the skin as possible so that the strips are not distorted too much by paring. The width of each leather joint is equal to the turn-in of 18 mm (0·7 in.) over the boards, plus the depth of the joint and 6 mm (¼ in.) for attaching to the coloured fly, and its length is the same as that of the endpapers. Cut out both joints as one piece and pare this thinly. Cut in half, if distorted trim evenly and run the paring knife along one edge to take away the thickness. The surface of the leather is pasted to the coloured fly and the white fold is tipped on just short of the back fold by the depth of the joint. This hides the edge of the leather and allows more freedom for the white fly leaves. The white waste is tipped on at the extreme edge of the folded leather and a compensating piece of pulp card equal to the thickness of the leather is touched with glue on to the waste. This endpaper is tipped on to the first section after the book is sewn. After rounding and backing it is sewn on through the joint. (For further details, see p. 137.)

SEWING

A book is not held together by thread alone: the strain is relieved by backing, linings, board positions and, in some degree, its covering. Sewing is, however, very important in the construction of a book, not only for the successful accomplishment of subsequent operations, but also for its durability. The thickness of thread is selected so that the resulting swell in the spine is taken up by the rounding and backing, giving the spine the shape of one-third of a circle.

Whim and fashion have altered spine shapes over the years: a flattish spine with weak shoulders was prevalent about 1900, but sixty years earlier the back had heavy shoulders with the remainder of the sections in a gentle curve. Both are poor constructionally. The former quickly collapses as only the first and last two or three sections are supported by the board. The earlier spines were lined heavily to take the lavish gold tooling, causing strain on the back linings when the book was opened, and a restriction at the shoulders. The present-day shape cannot be bettered, as each section to the left and right of the centre one is modelled against the next until the last is supported by the board.

Swell

Many factors must be taken into account to obtain the correct swell: the type and quality of the paper, the number of sections and of leaves to the section, the style of binding and the number of repaired folds. If the paper is soft, for example machine-made antique, the thread will sink into the paper and there will be little

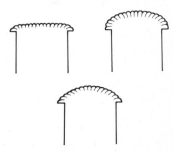

33 Spine and shoulder shape

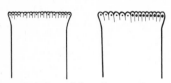

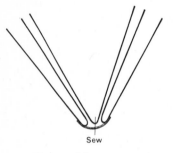

34 Relation of thread to swell

35 Groups of four-page sections guarded and sewn

swell unless a thicker thread is used. If the paper is hard, for example tub-sized ledger, handmade or art papers, the thread will give a fuller swell and so a thinner thread will be appropriate. Books made of soft text paper, with illustrations printed on coated paper grouped at the end, are sewn with two thicknesses of thread so that the swell of one half may equal that of the other. A book composed of a great number of thin sections with a limited number of leaves will, however, build up an uncontrollable swell whatever thickness of thread is used, and the swell is limited as follows. The first four or six sections are sewn 'all along', i.e. one length of thread for each section. This will ensure a good shoulder at the joint. But the middle part of the book is sewn 'two (or three) up', i.e. one length of thread used for every two (or three) sections. The last four or six sections are sewn 'all along' to retain the balance; include an extra tape or cord when sewing this way.

Similarly, to reduce swell, the first and last few sections can be sewn with a thick thread while the remainder is sewn 'all along' with a thinner thread. Sections of four pages only are guarded into groups of three and sewn through the middle fold.

Flat-backed bindings require no swell, while books that are rounded only require a swell in excess of normal to help retain the shape of the spine. For example, account books are sewn with thick thread for maximum strength and an exaggerated swell.

Sections in poor condition, that have been repaired on the backfold, will increase the swell of the spine by the number and thickness of the repair papers. The swell can be reduced, however, by repairing with strong, thin Japanese paper that can be beaten into the paper with a hammer, and by using a thinner thread. When sewing, judge how the swell builds up after five sections, and if it seems excessive change to a thinner thread or sew two up, but return to the original thread for the last five sections. Should there be no swell, resew the complete book with a thicker thread, to prevent the spine from collapsing after a short time. Slight excess swell is sometimes unavoidable but every three sections can be beaten with a loaded stick while sewing, to drive the thread into the paper and consolidate the sections. Swell is also reduced by using a knocking-down iron and hammer as in Fig. 136, p. 121, this applies only to books with too much swell. A book with too little swell may be rounded and backed easily but will collapse after removal from the lying press. It will become concave and the foredge will protrude beyond the protection of the squares.

Excess swell is much more difficult to control as the backing boards will not stay in position, backing will result in a deep joint and the spine will have a humped shape. Inside margins will be lost and the book will be difficult to open (see 'Rounding and Backing', p. 75). Sections sewn too tightly impose a strain on the thread and the spine is likely to become concave and will be difficult to round. Sections sewn loosely or unevenly will move out of position when rounded, causing 'starts' at the foredge and depressions on the spine. The linings and covering leather will not stick satisfactorily and gold letters will not take on the sunken parts. As there is limited movement in the backed spine of thin books the swell should be very slight.

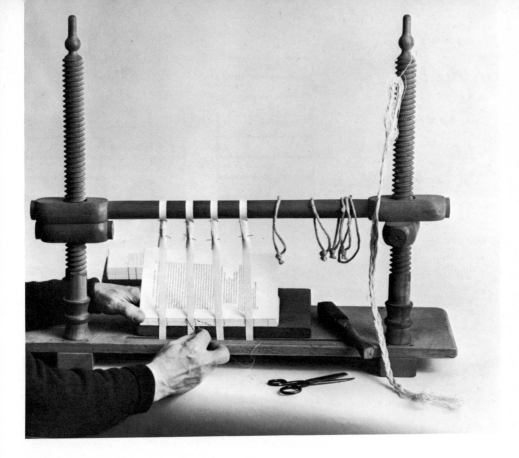

Tape sewing

All sewing should be done on a frame, apart from cheap, thin case bindings. The frame is arranged permanently for tape or cord sewing; loops of tape are pinned, and loops of cord tied round the crossbar. If only one book is to be sewn, lower the crossbar and estimate the length of the tape needed. The tape is wound round the sewing key and pushed into the slot in the frame. Pull the tape up tightly and pin it to the loops. Fix all tapes in position, lining them to the marked-up sections, and screw the crossbar up until the tapes are taut. See Fig. 98, p. 99.

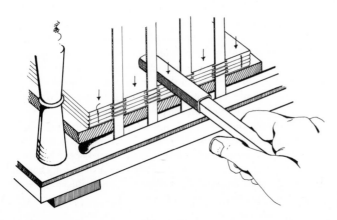

37 Consolidating sections with a loaded stick

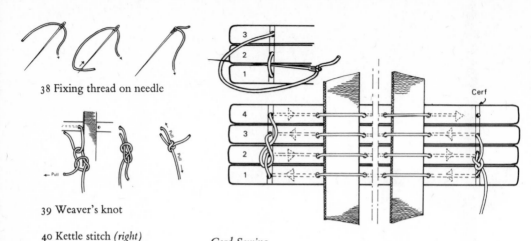

38 Fixing thread on needle

39 Weaver's knot

40 Kettle stitch *(right)*

Cord Sewing

When cord sewing, cut a length of cord and tie it to the loop. Measure it by pulling it tight against a sewing key held flat under the frame. Attach the cord to the key and slip it in the slot of the frame. Half-tighten the screws, check that the cord positions correspond with the marked-up sections, and stand a carpenter's square on the frame to ensure that the cords are vertical. Raise the crossbar until the cords are rigid.

The work is placed near to the binder so that the left hand is kept inside the sections and the right hand outside. A pressing board under the work will facilitate sewing. Be comfortable, sew calmly, and sew the whole book at one time. Develop a rhythm of sewing movements and the tension will be even. Do not jerk the thread but keep a steady pull to tighten the thread between sections.

Place the complete book on the frame with the head to the left and the front on top. Turn the book over and remove all but the last section: this is the back endpaper and should be sewn first. It should be marked up already with the tape or cord positions but the cerf is not sawn in. (The cerf is the channel cut into the backs of sections with a fine saw to accommodate the kettle stitch.) Fix the needle on the thread. When it is necessary to join threads together use a weaver's knot, made outside and pulled to the inside. The knot will not come undone and can be tied exactly where required. Different thicknesses of thread may be joined and a knot can even be made if one end is only 6 mm ($\frac{1}{4}$ in.) long. Push the needle through the cerf mark, take it with the left hand and push the needle out at the first tape mark, taking the needle with the right hand. Push it through on the other side of the tape and continue along until the needle comes out at the other cerf. Pull the thread steadily through in the direction of sewing, leaving 50 mm (2 in.) outside. Find the middle of the second section, turn it over, knock it up to the head and line it up on top of the endpaper. Push the needle into the cerf and sew all along until the end, where the thread is pulled through so that no slack lies between the sections. Tie the two ends together with a reef knot. Check the number or signature of the third section, turn it over, knock it up to the head, place it in position and sew to the end. On completion of the third section, the kettle stitch is made.

Except in overcasting, pamphlet sewing and account-book work the kettle stitch or knot, used to join one section to another, is formed in the cerf. (The term 'kettle' is a corruption of the German word *ketteln*, meaning 'to catch up a stitch'.) Bring the needle out of the cerf and take it under the section sewn previously on the inside of the linking thread, to emerge on the outside of the book. Hook the loop over the needle and pull the needle through to make a knot that sinks into the cerf. Just before the knot is formed, pull the thread tight through the sections. Sewing is continued, forming a kettle stitch after each section, until the last when two kettle stitches are formed. Cut the thread off, leaving 20 mm ($\frac{7}{8}$ in.) which is subsequently glued down.

Some useful stitches

The following are the commonest methods of sewing sections and sheets together.

In *single-section pamphlet sewing* small, thin books are sewn with three holes, larger books with five, seven, nine or eleven holes. The thread is pulled tightly and a reef knot is used to hold the middle thread down. Sewing may be started from the middle, the outside or the inside.

Side stitching is suitable for single sheets and work of little value, as the opening is restricted by thread in the inner margins. Some oriental books are sewn with silk in this way.

Blanket stitching is a variation on side stitching. Holes are made, with a drill if necessary, and not more than 9 mm ($\frac{3}{8}$ in.) in from the spine.

Overcasting is a method of sewing together a number of single sheets. The thread should be thin and if possible the holes should not lie more than 3 mm ($\frac{1}{8}$ in.) from the edges, otherwise opening will be restricted. Books of single sheets or sections too numerous to repair are knocked up square and glue applied to the backs. The sheets are separated into groups of six or eight leaves and each overcast. Normal sewing is continued, the thread passing through the 'centre' of the section. The method is not very satisfactory as

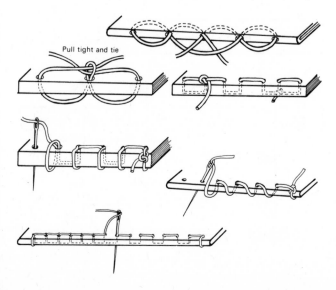

Pull tight and tie

41 Single-section pamphlet sewing

42 Side stitching (two methods)

43 Blanket stitching (*far left*)

44 Overcasting (*left*)

45 Side stitching and overcasting

the book tends to open in groups of sections and, should the paper be disproportionately thick in relation to its size, there is a strain on the back margins. An alternative is to overcast single sheets on tapes or cords as described below.

Side stitching and overcasting is also a method of strengthening the first and last sections of the library style. A saddler's stitch is made with holes 4 mm (⅙ in.) apart and 3 mm (⅛ in.) in from the edge. Thin sections may be put through a domestic sewing machine.

In *French sewing*, or sewing without tapes, the sections are linked together by passing the thread under the loop of the preceding section. Although a number of limp bindings are sewn in this way, without tape or cord, it is not strong enough for craft binding and should be used only for casual work. When sewing a heavy book this type of sewing can be combined with tape sewing to link sections closer together. The thread should not be too tight as the book could be pulled into a concave shape and be difficult to round. For added strength, this method has been adopted for the first and last three sections of large library-style books.

Tape sewing for case and library work: sewing with one length of thread for each section is known as 'all along' sewing and should be used whenever possible. The exposed linen-jointed endpaper for the library style is sewn with the thread going twice round the tape for extra strength. A continuous line of thread appears on the cloth reinforcement of the endpapers. 'Two up' or 'three up' sewing is the method adopted to reduce the excess swell that will occur if numerous or thin sections are sewn 'all along'. Add extra tapes or cords when sewing three up. This is not as strong as 'all along' sewing and not all the sections are held with a kettle stitch, but backing and back linings support the sewing. *Overcasting on tapes* is a sound method of sewing where the book is made up of single sheets or where repairs are impossible because of the build-up of swell in the spine. The first section is overcast with the thread passing diagonally across the tape. The second section is overcast through the first, and the third section through the second; sewing is continued in this sequence. Push the needle

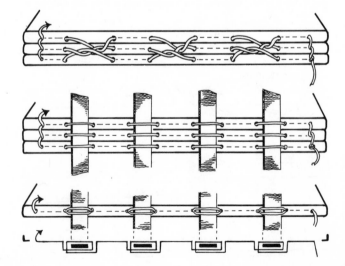

46 French sewing

47 Tape sewing for case and library work

48 Exposed linen-jointed endpaper

through the section being sewn, and tilt the needle to come out at the section below. Keep the sections lined up at the head and pull the thread tight. This method reduces swell and the need to overcast every group of leaves first. The backing will consolidate the stitching.

In *sunk cord sewing*, channels are cut into the backs of the sections with a fine saw to accommodate the cord. The thread passes over the top of the cord and sewing is therefore quick and easy. Avoid deep and wide channels as cuts and cords will show when the book

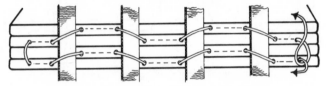

First few and last few sections sewn all along

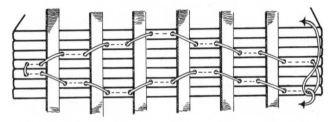

49 'Two up' and 'three up' sewing

50 Overcasting on tapes

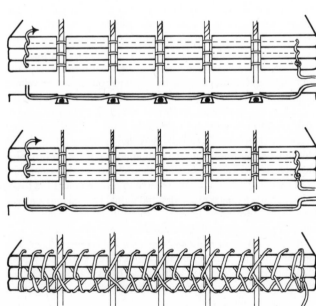

51 Sunk cord sewing. *Top*: usual method. *Centre*: shallow cuts. *Bottom*: single sheets overcast on sunk cords

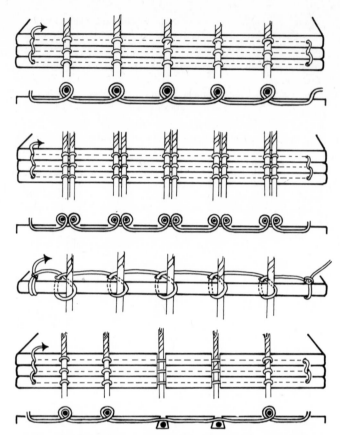

52 Raised cord sewing. *From top to bottom*: normal method; double cord sewing; single sheets sewn on raised cords; combination of raised and sunk cords

is open. The channels cut in the backs of the sections for sunk cord work may be made very shallow so that they are not seen when the book is opened. The book is sewn on thinner cord; half the thickness will be above the spine surface and it is flattened by the hammer when backing. Any remaining bumps are lost in the linings. Sewing on thin cord for the sake of appearance is poor craftsmanship and is not recommended. Single sheets in groups are overcast across the cords in a similar way to tape sewing.

Raised cord or flexible sewing was the usual method until the mid-eighteenth century, apart from sewing on thongs or vellum strips. It is difficult, almost laborious; as each cord is sewn, the preceding loop is pulled tight. It is more expedient to leave a small loop round each cord and tighten the loops one after the other before the kettle stitch is made. A common fault is to pierce the thread when returning into the section, so that it cannot be pulled through. If the sections are thick the thread may pass round the cord twice before entering the section, to make a more solid band.

Double cord sewing is rare today and should be used only on very large books of handmade paper. Originally the headband was an integral part of the sewing on both single and double cords.

A combination of *raised and sunk cords* has no merit other than decoration. The title can be lettered between two closely positioned raised bands to give a distinctive effect, although it would be equally satisfactory to sew on sunk cords and attach false bands.

THE PLOUGH AND GUILLOTINE

The lying press is an essential piece of equipment in the bindery; it should be professional-size, 600 mm (24 in.) between screws, as smaller ones are inadequate for good work. The flat side is used for backing, edge gilding, headbanding and the finishing of large books. The side bearing the runners should be used only for cutting edges and boards with the plough.

The design, which has hardly changed in four hundred years, is perfect for the work. The wooden cheeks are sympathetic to books and those with wooden screws give considerable pressure. A modification introduced by French manufacturers in the last fifty years consists of an extra cheek to the press with a centre wheel and iron screws which make adjustment convenient. The wooden press will give good service if carefully maintained; it is necessary to rub it over occasionally with a liquid wax polish and give a thin coat of linseed oil every year. The plough runners should be firmly screwed down. The plough blade must be sharp, ground to a spear shape, with a slightly rounded point and a long bevel on the upper side only. It is never sharpened underneath. When set in the plough the flat of the blade should run absolutely on the top of the press.

If the edges of a book require cutting, plough off the minimum as overcutting spoils the appearance of the printed page. The spine is the only square edge after sewing and is used as the lay edge for

Poor shape blunts easily

Good shape remains sharp

53 The plough blade: right and wrong

54 The lying press

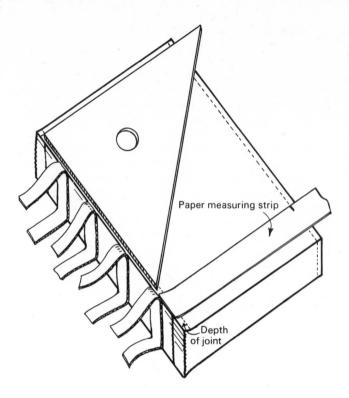

Paper measuring strip

Depth
of joint

55 Marking the guide lines for
cutting with the plough

measuring. To mark a guide line to cut the foredge, select the
smallest page in width and place a mark just within this distance
on the waste sheet. Line a strip of paper against the spine edge and,
following the profile of the book, mark off the cutting width.
Place the same mark at the bottom of the book and draw the
cutting line. Place a set square against the spine edge on the front
and draw a line at right angles as a guide to cut the head and draw a
similar line on the back to cut the tail. Mark off the depth of the
joint along the spine on both sides.

Hold the book fast between waste card in a finishing press and
lightly glue the spine with flexible glue, working it into the
channels between the sections. Knock the spine up square by
bringing it down hard on to a flat surface; also check that the head
is square. The glue holds the sections in place and imparts enough
moisture to the spine for the sections to be modelled by the
hammer without damage.

Cut the foredge first, with the cutting side of the press open and
the runners to the left. Lay a cutting board a little longer than the
book on the press and face it with a protective piece of millboard.
Place the book on these with the cutting line below the top of the
board; position a second cutting board on the guide line. Slide
them free from the press and pick them up in the middle with the
left hand without disturbing their positions. Transfer them to the
centre of the press and put them in as far down as the fingers will
allow. With the right hand, tighten both screws to hold them – the
wedged boards will prevent slipping. Open both screws a little at
a time and push all four down together with both hands. Develop

a rhythmic movement – unscrew and push, unscrew and push – and the book plus the boards will ease into the position illustrated in the diagram.

Screw up the press as tightly as possible with the press pin and measure the distances between the cheeks of the press for even pressure. In order to check for accurate positioning, draw the guide line on both sides of the book when marking up, and after knocking up pencil a line from one point to the other across head and tail. If this line is straight and continuous along the top of the press when the book is in position, the cutting will be accurate. Set the plough into the runners and turn the handle until the blade is running along the top of the cutting board and just short of the book. Push the plough forward, pull back and, on completion of the back stroke, advance the blade by a fractional turn of the handle. Cut on the forward stroke only; never on the return. Do not turn the handle back as it will be difficult to judge how much to advance the blade for its next cut. Cut only two or three leaves

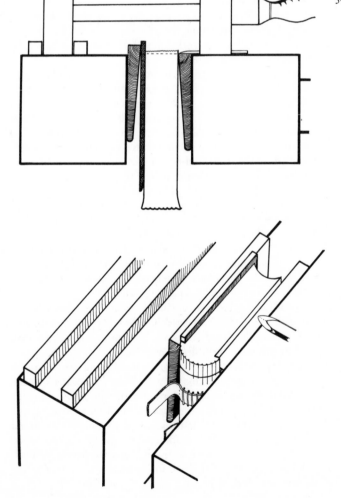

56 Book in position for cutting

at a time: forward cut, back, turn, forward cut, back, turn – and so on. Again a rhythmic movement results in a well-cut edge, and less effort is required.

Poor paper requires hard pressure and a sharp blade. If the paper shavings are corrugated either the plough blade is blunt or an attempt has been made to cut too many leaves at one stroke. If the cut edge is broken, it is an indication that the press is not tight enough or the pressure is uneven. Depressions on the surface of the cut are caused by incorrect positioning in the press, a poorly fitting blade, an uneven surface to the cutting board or shavings caught under the plough.

Head and tail are cut after rounding and backing, otherwise the swelling at the spine will cause distortion under pressure. On cutting the head and tail, the importance of taking off as little as possible at one time, and on the forward stroke only, becomes evident. The back folds offer resistance if cut on the return stroke and tend to break away. When the last section is cut, run the blade into the protecting millboard so that the endpapers are trimmed. The shreds of paper hanging from the joint are cut against the edge of the cardboard with a knife, either with the book in the same position or after loosening the press and raising the book up.

On completion of cutting the screws are only half undone and the book is pushed up from below for removal, as it will be damaged if it falls through.

Cutting can be achieved accurately and simply by using millboards only. Two millboards, thicker than the depth of the joint, have adjoining edges cut square in the plough and are positioned as in the illustration, one acting as a guide for the blade. When cutting boards are used the pressure is concentrated at the widest point of the wedge but without boards pressure is exerted by the whole side of the press. Cutting without boards is unwise if plates or folded maps increase the thickness of the middle of the book, or in manuscript work if there is decoration or raised gold initials which will be damaged under pressure. Edges without the necessary intense pressure will tear under the action of the knife. Large weighty books are cut using cutting boards as they assist in lowering the book in the press. Very small books may be cut with millboards, which must be longer than the depth of the cheek of the press, otherwise the book will be marked under pressure. Cutting instructions for the flexible style are given on p. 124.

Boards for fine bindings should be cut in the plough as heavy millboards cut in the board cutter have broken edges. Cut the two millboards in the board cutter about 12 mm ($\frac{1}{2}$ in.) larger than required and mark them 'front' and 'back'. Place them together and fix them with adhesive tape at the foredge and tail. Cut 3 mm off the spine edge with the plough. Place a carpenter's square against this cut edge and mark a right angle with a knife cut at the head. Tape the spine edges together and cut the head, making sure that the plough blade runs in the knife cut. Measure the width and length of board required, working from the two square edges. Tape the cut head and mark knife-cut lines at the foredge and tail. Cut these accurately and check for squareness by removing the tape and reversing the boards.

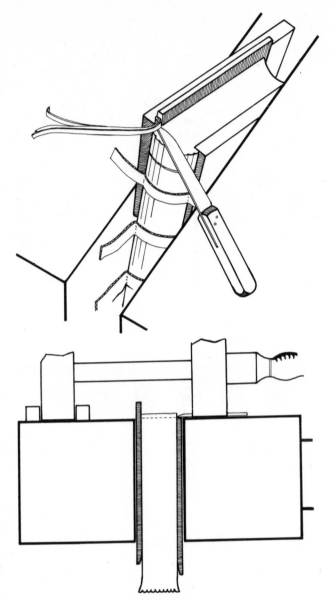

57 Cutting away the last few pages

58 Cutting without wedges

The small power guillotine is the most expensive piece of equipment in the craft bindery, yet it is little used. The edges cut with it are inferior to those cut with the plough, but it is accurate, efficient, fast and effective for cutting sets, or copies of the cheaper range of books, and for cutting paper in bulk. Boards should never be cut in the guillotine unless the blade edge has been ground at the correct angle for board cutting. Various safety devices are fitted so that the machine becomes inoperable if there is danger to the operator. Other safety factors must be observed; these include strict regard for instructions on maintenance and knife change, the caging of all moving parts and keeping the bed of the machine free of all tools. The machine consists of a blade which has a

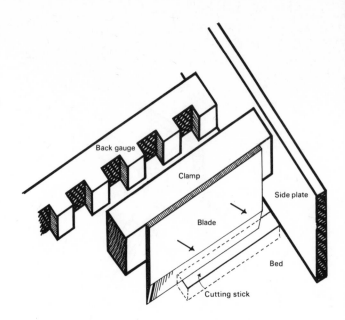

59 Main parts of the guillotine

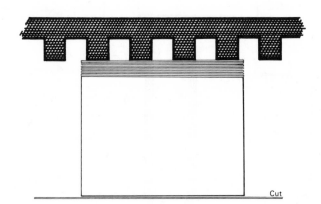

60 Cutting wedge

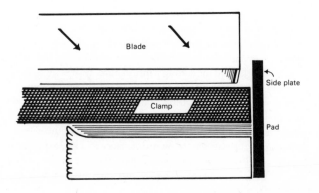

61 Cutting wedge in position

shearing action from left to right running into a cutting stick let into the bed of the machine. Parallel to the blade is the back gauge, which is adjusted to the length of the cut, while the side plate is at right angles to it and acts as a lay edge for squareness. The work is held fast by a clamp which can be operated independently or is brought down when the blade is in motion.

The guillotine will cut satisfactorily only if the work is solid, therefore books are cut all round before rounding and backing. The procedure is to mark up for cutting in the same way as for the plough. Glue up, knock up and allow the book to dry. Set the back gauge to the measurement required for cutting the foredge. Operating the foot clamp to hold the work firm, place the spine so that all the sections are flush with the back gauge. Cut the foredge. Remove the clamp pressure and take away the book but do not alter the setting. Fan out a wad of waste paper thicker than the swell at the spine and cut it so that the widest piece is as wide as the book. Now cut the tail by positioning the foredge, which is now a true lay edge, against the side plate with the folds of the sections facing to the left. Lay the wad of fanned-out paper (called a 'cutting wedge') on top of the book and adjust all to the cutting line. Bring the clamp down and the blade will cut just in front of it. If the spine distorts and pulls away from the side plate under clamp pressure the cutting wedge is not thick enough to compensate for the swell. Cut the tail. Set the back gauge to the final measurement to cut the head; turn the book over and, using both back gauge and side plate as lays, position it with the cutting wedge and make the cut.

ROUNDING AND BACKING

Correct sewing, as we have seen, is one of the main factors in the lasting qualities of a book and will make forwarding easier, particularly in the operations of rounding and backing. A flat-backed book that is unrestricted at the folds opens well, but to its detriment when standing on the shelf, as the sections are suspended between boards and held in position by tapes, mull and endpapers. In time gravity will affect the sewing and the threads will loosen. The further the sections are away from the boards, the more they will sag. The foredge will fall forward and the tail will rest on the shelf. Eventually the sewing breaks down and the binding collapses.

A book required to last must be rounded and backed. The amount of swell can be judged only from experience and this swell is distributed by rounding and backing (jointing) the book so that the spine is approximately one-third of a circle. The width at joint and foredge should then be the same.

The sections are moulded by a backing hammer, each section modelled over the next until the first and last are at right angles. The middle section is straight, but to the left and right the sections progressively lean against each other until the last is flush with the edge of the board. Thus the sections are not suspended between boards as in a flat-backed book, but are supported by the 'columns' of the boards. Thus the strain on the sewing is relieved and

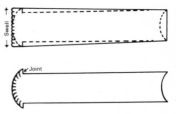

62 Correct rounding and backing

63 The sections supported by the boards

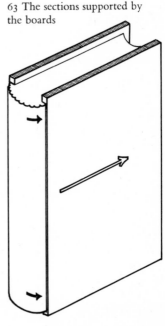

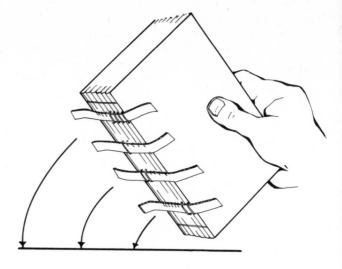

64 Knocking up the spine

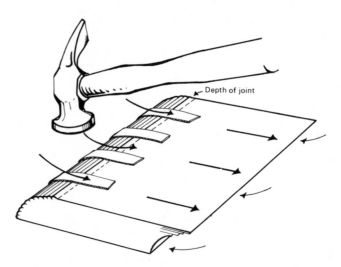

Depth of joint

65 Rounding the sections with a backing hammer

the spine will retain its shape longer. Support is given also by the linings and the covering.

After sewing, the endpapers are tipped into position and the depth of the joint marked. The spine is glued with flexible glue, knocked up square and work commenced immediately. To round the book, place it on a firm surface with the spine away from you. Spread the fingers across the book with the thumb on the foredge; push with the thumb and pull with the fingers, and assist the movement with glancing blows of the hammer directed on to the first few sections. When a regular half curve has been made, turn the sections over and repeat the movement, and a symmetrical round will result. Hold the book in this shape. (If sections start out of place or the curve is irregular it is the fault of uneven tension when sewing.)

Backing is commenced before the glued spine is dry. The lying press is opened to take both the book and the wedge-shaped backing boards. Hold the book – still in its rounded shape – on

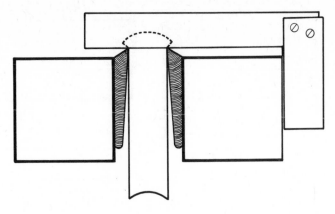

66 Checking for symmetry and squareness

the bench and place one backing board on the guide line, with the tapes or cords outside. Grip firmly, turn both over and position the second board. Pick up the book and boards in one hand and hold them at eye level to check that the boards are parallel to each other, the spine symmetrical and the book square. Lower them, foredge down, into the middle of the press as far as the finger-tips will allow, tightening or loosening the press as necessary. Push the book and boards into the press, loosening it gradually to accommodate the width. The book must fulfil the conditions shown in the diagram; if it does not, it is wrong and the process must be repeated.

A book is symmetrical and any deviation from a centre line will cause it to be out of square, greatly affecting its appearance and life. The backing boards must be an identical pair and their position on the joint the same. The spine should have identical curves on either side of centre. In order to check the symmetry, place a carpenter's square against the side of the press; the blade must touch the tops of the backing boards. Tighten the press with considerable pressure and check the measurement between the cheeks of the press at either end to make certain they are the same. Backing is continued by striking glancing blows on the sides of the rounded spine, beginning at one end and progressing to the other in a rhythmic pattern. The face of the hammer is held parallel to the plane of the spine. If the sewing is regular, not too loose nor too tight, the sections will pull each other leaving the middle section upright and untouched by the hammer while those towards the backing boards will have a definite fold in them. The angle of the face of the hammer is changed as the shape is formed and backing is not complete until the last sections (endpapers) are knocked flush with the oblique face of the backing boards. Often it is necessary to use the claw side of the hammer to complete the backing, but grooves should be avoided. The backing boards are shaped to overcompensate the angle of the joint so that when the book is removed from pressure the joint will fall back to a right angle.

Methods and books vary; a thick book with more movement in the spine is easier to back than a narrow one, but as long as the result is achieved it does not matter how the hammer is held nor

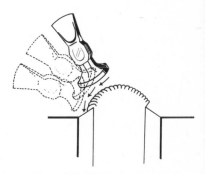

67 Action of the backing hammer

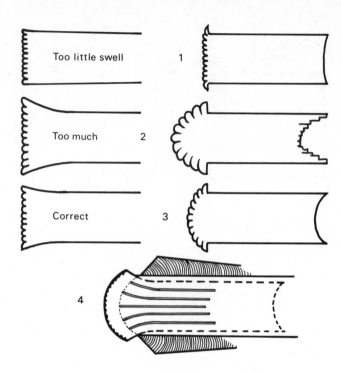

Too little swell 1

Too much 2

Correct 3

4

68 Swell

which side is used. A little paste can be rubbed in if the spine dries out before completion of backing, as hammer blows on dry sections will have little effect except to break up the paper. Backing should be accomplished in a few minutes while the spine is moist.

Faults and their correction

A spine with insufficient swell will collapse after backing. Too much swell gives an exaggerated round, the inner margins are lost and the book is difficult to open without splitting the linings. The correct swell for an ideal spine is shown in the figure above. Swell can be reduced by hammering the spine before gluing, to drive the thread into the paper. If, on sewing, excess swell is unavoidable, backing can be achieved by packing with strips of pulp card. These need to be 75 mm (3 in.) wide and a little longer than the book; they are placed at regular intervals parallel to, and the depth of the joint away from, the folds. The number required will depend on the amount of swell as their object is to pack out the rest of the book away from the swell at the folds. The backing boards are then retained in position (Fig. 68, *4*). Narrow books will not round satisfactorily, but they can be backed without rounding first and a joint can be formed with a bone folder. Small books and those sewn in the flexible style are better backed with a metalworker's small hammer, working between the bands. (See p. 121 for backing books sewn on raised cords.)

The depth of the joint is governed by the thickness of the boards used. The thickness is decided firstly by the weight of the book – as a heavy book will need a proportionately thicker board – then

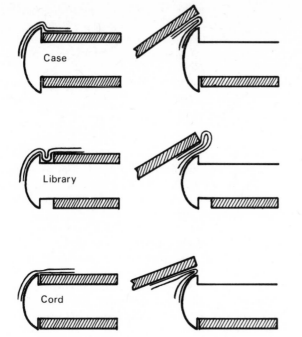

69 Depth of joint in three binding styles

by the binding style and finally by the personal preference of the binder. In a case binding the joint is one and a half times the thickness of the board, and this freedom at the hinge enables the cloth to fold back in a tight curve rather than at an acute angle. In the library, flexible and sunk cord styles, the joint is equal to the thickness of the board. In the library style the french groove gives a free opening even with thick leather. In the flexible and sunk cord styles, the leather has to be pared thinly for the boards to throw back.

EDGE GILDING

The early printer bound his own books, but as printing and binding became more specialized they were separated, and the binder concentrated on his own craft with its associated skills of gold tooling, marbling, box making, tree calfing, foredge painting, gauffering and edge gilding. In the early nineteenth century, as the demand for bound books grew, further specialization was necessary, and craftsmen set up to work in one aspect only of the craft or an attendant skill. Edge gilding became a separate trade, with high standards and efficiency, and as recently as the 1930s numerous London workshops were competing for work contracted by the trade. Few specialist edge gilders have survived, however, because of high costs, the reduction in the number of fine bindings and the invention of machines for gilding.

A perfect gilded edge is no mean achievement and today the binder must gild his own edges – not always to his satisfaction and certainly not economically. The decorative appearance of gilding is incidental to its worth in sealing the edges of paper against damp and fingering. Different craftsmen have different working methods but the better the paper and the more thorough its preparation, the better the result will be.

Before discussing equipment and methods, let us take a look at the principal material.

Gold leaf

Of the many ancient trades involved in the craft of bookbinding the most fascinating is the beating of gold leaf. This art has been practised for five thousand years: Egyptian coffins and monuments were plated with gold one fifty-thousandth of an inch thick, but the gold leaf used today is five times thinner. Gold of $23\frac{1}{4}$ carat fineness, with the addition of $\frac{3}{4}$ carat silver or copper to 'colour' the leaf, is cast into an ingot measuring $11 \times 1\frac{1}{2} \times \frac{1}{4}$ in. This is passed through steel rollers under pressure until it makes a ribbon of gold $1\frac{1}{2}$ in. wide, 230 feet long and $1/1000$ in. thick. From this ribbon 220 pieces $1\frac{1}{2}$ in. square are cut, and interleaved with $4\frac{1}{2}$-in. squares of tough Montgolfier paper. This is bound with parchment sleeves to form a parcel or 'cutch', and beaten with a 14-lb. hammer on massive stone blocks.

The weight and shape of the dome-headed beating hammers have changed through the centuries but always the beating is a rolling, thrusting, rhythmic action, performed with great concentration and dexterity. The cutch is turned and twisted as it is beaten, and middle leaves are replaced at intervals by the outer ones.

After 30 minutes each sheet of gold has extended to the edges of the paper squares. Gold and paper are separated; the gold is cut into quarters and interleaved between 4-in. squares of goldbeater's skin, prepared from the skins of ox intestines. A second parcel is made, forming a 'shoder', which is beaten for a further $1\frac{1}{2}$ hours. From the shoder each gold sheet is quartered and a 'mould' prepared of 1100 goldbeater's skins $5\frac{1}{4}$ in. square; between each pair of skins is placed a leaf of gold. The beating of the mould with an 8-lb. hammer is continued for $3\frac{1}{2}$ hours; this is a crucial stage. The skill lies in beating the gold from the centre outwards, until it is thin in the middle and thick towards the edges, which could extend almost to the outside of the package.

After this final beating the leaves, now approximately $4\frac{3}{4}$ in. square, are lifted from the skins with boxwood pincers and cut into squares of $3\frac{1}{4}$ in. by a frame of sharpened rattan cane called a 'wagon'. This work, and the transfer of each leaf between rouged tissue paper to make up a book of 25 leaves, is done with bewildering dexterity. It is estimated that the leaf beaten from the original bar of gold could cover an area of 7160 square feet.

The beating of gold leaf by hand is slow and costly; the first attempt to design a machine for this purpose was made by Leonardo da Vinci. Very little beating is now done by hand; the present-day machine is a curious arrangement of metal rods operating a hammer and anvil. Its design was made possible by photographing every movement of a gold beater at work. The machine produces gold leaf comparable to that beaten by hand, but the art is lost.

Equipment

The equipment is simple and the materials easily obtained. The most important item is a burnisher of some semi-precious stone such as agate, haematite or bloodstone, flat or dog-toothed to suit the edge profile. Gilding boards are the same as cutting boards; the grain direction of the wood should be indicated so that scraping can be done the way of the grain. Scrapers are shaped to suit the particular edge and can be home-made from steel plate, mounted in wood for comfort in handling. The edges are filed almost to a cutting edge then burred over by a sharpening steel. (Old spoke-shave blades are excellent.) Other items required are a soft bristle brush, a large water-colour flood brush and a gilder's tip. Materials required are french chalk, Armenian bole, black lead, beeswax and glaire. This is made of one part white of egg to four parts of water, shaken vigorously, left to stand in a jar overnight and well strained before use. Finishers' tooling glaire can be thinned by five times as much water and strained. One well-known binder uses the old-fashioned boiling-water starch with fine results.

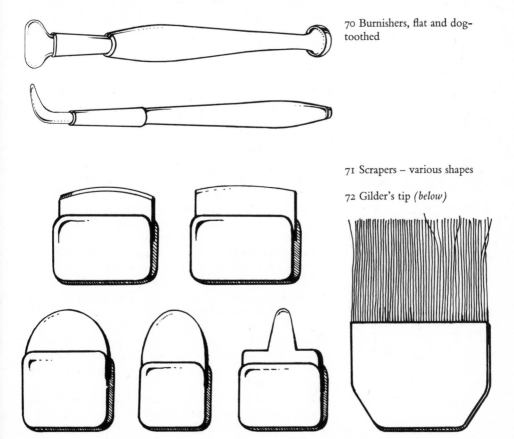

70 Burnishers, flat and dog-toothed

71 Scrapers – various shapes

72 Gilder's tip *(below)*

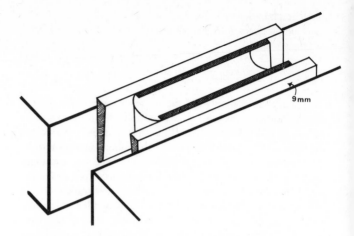

73 Book ready for gilding

Preparation

Head and tail edges are gilded after backing and cutting. Foredges can be gilded in the round or while flat, before rounding. Sections can be cut to size before sewing, knocked up evenly and gilded, which is known as 'gilding in the rough'. This seems to be an untidy method as the uneven pages soon collect dust and become dog-eared. Strips of paper are inserted where maps, diagrams and smaller leaves are short of the edges, to bring them up solid. Any edge to be gilded must be well cut with a sharp plough blade to lessen the work of scraping and smoothing.

The English method

There are two ways of gilding, the standard English and the French method. Study the paper to be gilded. Art or loaded paper contains glue and china clay and, as it is a wet preparation that sets the gold leaf, the loading will dissolve and the pages will stick together at their edges. This paper must be 'chalked'. Flick through the pages, shaking over them cotton wool impregnated with french chalk so that sheets receive a fine dusting. Good tub-sized paper needs no chalking, and less pressure is required in the press. Poor paper is more satisfactory if it is chalked and heavy pressure is applied. It is advantageous to cut two heavy millboards to a right angle in the plough and to place these in the joints. Any unevenness in the gilding boards is counteracted by the millboards and gilding is confined between them. Position the gilding boards, knock up level, screw up in the middle of the lying press, 9 mm ($\frac{3}{8}$ in.) above the top, and apply pressure.

Select a scraper and hold it at an angle so that the burr will take off fine, dusty shavings from the edge. Starting from the spine, scrape with a continuous shallow curved movement, finishing the stroke clear of the pages. Scrape until the edge is smooth, the line of the coloured endpapers is well defined and the millboard shiny and black. Rub vigorously with fine clean sandpaper until the edge is glossy. Do not touch the edge but brush the book and press free from dust and scrapings.

Although the edge has been scraped and sandpapered, the pores of the paper need a filler. A preparation of either black lead or Armenian bole is applied to fill the surface and to colour the gold. The bole gives a warm glow and the black lead a hard, bright appearance. Take a piece of cotton wool, wetted in water and squeezed out, and dip it in the filler. When the cotton wool is rubbed on a piece of waste paper, the consistency of the filler should be smooth, neither thick nor watery. Immediately, in a single movement, wipe over the edge. To assist the gilding of poor paper, which will absorb readily, add a little paste to the filler, but this is unnecessary for hand- and mould-made papers.

While the filler is drying, prepare the glaire and cover the jar to keep out dust. Cut pieces of cartridge paper 100 × 70 mm (4 × 2¾ in.) and handle these only by the edges. At this stage, set out a gold cushion (see p. 162) and knife, select a sheet of gold free from cracks or folds, and lay it carefully on the cushion. Cut sufficient pieces to cover the edge completely, 9 mm (⅜ in.) wider than the width of the edge. Rub a piece of the cartridge paper on the hair at the back of your head and place it firmly across the gold, so that the extreme edge shows at the edge of the paper. Using a zigzag movement, rub down gently with a finger and the gold will adhere to the paper, which can be lifted and laid face upwards ready for application. Prepare as many as required.

When it is dry, the filled edge is brushed vigorously to a high polish; poor-quality paper is burnished with the burnisher to a hard, polished surface. Dip a flood brush into the glaire and quickly flood the edge. With both hands, pick up the piece of paper with the gold adhering to it and approach the edge with the paper held tightly parallel to, and a few millimetres from, the wet surface. When the edge is in position over the far millboard, tilt the paper down and the glaire will suck the gold off the paper in an unbroken piece. Do not push the gold through the paper or touch it at all, or the glaire will penetrate the leaf and dull the gold. Cover the remainder of the edge in the same way, overlapping each piece by 4 mm.

Some prefer a gilder's tip to lay on the gold and this is recommended for applying small pieces to uncovered areas or cracks.

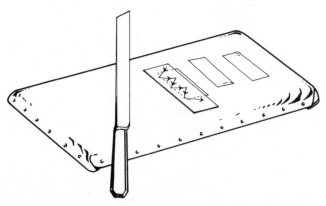

74 Lifting gold leaf

The tip, passed across the hair, will pick up enough grease to hold the leaf. Should the edge be long or large, apply glaire to one half at a time, and for patching, a hot breath will 'liven' the glaire enough to settle the gold on the breaks. The edge is left to dry for about half an hour, depending on the humidity. Condensation caused by breathing on the edge should disappear within ten seconds, and it will then be ready for burnishing.

The edge is 'set' by covering it with clean paper and, using gentle pressure, rubbing it with the burnisher to cover the surface across the width in a gradual zigzag movement. The second burnishing is done directly on the edge; the burnisher is dug into the shoulder, held tightly halfway down and controlled near the stone by the other hand. Pressure is applied by bearing down with the shoulder and moving the body. The burnisher should be held parallel to the surface, otherwise grooves will appear. If a sticking sensation is felt or dark streaks appear, the edge is not dry enough; it can be patched by breathing on it, laying on gold with the tip and burnishing immediately. Considerable pressure can be used for the final burnish. The burnisher will run more easily, and extra brightness will be gained, if you rub a piece of beeswax on the flat of the press and touch this with a piece of soft leather or cotton wool, which is then passed lightly over the gold surface. (Some gilders loosen the press slightly to give a cushioned pressure.) Finally, remove the book and tap it gently on the side of the bench to free the leaves.

The French method

The French method is similar, except that, after scraping and sanding, the edge is washed over with a thin paste wash to seal it. When this is dry, a further wash of Armenian bole and egg glaire is given. Again it is left to dry, brushed vigorously and the gold is laid on with glaire. The first burnishing is made through a scrap of thin vellum, beeswaxed on one side. In addition to the cross-movement with the burnisher, the gilder may 'sweep' the length

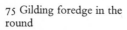

75 Gilding foredge in the round

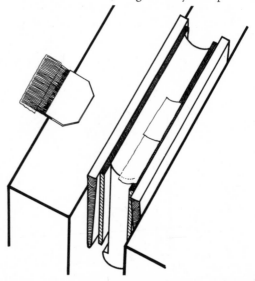

of the edge and sometimes damp it with a rag. The results of the professional gilder's work are enviable and come from mastery of tools and materials.

Foredge gilding

Foredges can be gilded either in their flat state or after rounding; in both cases the edge will look solid enough. To gild edges in the round, after scraping, sanding, filling and brushing, the press must be canted and glaire and gold leaf applied along the length, but only half the width at a time. The press is then tilted the other way and the other half applied, overlapping the glaire and the gold. This angling of the press is essential because otherwise the glaire will flood the channel and the gold will adhere to the middle but not to the sides.

Staining

As an alternative to gold edges, adequate protection can be given by scraping, sandpapering and rubbing over with beeswax before burnishing. Colour can be applied before waxing, and, as colour will not take on an edge under heavy pressure, after the edge has been prepared it should be removed from the press and placed between thick boards with a heavy weight on top. Apply the colour with cotton wool, sweeping the wash from end to end without stopping.

Book edges are coloured with aniline water dyes, as those dissolved in spirit penetrate the edges of the paper too easily and colour will appear on the faces of the leaves. Any good water colour that is transparent and does not contain china clay is satisfactory. It is far better to apply several layers of stain in succession, for subtle colouring, than one thick layer of vulgar tone. When it is dry, return the book to the press before waxing and burnishing.

HEADBANDS

In early bindings, headbands consisted of extra thongs sewn in with the others, resting on the top and bottom of the sections. These were either laced in the upper corners of the boards or cut off flush with the end threads. The separate embroidered headband was introduced when books became smaller and the kettle stitch joined sections together. Sewn headbands are not only decorative but also constructional, as books are often removed from the shelf by an indiscriminate finger hooked under the headcap, resulting in torn leather at the head.

The headband strengthens the headcap and makes up the difference between the top or bottom of the sections and the edges of the boards. The quality and decoration vary according to the time spent on them and the value of the binding. Single and double headbands worked in coloured silks are sewn on all but the thinnest

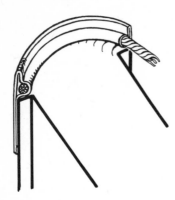

76 Two simple headbands for limp bindings

fine bindings. They can be sewn on the library style, if full leather but for half- and quarter-bound utility bindings an inserted cord is adequate. Ready-made false headbands are available, consisting of a core of cane covered by machine-embroidered stitches. They should be avoided except where costs are low. They are cut to size and stuck on, but they bear little relationship to the height of the squares; they are solely for decoration. A number of bindings from the cheap workshops of the nineteenth century were head-banded with pieces of men's striped shirting material folded in half and stuck on.

Where no additional strength to the spine is required – as, for example, in limp work – simple headbands can be made by pasting a strip of thin leather round cord and attaching this to the spine with glue.

Headbands should be bright and simple; a single headband worked in two colours is adequate for most books, while double headbands look disproportionate unless on large or thick volumes. Embroidery silks should be corded and of good quality. The straight or rectangular core, which is suitable for most books, is made from a piece of unpared leather glued to thin vellum, and cut to size as required. Core used on old books was round, and the thread was ordinary sewing linen. If an old book is to be head-banded, thin thread is used, stained with red, blue or green dye and with plain thread as the second colour.

A standard straight-core two-colour headband is worked as follows. Choose coloured silks that harmonize with the colour scheme of the book. Generally gold and one other colour are used but for this description I shall confine myself to black and white thread.

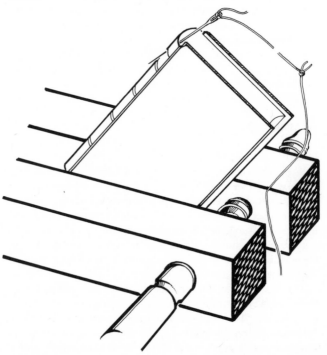

77 Book in finishing press for headbanding

Cut a strip of core 12 mm (½ in.) longer than the round of the spine (so that it can be held) and equal in width to the depth of the squares. Cut lengths of black and white silk, enough for the work but not too long to be manageable. Knot these together, cut off the ends close to the join and flatten the knot. Thread a needle with the black silk. Set up the book in the finishing press with the foredge towards you. Push the needle between the leaves just past the endpapers until it comes out at the spine immediately under the cerf and pull the silk through until the knot catches in the kettle stitch inside the book. Take the needle over and through the same position and place the core through the resulting black loop; pull the thread tight so that the core stands firmly and upright on the extreme back edge of the spine. Bring the black thread over the core for the second time and hold it taut. The white, held firmly, crosses over the black, passes under the core and round it twice. (This cross-thread is known as a 'bead' and locks the previous turns down on the surface of the book.)

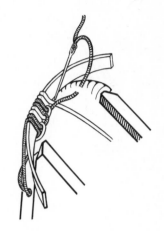

78 Sewing on headband

Keeping the white thread taut, cross with the black and make two turns, beginning under the core. Form another bead with the white and make two turns. Cross with the black and this time a tie-down is made, by pushing the needle between the leaves directly at the end of the last two white turns, to come out under the kettle stitch. Bring the black up, over and round the core twice and continue crossing and turning twice for each colour, forming the beads and tying down at alternate blacks until the end is reached. The colour which completes the band is taken down under the cerf; the other colour crosses to form the bead and is then taken down through the same place but comes out above the cerf. If this is the white silk, thread it into a needle, tie the two ends in a reef knot across the kettle stitch, flatten the knot and cut off any excess thread. Glue the knot, the tie-downs, loose ends and the extreme ends of the headbands to hold the first and last turns in place. Excess core should now be cut off.

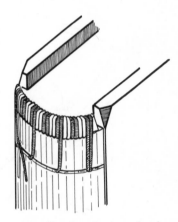

79 Headband sewing completed

The threads are held with even tension throughout so that they fit snugly together, and the beads are all the same size. To get even tension and regularity, headbanding must be carried out with quick, rhythmic movements. If the silks are held too loosely, the beads will form halfway up the core, and if too tightly they will disappear under the core. It may help to slip the threads alternately between the leaves of the foredge while working, to hold them taut. Joins in the thread are made using a weaver's knot on to the tie-downs at the back of the book.

New colours can be introduced by joining to the tie-downs with many decorative possibilities. For example, a third of the spine width may be in red, then a change can be made to black, and on reaching the centre three white threads can be introduced; the arrangement is completed in reverse order.

Double-tiered headbands are worked with a straight core and a narrow, round one: a 'cello string or a thin cord stiffened with paste is suitable. To facilitate sewing, these may be bound together with thread at one end. Again, for the purpose of this instruction we use black and white thread and in some of the diagrams the boards are omitted for clarity. Thread the needle with a length of

80 Headband colour variation

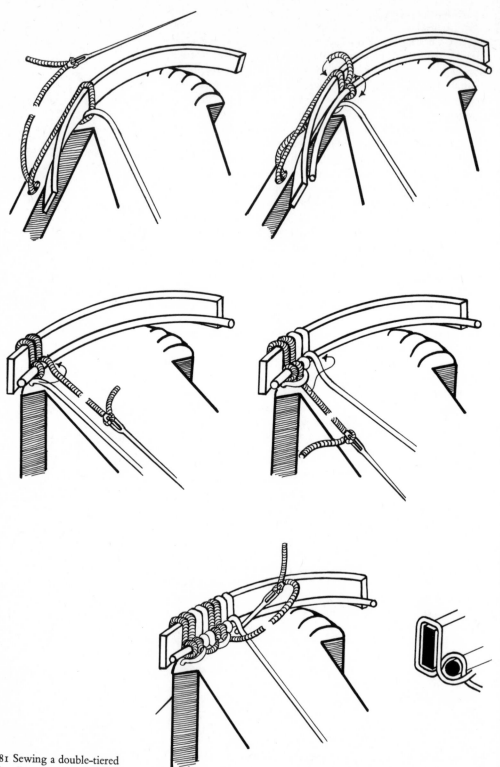

81 Sewing a double-tiered
headband

black thread knotted to a white one as before. Push the needle into the section just past the endpapers so that the point comes out of the spine under the kettle stitch. Pull it through so that the knot catches at the kettle stitch inside the book. Put the needle through the same entry and pull to leave a small loop. Place the rectangular core into the loop and tighten, so that the core sits firmly upright on the back edge of the sections.

Place the small core at the base of the large one if it is not already attached to it. Bring the black thread up under the large core and between the two, then over and round the small core. Continue the thread between and over the top of the large core and round it, then between and over the top of the small one. Cross the black with the white thread, taking it under the small core, between and over and round the large core. Again pass between, then over and round the small core, continuing between, then over and round the large core and, as before, between the two and over the small core. Cross over with the black and repeat movements as for the white. Cross over with the white and repeat, until there is a sequence of black, white, black, white and then push the needle in the section alongside the last white to cross it to form the bead. Insert the needle so that it comes out at the kettle stitch. Pull the bead tight, bring the black thread between the cores and up and over the large one. Continue the sequence.

Complete the sewing as for a single headband. Use a spare needle to close up the gaps between the turns and to tease out the beads to the same size. It is a common fault to make the headband too wide, and as this will obstruct the hinge it should be a little short of the round of the spine.

LEATHER PARING

One of the most admired skills in bookbinding is the paring of leather, yet only sharp tools and confidence are required. Confidence is gained by experience, and sharp tools by a zealous consideration and care for knives.

For centuries, only the French knife was used. Edges were pared by pushing the blade in a continuous movement and at the same angle through the leather. Broad areas and narrow channels were reduced by a forward scraping action. In this century the German or English knife has gained popularity and with the spokeshave is used for all paring work. The spokeshave has been adopted in the last fifty years and the binder has modified the tool to suit his requirements. Only the flat-based type can be used, the slot for the blade being filed a little wider so that parings will not collect round the blade. The blade is given a longer bevel and is slightly curved so that its corners will not gouge into the leather. Only the centre of the blade is used for cutting. The spokeshave is a safer and quicker paring tool than the French knife.

The cutting edges of paring knives should have a long bevel on one side, the underside being left flat so that the angle of cutting is low. The French knife is used in the same way by the right- and left-handed, but an English knife is held by a right-handed person

82 (*Above*) Leather paring tools, displayed on a paring stone: *1* spokeshave, *2* French knife, *3* right-handed and *4* left-handed paring knife, *5* scalpel, *6* G–clamp

with the bevel on top and the point of the knife to the left, and by a left-handed worker with the point to the right. A perfect paring knife, or any other cutting blade, can be made from an engineer's wide hacksaw blade, as the metal is of good quality, and indeed some craftsmen argue that any knife can be used, if the metal is good.

Regrinding to a long bevel need not be done very often, though the knife should be touched up on a fine oil stone and frequently stropped. Knives should be kept in sheaths to protect the edges, and for safety.

A large lithographic stone is the best base for paring. Exercises in knife control are worth while before serious paring is undertaken. Lay a strip of leather on the stone and hold the knife the thickness of the leather away from its edge. Push down at an angle of 45° to take off the edge (1 in the diagram). Place the leather on the stone with its pared edge to the right, holding it with the left thumb against the front edge of the stone. Hold the blade rigidly at a lower angle and penetrate the leather about 6 mm ($\frac{1}{4}$ in.) from the edge. Push forward in a continuous movement until the hand touches the stone. Without withdrawing the knife or altering its angle pull the leather back and continue with the blade and remove area 2. Finally, lower the angle of the blade again to remove area 3 so that a continuous and even strip is pared about 15 mm ($\frac{9}{16}$ in.) wide. The fingers must spread the leather flat to prevent wrinkles appearing and the point of the knife from penetrating. With practice and a sharp knife areas 1, 2 and 3 can be removed with one sweep of the knife.

83 (*Below*) Leather paring exercise

84 (*Opposite above*) How to hold leather for paring

85 (*Opposite below*) Alternative method: paring from left to right

86 Paring with the spokeshave

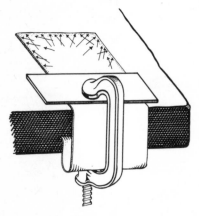

87 Direction of movement of
the spokeshave

Some prefer to lay the leather in the centre of the stone and to pare with the knife held almost parallel with the leather, removing the edge by sweeping the blade from left to right in one movement. In both methods, hold the knife rigidly to keep it under control; it is the sharpness of the blade which does the work. If the cut is woolly and force is needed, the knife is blunt; this makes it unsafe, and paring a waste of time.

When using the spokeshave, first the leather must be edge-pared with a knife, otherwise the spokeshave blade will catch in the edge and tear the leather. Fig. 86 illustrates the set-up for paring with the spokeshave. The leather is held firmly by one or two G-clamps and a strip of thick millboard or a slat of wood protects the grain from being crushed. This should be clamped close to the area to be pared as any free movement will tear the leather. Set the blade finely and evenly, cut with the centre and push against the leather in a continuous curved movement. Change the length and angle of direction at almost every stroke and if working towards the edge, press more heavily on that side of the spokeshave until there is a gradual change from thick to very thin at the edges in the pared area. Strop the blade frequently. Parings that get under the leather must be removed every so often or holes will appear as the spokeshave pares away bumps.

Even paring is of the utmost importance. This can be achieved by noticing the similarity of dye colour as paring progresses, or alternatively by folding various parts of the leather at different angles and running the finger and thumb tightly along the crease, when any unevenness will be felt. Mark these areas with a chinagraph pencil and pare away the markings. The amount to be pared away depends on the thickness and type of leather, the binding construction, the quality and subsequent use of the book.

6 Binding styles

CASE BINDING

The publishers' edition, or case binding, is not a true binding but a cheap and acceptable method of giving temporary protection to books of casual worth. To supply mass demand and reduce cost, machines have been devised to do all the operations efficiently. The sections are sewn, cut, rounded, backed and the spine lined up with the first and second linings. A separate case is made from two boards held together by a cloth cover with a strip of paper or card glued to the back as a stiffener. The sections are pasted into the case and held by tapes or linings and endpapers.

Some very fine examples of printing and works of universal interest are casebound. False headbands, unusual covering materials and elaborate gold blocking make the cases interesting but, regrettably, give no additional protection to the contents. Case binding is unsuitable for books of value and those in daily use.

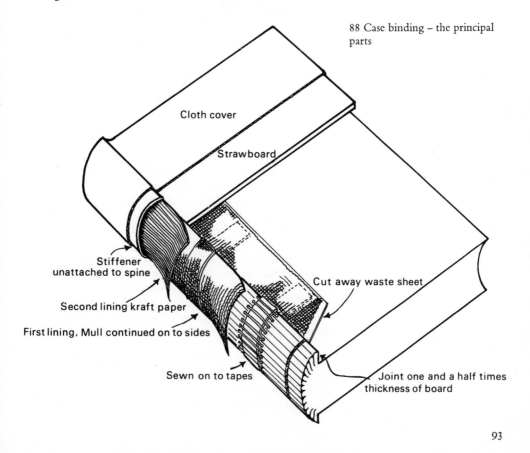

88 Case binding – the principal parts

Cloth cover

Strawboard

Stiffener unattached to spine

Second lining kraft paper

First lining, Mull continued on to sides

Sewn on to tapes

Cut away waste sheet

Joint one and a half times thickness of board

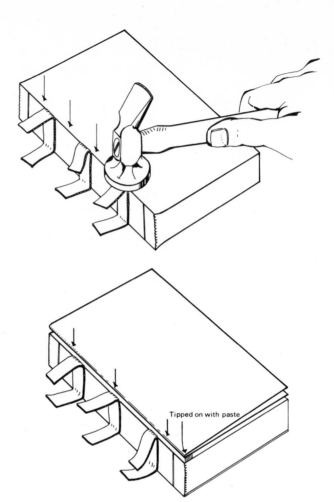

89 Hammering the thread into the paper

90 Tipped-on endpapers

Flat-back case binding

Sections are folded or, if it is a repair and rebind job, the book is pulled, the groove knocked out, repaired and pressed as explained on pp. 49–54. Endpapers can be a single fold tipped on or the common made style, depending on the weight and quality of the book. To identify the work, title or number them on the front of the endpapers. A flat-backed case should be marked up for either French or tape sewing; the number of tapes is determined by the size of the book. If the sections are few, sew without a frame. In order to reduce the swell caused by stitching, beat the spine with a hammer to drive the thread into the paper.

As the single-fold endpaper has no protective waste sheet it is tipped on after reducing the swell. Paste both folds for 5 mm, line them up with the spine edge, rub them down and leave them to dry under a weight.

Next, mark up the book for cutting. Glue up the spine with flexible glue and knock up. Cut the foredge, but before cutting head and tail, pack the book with waste paper if necessary, as explained on p. 156. Strawboards are now cut, to overhang the size of the book by 3 mm at head, tail and foredge but 7 mm short from the spine. The back strip (of the same weight of board) is cut as wide as the spine and as long as the boards. Board is selected to accord with the weight and thickness of the book. As a guide, a thin book requires a strawboard of 1000 gsm and a book that is 50 mm (2 in.) thick a board of 1800 gsm. If the book is out of square, the boards must still be cut true and to the same size, because boards of different sizes cause a strain on the sewing and hinging.

Place the book between its boards in a finishing press and cut a first lining of mull long enough to cover both cerfs and overlapping each side by 30 mm (1¼ in.). Glue the spine thinly with flexible glue and position the mull. Lightly glue again before rubbing down with a folder. The second lining, of kraft paper, is cut to the same size as the spine and is glued on to it, damped with a sponge and rubbed down with a folder. The damp paper moulds readily, excludes the air and on drying will contract to make perfect adhesion.

Position the boards on the book with the squares set and make a template for the covering cloth by placing the book 18 mm (¾ in.) from the top and right-hand edges of a sheet of waste paper. Position the spine strip and wrap the waste round, holding the

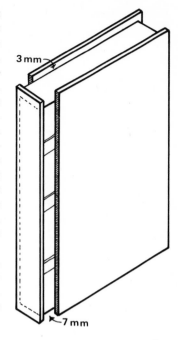

91 (*Above*) Strawboards cut to size

92 (*Left*) First and second linings glued on

93 (*Below left*) Making a template for the cloth

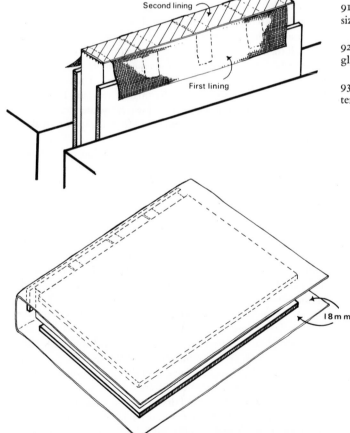

boards firmly in place. Allow the extra 18 mm turn-in on the other two edges and cut the cloth using this template.

Position one board on the cloth 18 mm from the top and right-hand edge and with this as a guide make two pitching lines down the foredge and along the top of the cloth. Place the boards on the book, setting the squares at the foredge but knocking them up to the tail of the book. Put it down so that the foredge projects over the edge of the bench where it may be picked up without disturbing the boards. (When making the case the concern is with the thickness of the book and the distance between the boards and not with the squares at head and tail.)

Lay the cloth out on a waste sheet and, using cold or hot thin glue, brush from the middle outwards until the cloth is evenly glued. Pick up the book and line it up on the pitch marks. Hold the top board, place the spine strip and wrap the cloth over, only removing the retaining hand when the cloth is in position. Throw back the board and remove the book. Centre the strip, and if the boards do not line up to the pitch marks lift or slide them into position. Rub the boards down with a folder and as each corner is turned off the edge of the bench, cut off the cloth at an angle of 45° and at a distance that is one and a half times the thickness of the board. Turn in at head and tail, modelling the cloth to the board with a folder.

Nip in the corners and turn the foredges. Turn the case over and rub it down with the fist or a folder, but do not use a folder too vigorously unless through a paper shield, as thinner cloths will mark easily. If the cloth is hard and resistant, nip the case flat in the press between boards. Run the folder down the edges of the strip and the inner edges of the boards to firm down the cloth. The turn-in may be irregular; if so, trim out to the smallest margin. The case is titled more easily at this stage. Trim down the waste sheet, if used, and also the tapes and mull 25 mm (1 in.) from the spine to make a flange.

As in all binding operations, the equipment and materials should be assembled before the work is begun; for casing in, apart from the usual tools, two sheets of waste paper, paste and two pressing boards will be needed.

Lay the case on the bench with the front to the left and the book with the back uppermost. Put a sheet of waste under the board paper and paste the board paper, tapes and mull. Remove the waste, pick up the book and pitch it on to the back cover, setting equal squares at head, tail and foredge. Place another waste under the front board paper and paste up. Remove the waste, pick up the whole book and turn it over on to the front board. Look directly down, so that the back board can be placed exactly over the front board, and all squares will be the same. Do not open the book but place it between pressing boards with the back strip outside; nip in the centre of the press for a few seconds.

Remove the book and examine it; if the right amount of paste has been used the endpapers will be stuck firmly and cleanly, and it may be left in the press until dry. To avoid unsightly marks on the fly leaves made by the tapes under pressure, slip a thin pulp card between the boards and the leaf before pressing. A common fault is the loss of a square at the foredge and this occurs when the boards are out of square or the distance between the boards is incorrect. A flat-backed case opens well but it is not as durable as a case binding with a rounded spine.

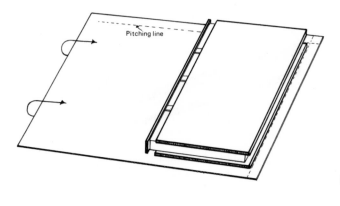

94 Glued cloth wrapped round

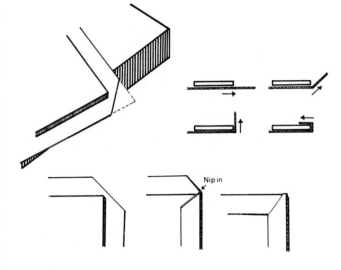

95 Turning in the cloth round the board (case binding)

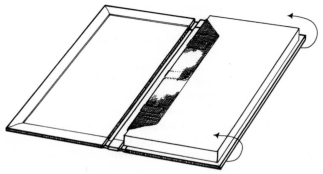

96 Casing in

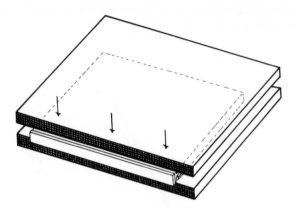

97 Book between pressing
boards

Better books should be forwarded as follows. Prepare the book,
press it, and make the common made endpapers. Mark it up for
sewing on tapes (heavy books are best set up in a sewing frame).
Pin loops of tape round the crossbar. Cut a length of tape, wrap it
round a tape sewing key and insert it into the platform slot. Pin
the tape to the loop and when all tapes are attached, in positions
corresponding with those marked on the spine, tighten the screws
until the tapes are rigid. Selecting the thread carefully for thickness
(see p. 62), sew the sections, keeping an even tension on the
thread. Release the sections from the frame and trim down the
tapes to 30 mm (1¼ in.) on either side. Endpapers differ in quality
and thickness from the text paper, sewing tends to be looser, and
they are apt to become misplaced when backing, so it is safer to
tip them in. Lay the book on the edge of the bench with the endpapers thrown back. Paste an area 3 mm wide, protecting the
adjoining section with waste, and pull the endpapers over flush
with the fold of the first and last sections. Leave this to dry under
a weight. The book should not be pressed as the spine would be
distorted under pressure because of the swell. Mark up for cutting
and indicate the depth of the joint, which should be one and a half
times the thickness of the board.

A limitation of cloth as a covering material is its inability to fold
back sharply on itself at the hinge, hence the extra-deep joint. If
the joint and the board are the same size the board will open only
halfway and this places a strain on the first few sections. The hinge
will split and the endpapers pull up.

Glue the spine with flexible glue, rubbing it into the channels
between the sections. If possible before the glue is dry, knock up
to the head and spine, cut the foredge, round and back; smear a
little paste on the spine if you need to keep it moist. Cut the head
and tail. The boards should be cut flush with the joint with 3 mm
squares on all three sides. Cut a stiffener, the width of the spine and
as long as the boards, for the back of the case. The material varies
according to the book: for example, kraft paper is ideal for thin
books but thick books will require manilla or pulp card. Next,
glue on the first and second linings.

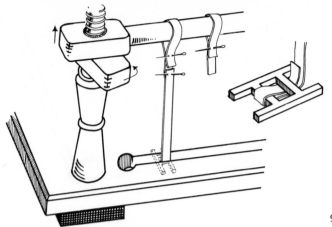

98 Sewing frame with tape key

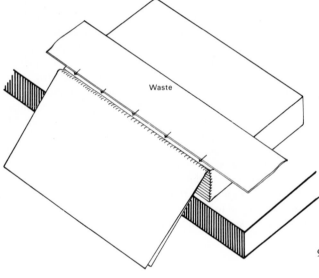

Waste

99 Tipping on endpapers

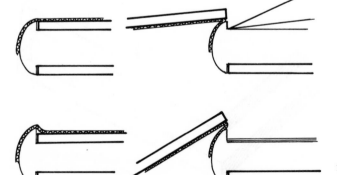

100 Reason for the depth of a
cloth-hinged joint

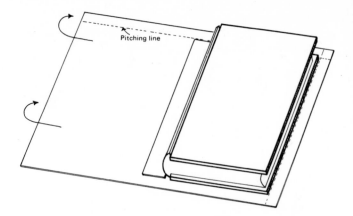

101 Folding the cloth round the board

Make a template for the covering material by setting the boards in position on the book and placing it on a sheet of waste paper, 18 mm (¾ in.) from the top and right-hand edges. Wrap the paper round, mark off the 18 mm turn-in on the other edges and cut the cloth using this template. Mark the pitching lines on the cloth as previously described and apply the adhesive. Glue is satisfactory for book cloth but buckram and other stiff cloth should be softened first with an application of paste and then glue. (Some binders prefer to work with a paste and glue mixture; both methods give a longer working time as the adhesive sets more slowly.)

Remove the glued cloth to a clean surface and position the book with the boards flush with the joint and the tail. Line the stiffener against the spine and wrap the cloth tightly round the curve of the spine and on to the top board.

Remove the book, line up the boards to the pitch marks, centre the stiffener, cut off the corners and turn in the edges. Nip the case flat between boards, trim out the uneven turn-in and allow it to dry under a weight. Lettering (see next chapter) can be done at this stage directly on to the cloth, or a leather label can be tooled and put aside to be pasted on to the spine later.

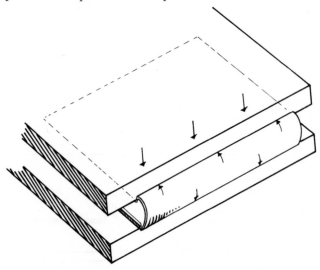

102 Forming the back of the case

Trim down the waste sheet, tapes and mull to 30 mm from the joint as in the flat-backed case. Before casing in, the joints of the book are hooked over the inner edges of the case and put between boards in the press. Sharpen up the joint edges against the pressing boards and form the back of the case to the rounded spine by rubbing with thumb and folder.

Now case the book in, taking care that the front cover and front of the book correspond, so that the book is not cased in upside-down. Put a sheet of paper under the back board paper and paste the board paper, waste, tapes and mull. Remove the sheet, turn the book over and hook the joint against the spine edge of the back board, setting the squares at head and tail. The foredge square will be right if the case has been made correctly. Place another sheet under the front board paper and paste up. Remove the waste and bring the front board over, hooking it into the joint and squaring it perfectly on top of the back board. The book should not be opened for examination, as the position of the endpapers would be disturbed, but is nipped immediately in the press with the pressing boards up to the joint. Examine it after a few seconds then replace it for several hours to dry. (The thickest part of the book, where tapes, mull and waste bulk, must lie directly under the screw of the press, otherwise the sloping platen will give uneven pressure.)

The case binding can be strengthened by overcasting the first and last sections, by sewing on extra tapes, by using linen-jointed endpapers and by making a hollow so that the back of the cover is glued to a tube on the spine (see p. 115). Heavier cloth can be used in cased work if the American groove is incorporated; this is explained in Chapter 9, p. 203. Another innovation is to extend the stiffener to the same size as the height of the cloth so that it is incorporated in the turn-in to make a firmer head and tail.

Full leather case binding

A single-section manuscript or presentation pamphlet can be bound attractively as a case binding in full leather with a leather joint. The section, with fly leaves folded round, is sewn on to a strip of leather with five-hole thread stitching. The leather, pared very thinly, should be as long as the book and 35 mm (1¾ in.) wide. After sewing, the book is cut square and gilded or, if handmade paper is used, is left uncut to retain the deckle edge. Thin mill-boards are cut with a 3-mm overhang and short of the spine by 7 mm; they should be lined on the inside with a well pasted sheet of bond paper to counteract the pull of the leather cover. The boards may be bevelled with a gradual slope on the outside edges, to give an elegant appearance.

A template is made by positioning the boards on the book, wrapping a sheet of waste paper around and allowing a 15-mm (⅝-in.) turn-in on all edges. Cut the leather from this pattern and pare it thinly all over, particularly down the centre and round the edges. (A case binding will not function properly unless the leather is pared sufficiently.)

Lay the leather out and glue it with a vegetable glue. Place the book, with the boards in position, 15 mm from two edges and

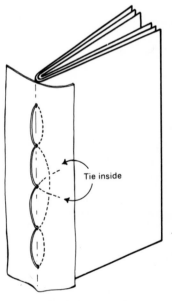

Tie inside

103 Leather joint on single-section binding

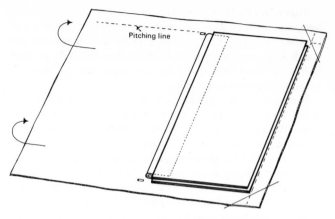

104 Single-section binding:
stage 2

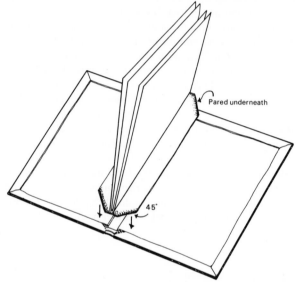

105 Single-section binding:
stage 3

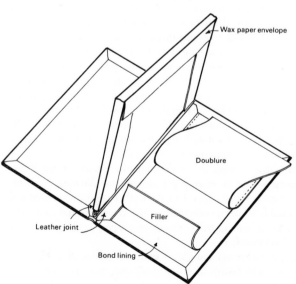

106 Single-section binding:
stage 4

wrap the leather round. Remove the book and pare off the corners at 45°, a little way from the corners of the boards. Insert small pieces of cord, as wide as the book, at both ends between the boards and turn in the head and tail. Leave it to dry flat under a weight. Pare away the corners of the leather hinge to a 45° angle and pare the turn in at the joints of the case. Protect the text with a wax-paper envelope and case the book in, as described in flat-backed work, but gluing only the leather hinge; the leather is moulded into the joint with thumb and folder. Trim out the turn-ins to an even margin.

As glue has been used and the boards lined to counteract the pull of the leather there should be no outward warp, but an extra lining of bond paper may be necessary. A filler of pulp card is glued in to bring the surface of the board level with the leather. Using the same type of paper as the fly leaves, cut doublures to cover the fill-in, leaving a generous margin for subsequent tooling. The paper is glued into position using divider lines as pitching marks. Finally, press the book between metal plates covered with paper on the inside and polished boards outside.

The operations for case binding can be summed up as follows:

1 Collate	16 Back
2 Pull	17 Cut head and tail
3 Knock out the old groove	18 Cut the boards and spine stiffener
4 Repair	
5 Press	19 Apply first lining of mull
6 Make the endpapers	20 Apply second lining of kraft paper
7 Mark up for sewing and saw in the cerf	
8 Set up the sewing frame	21 Make the template for the covering material
9 Sew	22 Cut out the cloth and make the case
10 Tip the endpapers into position	
11 Mark up the depth of joint and guide lines for cutting head, tail and foredge	23 Trim out inside of case
	24 Title the case
	25 Trim the tapes, mull and waste sheet
12 Glue up the spine	26 Shape and form the spine of the case
13 Knock up square	
14 Cut foredge	27 Case in
15 Round	28 Press

THE LIBRARY STYLE

From the middle of the nineteenth century the heavy demand for bound books to supply public and private libraries led to a deterioration of standards. Binders were more involved in the appearance of a book and less concerned with strength and durability. Costs of binding were reduced by dubious binding practices and the use of unskilled labour. Books were sewn by the sunk cord method on very thin cord and boards were placed flush with the joint. Calf was the fashionable leather and because of demand its tanning was simplified and speeded up by the use of injurious

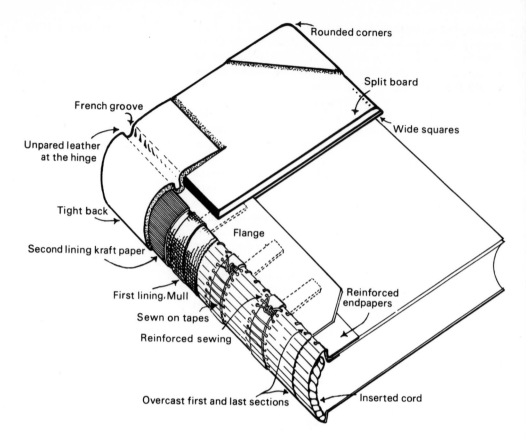

Rounded corners

Split board

French groove

Wide squares

Unpared leather
at the hinge

Tight back

Flange

Second lining Kraft paper

First lining, Mull

Reinforced
endpapers

Sewn on tapes

Reinforced sewing

Overcast first and last sections

Inserted cord

107 The library style: principal parts

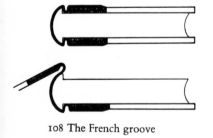

108 The French groove

acids. It was further weakened by the excessive paring necessary for the style of binding. Backs were stiffly lined to take gold tooling, and this made them inflexible and brittle. Endpapers were usually no more than a fold of weak marbled paper.

This style, with its thin boards and elegant finishing, was unable to withstand constant and heavy use by a public many of whom had no understanding of or sympathy with the books they used, and to overcome this problem a style of binding was evolved using many of the features of the binding of account books. The main strength of this style, termed the 'library style', lies in the use of thick unpared leather at the hinge, and the use of morocco instead of calf, as it is stronger and more durable.

As the diagram shows, a flush-jointed book can open well only if the leather is pared down the hinge to allow freedom for the boards. The library-style board is set away from the joint and the gap is known as the 'French groove'. The leather is moulded into this groove and when the board is opened it stands away and high off the joint, allowing a free opening even with unpared leather.

Sewing on to unbleached linen tape was introduced and proved more durable than hemp cord; other constructional features were the tight back, endpapers reinforced with linen, and the protection of the tape inside a double board known as the 'split board'. Endpapers and the first and last few sections were further strengthened by overcasting, guarding with linen and reinforcing the sewing. The library style is not an elegant style but it fulfils its purpose of withstanding heavy and constant use.

Books to be bound by this method are checked, collated, pulled, the groove knocked out, repaired, guarded and pressed as already described. Hidden or exposed linen-jointed endpapers are made as explained in Chapter 6 (p. 58). Mark up for sewing as before but include an extra tape. Saw in the cerf but without touching the endpapers. For heavy books or those in constant use, the first and last sections can be guarded with a 12-mm (½-in.) jaconette strip or overcast with a fine linen thread – or both. This will increase the strength at the first and last sections, which are the first to wear.

Set up a sewing frame (see p. 63). It is preferable to sew the endpapers at the same time as the sections, to give even tension of sewing. Both types of endpapers are sewn as illustrated on p. 59 (9 and 10). Sewing is continued until the third section when, on coming out at the tape position, the loops round the tapes of the previous two are hooked up by the needle and looped round twice before going into the section. This is only recommended for heavy books, however, as if the thread is pulled too tightly the spine becomes concave and difficulty is experienced in backing. The same is done on the completion of sewing, when the endpaper thread is hooked round the previous two sections.

Tip the endpapers and the first and last sections of the text in position with paste. Mark up for cutting and mark the depth of the joint, which is equal to the thickness of the board, and is therefore established by the weight of the book. The process of gluing up, knocking up, cutting the foredge, rounding, backing and cutting the head and tail is continued.

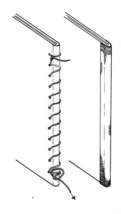

109 Two ways of treating the first and last sections

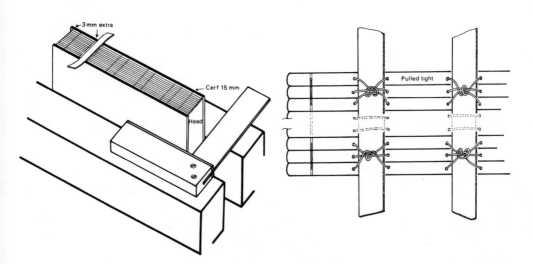

Library-style boards are on the thick side, and are known as 'split boards'. For most small books they are made of a light straw-board of 500 gsm inside, and a thick millboard on the outside. These are cut 15 mm ($\frac{9}{16}$ in.) larger than required and the heavier board is glued, to control warping, for two-thirds of its width.

110 Library style marked up for sewing

111 Reinforcing the sewing on first and last three sections

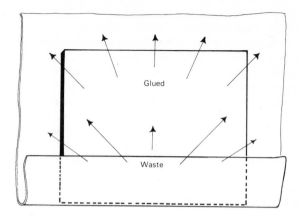

112 Gluing up split board

The strawboard is placed on top, knocked up to the open end, and both are nipped in the press. The boards can be cut to size in the board cutter almost immediately, leaving equal squares at head, tail and foredge but making an allowance for the French groove at the spine edge. This is determined by the size and weight of the book, as we have seen, and by the thickness of the leather to be used. Most standard books will need a groove of 5 mm. A thick knitting needle or similar rod of the required diameter can be laid along the joint as a gauge, and the board thrust against it.

The waste sheet is glued 60 mm (2⅜ in.) from the spine; the tapes are glued to this and moulded into the joint with the bone folder. The waste is then folded foredge to joint and boned down, trapping the tapes inside. The whole is trimmed as in Fig. 114, forming a flange to go into the split board. To attach the boards, the opening of the split board is glued thinly on both sides, closed, then rubbed down by hand to distribute the glue evenly. The gauge is quickly placed along the joint, the split board opened and the flange inserted into the split. The board is set against the gauge and head and tail squares set. Nip the book in the press immediately, placing the pressing boards up to the edge of the split boards (removing the rods), and position the whole thing in the centre of the press. Examine the squares after a few seconds to see if they are correct, then replace the book, in good shape, in the centre of the press.

113 (*Below*) Gauge for the French groove

114 (*Below right*) Flange formed from waste sheet

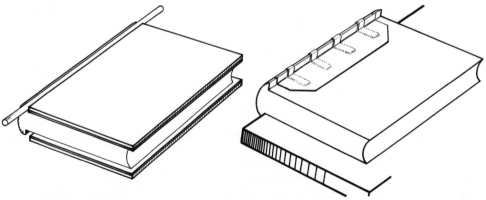

While it is in the press the back can be set and cleaned. The glue on the spine, put on for the cutting and backing, can be removed by smearing paste quite thickly on the spine and leaving it for five or ten minutes. The paste is then scraped off, leaving only thin lines of glue between the sections. This operation is important for the durability of the book, as not only does it clean the spine of dirt and excess glue but, on drying, the spine will retain its shape permanently.

At this stage the headbands are sewn. For the construction of first and second linings, set the book up in a finishing press. The first lining is mull cut a little longer than the spine and exactly the same width. Glue the spine thinly with flexible glue or cold vegetable glue. Position the mull, lightly glue again on top and bone it down firmly, removing any excess glue. The second lining is kraft paper, cut the same size as the mull. Glue the paper, position it, dampen it and bone it down firmly to exclude air.

A smooth spine will wear better than an uneven one, so when the spine is dry the second lining is sandpapered, but not so deeply as to cut the stitching. A repeat lining of brown paper is glued on top and this again can be sandpapered to produce a smooth back. Depending on the width of the spine, yet another layer of paper can be placed, but a lining of mull and three brown papers, even if sanded down, is like a thin card and can restrict the opening. Far better to have fewer linings and an uneven back than an inflexible spine.

Cutting out the leather

A library style can be bound in quarter, half or full leather: proportions are a matter of judgement but as a generalization there should be not less than 35 mm (1⅜ in.) of leather appearing on the sides, and the diagonal of the corner should be the same. Cut out the leather economically, using the templates for size. No paring is necessary down the hinge as long as the leather is not too thick but the rest of the leather can be pared in two ways. If a long bevel is pared (1 in the diagram above) the cloth or paper on the sides becomes part of the board and is below the surface of the leather and does not wear away so easily. If the short bevel is

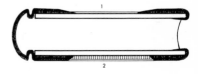

116 Long and short bevel in half-binding

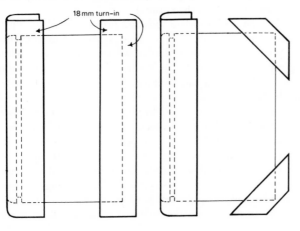

18 mm turn-in

115 Templates for half-binding

Board positions

117 Pared leather for both
methods

used(2), the sides are filled in with an inferior pulp card to bring
them up level with the surface of the leather, and the siding is
glued to this. Thus the boards are thickened and the bevel on the
boards is lost.

Covering

Prepare the book for covering by slightly bevelling the edges of
the boards and taking the sharpness off the corners with sandpaper.
Rub down any unevenness of the boards, clear out nubs of glue
from the French groove and trim the linings down to the level of
the top and bottom of the spine.

The corners or foredge strips should be pasted on first as a
matter of expedience, for once the spine is attached the book cannot
be opened until it is dry. Paste up the corners or strips thinly and
evenly with a beating motion of the brush and while these are
absorbing the paste arrange the necessary materials and equipment:
a damp sponge, a rounded heavy bone folder and a thin pointed
one, a length of cotton string and two pieces of woven cord (not
nylon). The last are cut as long as the round of the spine and equal
in thickness to the depth of the squares. (These will be inserted at
head and tail to make up the difference between the top of the
book and the edge of the squares.)

Work on a firm surface such as a paring stone. Paste up the
corners or strips again, using as little as possible because thick paste
lying on the surface of the leather will cause an uneven and unsightly appearance on drying. Position the corner or strip on the
board and, working only with the pressure of the fingers, mould
the leather firmly and tightly to the board. Wipe the corner fold
over with the thumb, assisted by a spot of paste and a tap with a
bone folder. Leather is an amenable material: it can be modelled
while wet and will retain its shape on drying. However, it is
marked easily in its wet state and excessive use of the folder will
cause scoring. Paste is not harmful on the surface, and excess paste
and fingermarks can be wiped off with a damp sponge.

Finally, look along the profile of the boards and if the line is
uneven tap the edges with a folder to consolidate them. Place a

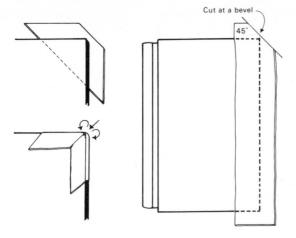

Cut at a bevel

45°

118 Moulding the leather to the board

piece of wax tissue or thin card between the corners and the end-papers to prevent the damp from penetrating, and then put the job aside for a while to let the corners dry off. Do not be in too much of a hurry to cover the spine: a binder always has a number of jobs going at one time and he turns to these when there is a waiting period.

Paste the leather for the spine twice, as for the corners, and also paste the spine of the book and down the sides to be covered. Hold the book by its foredge, and position the leather on the spine so that it is equal at the top and bottom and on the sides, moulding it to the spine as if fitting a tight leather glove on to the fingers. Check that the French groove does not close up, or the foredge square will be lost. Run a damp sponge over the surface; this will keep the paste moist and give a longer working time. (Note that there is a tendency to hold things with the finger nails, and this will cause unsightly marks in the leather. Remove your rings, keep your fingernails short, and learn to hold things with the balls of the fingers.)

Place the book flat on the stone, slightly raise the top board, and the depression of the French groove will show. Push the leather firmly into the groove with a thick-ended folder: this is the only time that a folder is used forcibly on leather. Repeat this on the other side, and then rub the spine with the part of the hand be-tween the finger and thumb to firm it down. Stand the book up-right with the spine away from you and the boards thrown out-wards. The turn-in of the leather at the bottom can be prevented from soiling the lower edge of the pages by covering the edge with a square of paper or turning the leather up at the spine. Rub some paste on the surface of the leather where it is to be turned in. Place the woven cord on the top of the spine and hold it in position. Fold the turn-in over and round the cord and down into the back so that the roll of leather containing the cord sits firmly and tightly on the top edge of the book (and make sure the leather is not wrinkled on the inside). Turn the sides into the gap between the French groove and the joint and model them down on to the inside of the boards. Rub the back again by hand and set the French groove with the folder, pushing out any wrinkled leather.

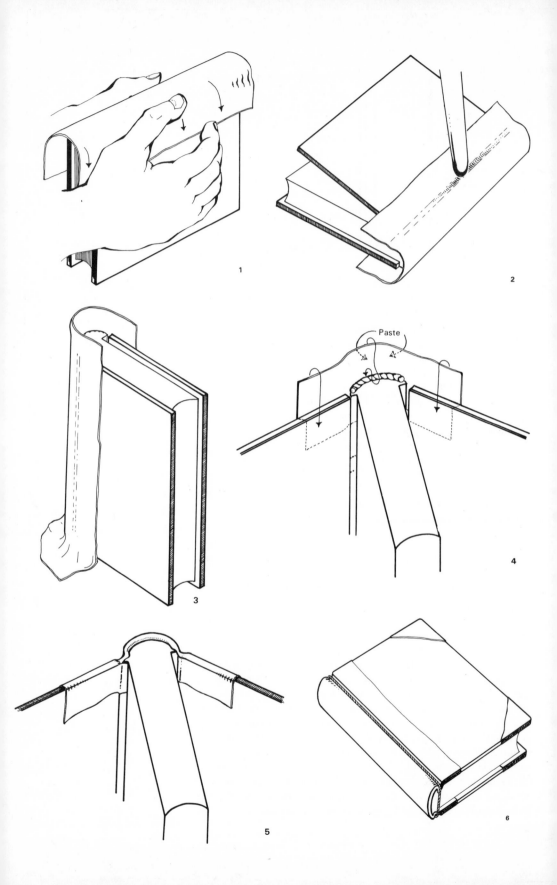

1

2

3

4

Paste

5

6

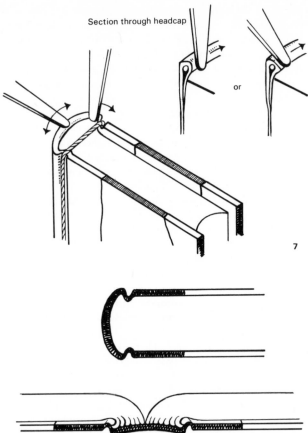

Section through headcap

or

7

119 (*Opposite and left*) Stages in leather half-binding

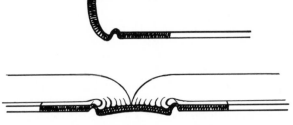

120 Completed binding open and shut

Turn in the other end, rub the back and set the groove similarly.

The book is tied up with cotton string to assist in forming the headcaps; these are shaped by standing the book up on a hard surface and tapping the bottom of the spine with a heavy folder to form a solid, uniform and pleasantly rounded shape. The leather at head and tail can be modelled with the pointed folder as shown in the diagram. Set the French groove again by pushing the tie-up string aside with the folder. Firm the leather everywhere with the hands. Wash over with a damp sponge to remove paste marks and put it between clean, smooth boards with a knocking-down iron as a weight on top. Allow it to dry and then remove the string.

Great care must be taken on opening the book: it must not be wrenched open indiscriminately as a certain degree of stiffness is usual in a newly covered book. Gently ease open the boards by opening and shutting a little at a time until the boards open freely. Place the book on the bench with the boards flat on either side of the vertical pages. Take a couple of sections at a time from either end and gently press down, applying pressure on the spine. Work towards the middle and the book will become flexible. A well-bound library style (if the spine is wide enough) will have the spine flat or slightly concave when opened in the middle and will fall into a regular convex shape when shut.

Trim out the leather on the sides evenly, straight and as wide as possible, measuring with dividers and using a knife and a straight-edge. Pull away towards the cut so that the surface of the board is not damaged. If the leather is edge-pared only, trim out at a 45° bevel with a paring knife. On the very edge of the board, pare away the leather to a long bevel; this will allow the siding material to 'settle' on the edge of the board without an unsightly drop.

The siding material is usually a strong cloth or buckram harmonizing in colour with the leather and it is cut so that it just binds down the edge of the trimmed-out leather. A turn-in of 18 mm (¾ in.) at head, tail and foredge is necessary.

To trim out for the corners, position the cloth on the side and place a pitch mark in pencil as a guide for attaching later; identify each side with a pencil mark. Glue the cloth thinly and evenly, pitch it into position and, using a folder, make certain that the cloth is stuck and follows the profile of the board, and that no 'tunnels' run between the edges of the board and its covering. Nip it in the centre of the press, with the pressing boards up to the edge of the French groove and with a thin piece of card, larger than the book, inside the covers to prevent the turn-over of cloth and leather marking the endpapers. Trim out the inside of the boards, leaving as wide a margin as possible and using dividers to measure.

The exposed board on the inside has to be filled in to bring it level with the trimmed-out leather and cloth turn-in. Cut a piece of pulp card or manilla a little larger than the exposed board and position it against the inner edge of the board. With a hard pencil 'feel' the other edges of the turn-in through the card and this, when cut out with scissors, will make a satisfactory fit. This must be done accurately because, if it is short or overrides the turn-in, the endpapers will go down, and show unsightly depressions or ridges. Glue the filler, position it on the inside of the cover and rub it down vigorously.

Endpapers are put down by the shut method. If the exposed cloth-jointed endpaper is used, place a sheet of waste paper under the board paper to protect the text, and glue the board paper from the middle outwards. Remove the waste and simply shut down the board. Without opening it, nip it in the press for a few seconds. Examine the ends and if stuck firmly place the book under pressure to dry out for some hours.

If using the hidden cloth-jointed end, the linen hinge, which is trimmed to fit between the head and tail turn-ins, may be put down first with glue. It can also be put down after trimming out the inside of the boards and before filling in. The filler is then taken only to the edge of the linen hinge and the board paper is put down on top. Alternatively, the hidden cloth hinge can be incorporated into the split board with the tapes and waste sheet.

Should a wider margin on the inside be preferred the board is thrown open and the endpaper, held between finger and thumb, is pulled tightly down into place. The required margin is marked off with dividers and the board paper is trimmed to size with a knife and straight-edge, with a piece of scrap card beneath it. The endpaper is pasted down by the shut method. As the grain of the

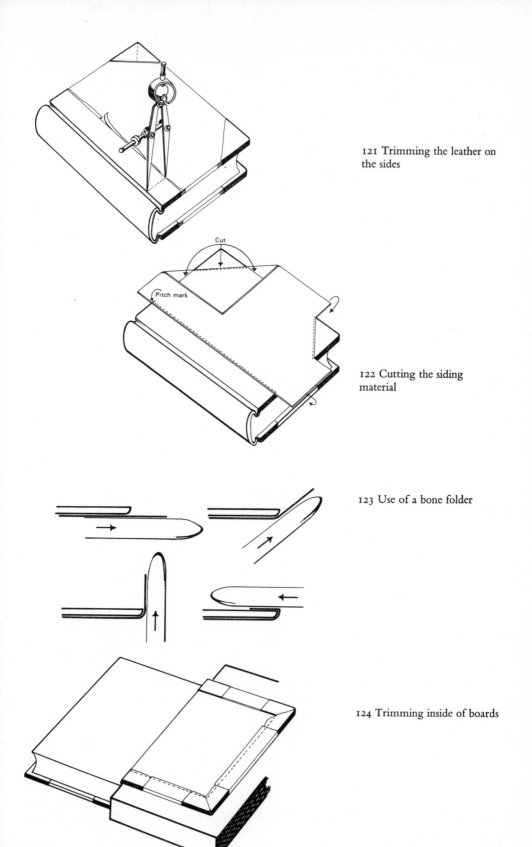

121 Trimming the leather on the sides

122 Cutting the siding material

123 Use of a bone folder

124 Trimming inside of boards

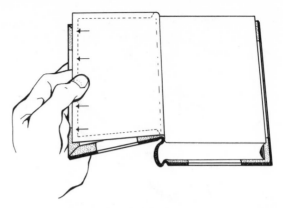

125 Trimming of endpaper

paper is going from head to tail the paper will stretch only towards the foredge when pasted. Thus a little extra should be trimmed off the board paper at the foredge to allow for this stretch. Experience can be the only guide as the amount it will stretch depends on the quality of the paper (a bookbinder must know his papers and tends to work with only a few so that he can control them), the thinness of the paper, the size of the sheet, whether glue or paste is used, the thinness of the adhesive and the speed and method of working.

Press for some hours, and the binding is ready for finishing.

Care of leather

The British Museum have tested and introduced an excellent preservative and polish for leather bindings. Although it is used chiefly by the restorer and refurbisher, it is common practice to treat newly bound books with it as well. It is used sparingly, rubbed well into the leather, particularly down the hinges. It contains 200 grams of lanolin, 300 millilitres of cedarwood oil, 15 grams of beeswax and 310 millilitres of hexane or petroleum ether. The lanolin makes the leather more supple and slows down the drying out, especially in a centrally heated atmosphere. The cedarwood oil is a preservative too, and resists insect pests. Beeswax remains on the surface and improves the appearance of the leather when polished with a cloth. Hexane is the medium which dissolves the ingredients and carries them into the leather.

After paring the cover, and before pasting, the conscientious binder wipes the leather over with a solution of 8 per cent potassium lactate in distilled water. This will replace the natural salts lost by the modern tanning process, the washing with water while covering, and the effect of time. An addition of 0·25 per cent paranitrophenol will preserve the solution and act as a fungicide in the leather.

Varnish made from shellac was once used extensively to disguise poor work and materials, as it gives the book a shiny appearance. It is not recommended, however, because although it is a protection against grime, it seals the leather and prevents it absorbing natural grease from the hands. In time, the varnish turns yellow, hardens and cracks down the hinges of the book. Nevertheless a clear cellulose varnish, sold under the trade name of 'Zapon', is sometimes applied to the leather turn-ins on the inside of the boards. This prevents the dye from the leather staining the endpapers.

Operations for the library style in leather

1 Collate
2 Pull
3 Knock out the old groove
4 Repair
5 Press
6 Make the endpapers
7 Mark up for sewing and saw in the cerf
8 Overcast first and last section
9 Set up the sewing frame
10 Sew
11 Tip the endpapers into position and also the first and last section
12 Mark up the depth of the joint and guide lines for cutting the head, tail and foredge
13 Glue up the spine
14 Knock up square
15 Cut foredge
16 Round
17 Back
18 Cut head and tail
19 Prepare the split boards
20 Cut the boards to size
21 Prepare flange for insertion into split boards
22 Attach boards
23 Press, set and clean off spine
24 Sew headbands if required
25 Apply first lining of mull
26 Apply second lining of kraft paper, sandpaper, apply subsequent linings
27 Make templates for the covering leather
28 Cut out and pare the leather
29 Prepare the book for covering
30 Attach the leather corners
31 Attach the leather spine
32 Tie up and form the headcaps
33 When dry, 'open' the book
34 Trim out the leather on the sides
35 Side with cloth or paper
36 Trim out the insides of the boards
37 Put down the hidden cloth joint of the endpapers if applicable
38 Fill in
39 Trim out and put down the endpapers
40 Title and polish
41 Press

THE LIBRARY STYLE IN BUCKRAM

The library style can be covered economically and successfully in buckram. The tight-backed leather spine opens flat or slightly concave, but as buckram is stiff and hard the spine is modified by the attachment of a paper tube called a 'hollow'. The back remains round and the sections throw up for an easier opening. Although the hollow back is necessary for covering in vellum or buckram, and for sections of stiff paper, there is more strain on the sewing, the back linings and the spine shape.

Operations are continued as for the library style until the first and second linings are placed. Sandpapering is unnecessary but a strip of kraft paper is cut for the hollow, 18 mm ($\frac{3}{4}$ in.) longer than

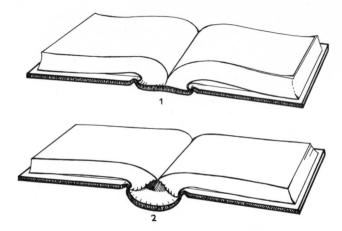

126 Library style in leather 1.
Library style in buckram 2

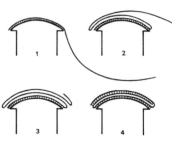

127 Stages in the making of a
hollow

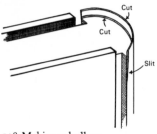

128 Making a hollow
(continued)

the spine and over three times its width. Set the book up in a finishing press, glue the spine, place the paper flush with the spine edge and gently rub it down. Fold it on the opposite edge, take it to the other side and fold it again. Finally, bring it back and make the third fold and cut it off at the crease. The kraft paper will now be exactly three times the width of the spine. Without delay, remove the paper from the glued spine and, if necessary, reglue the spine. Replace the centre portion of the hollow, dampen it and rub it down vigorously. Bring over the outside piece so that the glued side is on top and fold over the unglued third on to this; dampen it and bone it down firmly. One layer will be on the book, and two will be off; to stiffen the hollow extra single pieces can be attached and liberally coated with glue to give a firm, hard shape.

When dry, the hollow is prepared for covering by slitting down the extreme sides of the tube for 25 mm (1 in.) at head and tail. First and second linings and the part of the hollow glued to the spine are cut level with the edges while the free part is cut down level with the boards. Make a template for the covering material by placing the book 18 mm from each edge of a piece of waste paper. Add 18 mm extra from the tail to give the length. Wrap the paper round the book and add 18 mm from the foredge to give the width. Cut the buckram from this pattern.

Cut two pieces of cord equal in thickness to the squares and a fraction shorter than the round of the spine. Two rods, such as knitting needles, as wide as the French groove are linked together with elastic bands and put ready with two pressing boards.

Buckram is made pliable for covering by pasting and gluing immediately. The additional moisture in the paste will soften the buckram and act as a base for retaining glue on the surface; it will also slow the drying action. (A similar result can be obtained by applying a mixture of paste and glue.)

Glue the spine of the book and pitch it on the glued buckram, allowing the 18-mm turn-in. Draw the cloth round the spine and on to the top board and run a heavy bone folder into the French groove to set its position under the buckram. Clip the prepared rods into this groove, place pressing boards with their edges on the rods and nip in the press for a moment.

129 Buckram cover: first stage

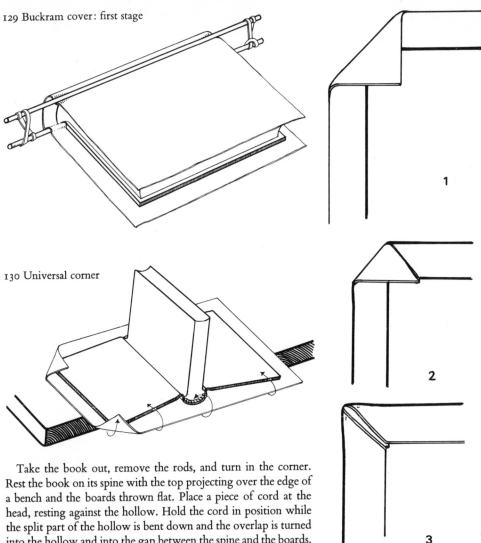

130 Universal corner

1

2

3

Take the book out, remove the rods, and turn in the corner. Rest the book on its spine with the top projecting over the edge of a bench and the boards thrown flat. Place a piece of cord at the head, resting against the hollow. Hold the cord in position while the split part of the hollow is bent down and the overlap is turned into the hollow and into the gap between the spine and the boards. Model the buckram over the boards along the head and over at the corners. The tail is turned in the same way. Turn in both foredges. The corner treatment is known as the 'universal corner' and the diagrams will make it clear. It is not an elegant method but it is hard-wearing and will not burst open on impact.

Tap the corners and edges to make them solid. Place an old piece of limp book cloth across the spine to prevent marking and rub down with a bone folder. Stretch a piece of string across from groove to groove and model the headcaps into shape. Replace the rods and boards and put in the press to dry.

The covering operations must be done quickly and efficiently as if the cloth is dry it will not stick and the cover will be ineffectual. It helps if the hollow back is glued up also, at the same time as the cloth.

The operations of opening, trimming out, filling in and putting down endpapers and final pressing are the same as for leather.

131 Turning the buckram over the boards

132 Modelling the headcap into shape

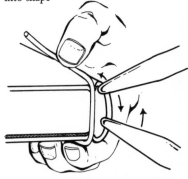

1 Collate
2 Pull
3 Knock out the old groove
4 Repair
5 Press
6 Make the endpapers
7 Mark up for sewing and saw in the cerf
8 Overcast first and last section
9 Set up the sewing frame
10 Sew
11 Tip the endpapers into position and also the first and last section
12 Mark up the depth of the joint and guide lines for cutting the head, tail and foredge
13 Glue up the spine
14 Knock up square
15 Cut foredge
16 Round
17 Back
18 Cut head and tail
19 Prepare the split boards
20 Cut the boards to size
21 Prepare flange for insertion into split boards
22 Attach boards
23 Press, set, clean off spine
24 Apply first lining of mull
25 Apply second lining of kraft paper
26 Attach hollow back and slit down the hollow
27 Make the template for the buckram cover
28 Cover
29 When dry, 'open' the book
30 Trim out the inside of the boards
31 Put down the hidden cloth joint of the endpapers if applicable
32 Fill in
33 Trim out and put down the endpapers
34 Letter direct on to the buckram or cut, pare, attach and title a leather label
35 Press

THE FLEXIBLE STYLE

Until the end of the eighteenth century almost all books were bound in the flexible style. The term 'flexible' refers to the spine, which becomes concave when the book is opened. Very early books consisted of folded vellum sheets sewn on double thongs of twisted pigskin, with the headband incorporated in the sewing. The book was rounded only and the thongs laced and pegged into shaped wooden boards. A wrapper of leather was glued to the backs of the sections and the boards, and turned in over the edges.

The introduction of paper in the fourteenth century and the invention of printing one hundred years later resulted in the style becoming sophisticated and bindings elegant. Single cords replaced thongs, card was used instead of wooden boards, and the headbands were sewn separately. Thick hide and pigskin were used for the larger books, and small printed volumes were covered in calf and sheepskin. Much later books were printed on machine-made paper, which could not withstand the strain of sewing the flexible way. For this reason, as well as for economic ones, the style was almost abandoned in favour of the sunk cord method.

The flexible style should be used only for books worthy of a fine binding, with strong paper and generous margins. Binding in

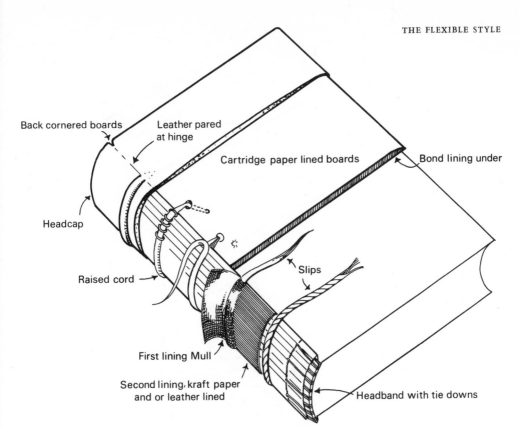

Back cornered boards

Leather pared at hinge

Cartridge paper lined boards

Bond lining under

Headcap

Raised cord

Slips

First lining Mull

Second lining kraft paper and or leather lined

Headband with tie downs

the genuine flexible style is difficult for the craftsman as it involves exceptional techniques in sewing, cutting and covering. The best materials are used and such refinements as headbands, edge gilding and decoration are lavished on the work. The style does not, however, lend itself to contemporary designing as any decoration should stem from or link with the bands across the spine. Traditionally, these raised bands are in odd numbers, five being most common, but seven or nine can be used, depending on the size of the book.

133 Flexible style: principal parts

Pull the book, knock out the old groove, and repair and strengthen the first and last two sections with bond paper or Japanese paper. Separate the sections into groups of five and put them between thick metal plates in the standing press for prolonged and intense pressing. After pressing, collate the book and, leaving out the endpapers, knock the sections up square to the head and spine between two pieces of strawboard; screw them up in a finishing press. Check for squareness with a carpenter's square, using this to knock the sections level.

Mark up for sewing. Within marks 3 mm from the head and 6 mm from the tail, make six equal divisions with dividers. (The addition at the tail gives 'weight' at the bottom, making the middle band optically central.) Use the carpenter's square to draw parallel lines across the book, marking each section with firm black dots. Saw in cerfs 15 mm ($\frac{5}{8}$ in.) from each end.

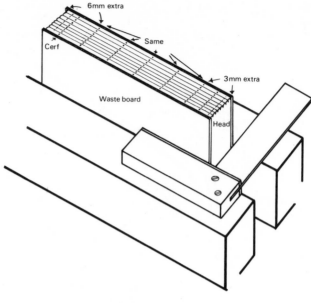

134 Marked up for sewing

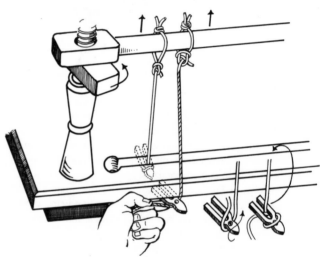

135 Setting up the sewing frame

The work described includes only the made endpaper, without the stiff leaf, as the leather joint and doublure are described later (see p. 136). Endpapers are made larger and the heads trimmed square with the sections. They are lined up with the head of the book and the positions of the cords and cerfs marked. (Endpapers are not cut with the saw.)

Sewing cord is selected according to the size and weight of the book, and if the cord appears too heavy a strand or two can be removed. It is better if the cords are a little on the thick side, provided that they are not clumsy, for thin, elegant bands are too weak and a 'neat' book probably means that the binder has concerned himself more with the appearance than with strength.

The sewing frame can be set up permanently for cord and tape sewing by pinning loops of tape and tying cord round the crossbar; loops not in immediate use are pushed to the right. Lower the crossbar as far as possible and tie lengths of cord to the loops, securing them with sewing keys. The key is held flat against the underside of the platform as a measure and the cord twisted round and held, as illustrated. Pass the key through the slot in the base of the frame and, when all are in position, tighten the screws until the cords are firm. Alternatively, the cord may be held in position without keys by wedging a cutting board into the slot to trap the cords.

Place the sections on a pressing board to the left of the frame to facilitate reaching the insides of the sections when sewing, and line up the cords to coincide with the marked lines. Stand a carpenter's square on the platform and adjust the cords until they are vertical. Tighten the screws further so that the cords are rigid from base to bar.

Sew the book as illustrated in Fig. 52, p. 68, pulling the thread tightly round each cord as the next is sewn; keep an even tension of thread from section to section. Beat down every two sections with a loaded stick to consolidate the sewing and should the swell build up too much after five sections, change to a thinner thread or sew two up, reverting to the original thread for the last five sections. After sewing, release the screws, undo the knots, remove the sewing keys and cut the slips down to 100 mm (4 in.) on each side. If the swelling is still in excess, beat it out with a hammer and a knocking-down iron.

Tip the endpapers and the first and last sections in position with paste and leave them to dry under a weight. Mark off the depth of the joint, equal to the thickness of the board to be used. Glue up the spine with flexible or cold glue, avoiding the bands by 3 mm on either side and keeping the glue clear of the slips. Knock up to the head and spine and round and back the book, keeping the slips outside the backing boards. As the method of sewing restricts the movement of the sections, rounding is sometimes difficult but will be achieved by perseverance. To keep the spine pliable, rub in a little paste. A light hammer with a square face is preferable for the backing operation as it can be used between the cords without crushing them, and the joint can be sharpened under the cords by lifting them and using the claw part of the hammer. If the cords are not at right angles to the spine, tap them into position with a band stick.

Leave the book in the press to dry.

Cut two millboards equal in thickness to the depth of the joint and 12 mm (½ in.) larger than the book either way. Mark them front and back and hold them together with strips of adhesive tape. Cut them with the plough to the same size as the smallest page of the book (as described on p. 70).

Line the front board up to the head and the joint and mark off the exact position of the cords on the spine edge of the board. Place the back board alongside the front and mark off the same positions. Set the dividers to 12 mm and scratch a line down the outside spine edge of each board. Turn them over and score a similar line 22 mm (⅞ in.) from the spine edge on the inside. Draw lines at right angles from the cord positions with a carpenter's

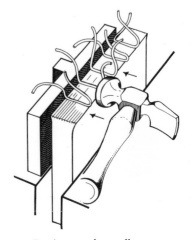

136 Beating out the swell

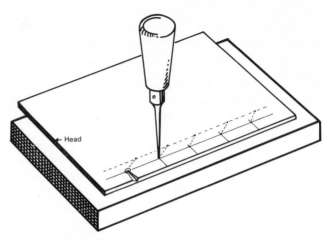

137 Making holes for the slips

square until they intersect the first vertical lines. At these points make pilot dents in the board with an awl. Place the board on a block of wood or lead and hammer the awl through the board, making a hole narrower than the thickness of the cords. Turn the board over and make a return hole at 45° towards the tail on the second scored line. The awl should be blunt, so that the hole erupts out of the board; this is hammered down later to trap the slips. The board is recessed to sink the slips into the board; the wedge-shaped cuts should not be too deep, as cord, when pasted, can be compressed into very little space.

Separate the strands of the cord and tease each one out with a needle to separate the fibres. Stroke the slips with a blunt knife, beginning at the bottom, gradually working up and around the fibres until they are full thickness at the base with a blunt point at the top.

For lacing on the boards, prepare the following: paste, hammer, a pair of shears, and an awl; two thin and two thick metal plates; two pressing boards; four sheets of wax paper; a knocking–down iron held in the end of the lying press. Clear the holes with the awl. Paste up the slips with the fingers, leaving the bottom 12 mm ($\frac{1}{2}$ in.) unpasted. Stand the board vertically against the joint, thread the pasted slips through the first set of holes and return through the others, pulling tightly each time. Ease the board down with a rocking movement until it lies flat without straining against the joint. The board should not be set tightly against the joint as a little play allows thicker leather at the hinge. (Some binders insert an L-shaped piece of manilla in the joint and line the board up to this.) Cut off the excess slips about 5 mm from the return holes, paste them, splay them out in rivet form and tap them with a hammer to secure them. Lace on the other board in the same way.

Support the book in the left hand with one board on the knocking-down iron and hammer the return cords with a knock-and-slide movement of the hammer until they are flattened. Turn the book over and hammer the trimmed off cord (Fig. 140, *1, 2*).

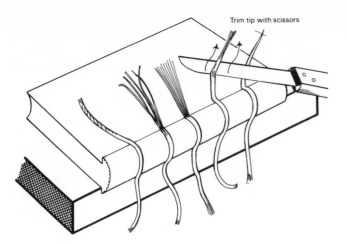

Trim tip with scissors

138 Trimming the slips

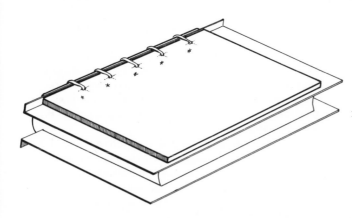

139 Board laced on

140 Hammering the cords

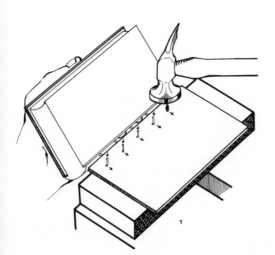

1

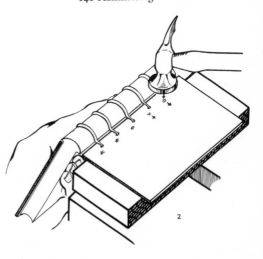

2

Without delay, place the plates and wax papers as shown in the figure and put the whole into the press directly beneath the screw under heavy pressure to dry. While in the press, old glue can be cleaned off the spine with the wooden scraper, and the bands pushed parallel to each other across the spine.

Free the board from the unpasted parts of the slips and prepare it for cutting. Draw a line within the edges of the boards as a guide for cutting the foredge square (3 mm); cutting is done with the aid of trindles. Cut two pieces of thick millboard longer than the book, one wider than the width of the book, and the other the same measurement as the distance between the joint and the cutting line. Push the trindles between the boards and the spine to flatten the back and, provided that the sewing is sound, the swell sufficient and the backing effective, no harm is caused by this operation.

Position the millboards and check that the foredge is flat. Lift and remove the trindles by their string and lower the book between the cheeks of the cutting press, letting the book boards hang free. Manipulate the screws, keeping them tight enough to hold the book firmly but allowing the book and boards to be pushed into the cutting position with the short millboard level with the top of the press. In this process, accuracy is essential. The plough blade can be taken from the plough and run along the top of the press to ascertain exactly where the cut will be made, for it is much better to repeat the operation half a dozen times than to make an incorrect cut.

Heavy books can be bound with tape before the trindles are removed, to prevent the sections from slipping, and in this case cutting boards must be used instead of millboards. In other styles, the foredge is cut before rounding and backing so the shape of the foredge is governed by the movement of the sections. Cutting with trindles after the spine is backed, the foredge is shaped by the movement of the leaves and repeats the curve of the spine. As a matter of interest, there is no reason why trindles should not be used to cut the foredges of the sunk cord and library styles but with the latter the trindles are modified to flat bars and must pierce the flange. Undoubtedly foredges cut this way are far better and more even. If the trindles are not thick enough to flatten the back sufficiently they may be thickened by the addition of thin millboards or metal rulers.

Drop the front board by a 3 mm square at the head, and bring the top of the board level with the surface of the press as a guide for cutting. Protect the other board by throwing it back, and cut into a piece of thick waste board placed flush with the joint. As an alternative, insert a millboard between the book and its board. Drop the back board by the distance of the square and cut the tail.

Edge gilding is carried out at this stage, and trindles may be used to flatten the foredge. This is also the stage at which headbands are sewn.

A genuine flexible style has a tight back, and the movement of the spine should not be restricted by excessive lining. Much depends on the width of the spine, the size of the book, the stiffness of the paper and the covering leather.

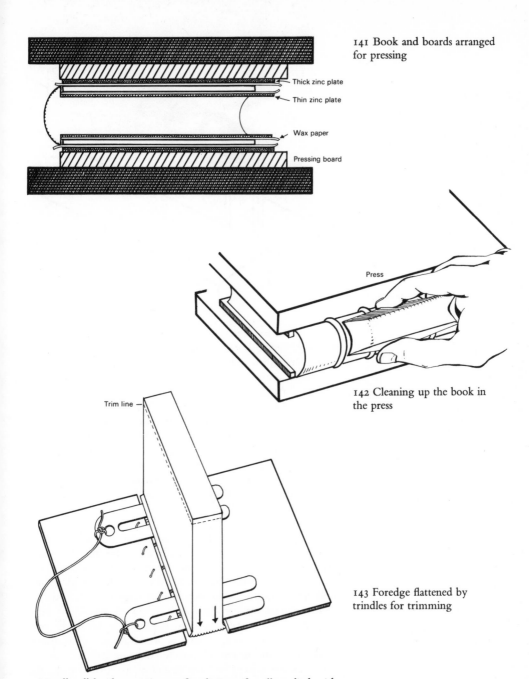

141 Book and boards arranged for pressing

Thick zinc plate

Thin zinc plate

Wax paper

Pressing board

142 Cleaning up the book in the press

Press

Trim line

143 Foredge flattened by trindles for trimming

Usually all books are given a first lining of mull applied with flexible or cold glue. Place the book in a finishing press and model the mull on the spine, covering the bands and allowing it to project a little above the headbands to strengthen them. A second lining of kraft paper is cut as wide as the spine and laid between the bands. The paper is glued, positioned, dampened and rubbed down with a folder. The entire spine may be covered in kraft paper but it is applied in pieces because of the difficulty of modelling over the bands.

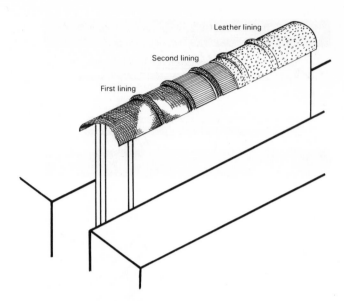

First lining
Second lining
Leather lining

144 Linings laid and moulded on the spine

Nip up the bands to good shape with the band nippers. When the second lining is dry, sandpaper away any unevenness and if further strengthening is needed apply more kraft paper.

Today it is usual to line all but the thinnest books with leather after the first and second linings and this is particularly recommended for large books. Cut a piece of unpared morocco exactly the width but longer than the length of the spine. Paste it twice and glue the spine thinly. Apply the leather, damp it well, and rub it vigorously with a bone folder. Model the leather over the bands with band nippers and beat it down to make it stick thoroughly before it is allowed to dry. The spine can be sandpapered and the bands shaped with a scalpel to give a pliable yet smooth and solid spine.

The insides of the boards are lined with pasted and stretched bond paper to counteract to some degree the pull of the covering leather. The free parts of the slips are pasted into the wedge depressions and rubbed down into position. The outsides of the boards are lined with thick cartridge paper which is glued and well rubbed down. When dry, the cartridge is sandpapered to remove the unevenness of the laced-in slips. As has already been stressed, the practice of achieving a neat result by sewing on very thin cord and leaving the boards unlined leads to a fundamental weakness in construction. The method of lining and sandpapering allows thicker slips to be laced in and is less obvious under the covering leather.

On covering, a head cap is formed at head and tail and, to enable it to be shaped, the corners of the board nearest the spine are cut away; this is called 'back cornering'. As a guide, the cut should be as wide as the thickness of the board and three times as long. A less common alternative is to cut away the inner side of the board in a similar way, but this is more suitable for early books. Boards are very clumsy if left thick at the edges, and bevelling will give a cushioned appearance which is pleasant to see and to handle. It is unnecessary to use very thin boards and overpared leather to achieve elegance. Draw a line 4 mm from the outside edges of the board. Hold a very sharp cobbler's knife at such an angle as to cut along this line and remove almost half the thickness of the board. Finish off with sandpaper to a long curved bevel. Some binders prefer to shape the boards before lacing them on, and this is easier and safer as the sandpapering may damage the headbands and edges. The book is now ready for covering.

When covering, the sections are enveloped with a wax or kraft paper to protect the edges against paste and fingering. The making of templates and the paring of leather for half and quarter bindings have already been explained (p. 107), but for the flexible style the leather must be thinned down the joints with the spokeshave or French knife so that the boards may open freely. The amount to be pared away depends on the original thickness and quality of the leather, the size of the book and the freedom of the boards against the joint; therefore it can only be judged by experiment and experience. The exact position of the joint is found by wrapping the dry leather round the book equally on either side and rubbing the spine with the palm of the hand. The joint and bands will leave an impression which is then marked with a white chinagraph pencil.

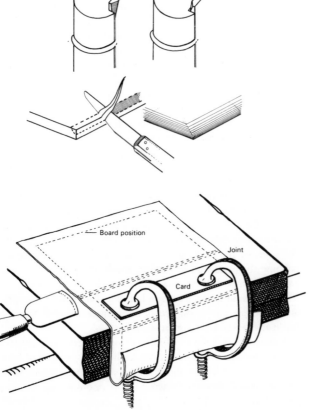

145 Back cornering and bevelling

146 Paring the leather with the French knife.

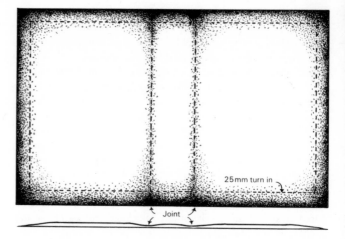

147 Full leather cover pared all round and at the joints

A full leather cover is cut from a template made by wrapping paper round the book with 25 mm (1 in.) extra for the turn-in on the sides. The leather is pared down the joint, as already explained, and the paring eased off, to leave an oval of unpared leather in the centre graduating to minimal thickness at the edges. (A test for evenness in paring is to fold the leather over down the board and joint positions and run a finger and thumb along this fold to feel if there is any irregularity of thickness.) Leather should not be pared too much where the edges of boards occur, for thin leather gives little protection. Slender boards may be elegant but the aim of binding is preservation rather than appearance. Avoid sudden changes in thickness, and test constantly by folding in all directions and feeling for unevenness. On completion of paring, draw pitching marks on the leather to indicate the joint and board positions, and mark the better side for the front.

The following are needed for covering: paste, water, sponge, heavy and pointed thin bone folders, bandstick, band nippers, 45° set square, paring knife, thin thread, blanket, backing board and a clean litho stone. Paste up the leather, brushing vigorously so that no paste is visible on the surface; while this is soaking, check the book, trim down the back linings to the level of the headbands, cut off excess headbanding core, clear the back corners and make sure that the board linings are stuck down firmly.

Paste the leather again. Depending on their type, thickness and hardness, some skins may need three applications of paste. Paste the spine of the book and down the spine edge of the boards, rubbing the paste well in with the hands. Hold the leather in the middle with both hands and gently stretch the way of the spine. This will cause slight distortion but will also give extra length to accommodate the bands. It may not be necessary for all leathers, but it is essential for resistant ones.

Some binders prefer to work on a stone, others on a blanket; the latter is perhaps preferable as wet leather is easily marked by grit or other matter left on the stone. So if you use a stone, wipe it frequently and use it for corners only; carry out the main covering on a blanket.

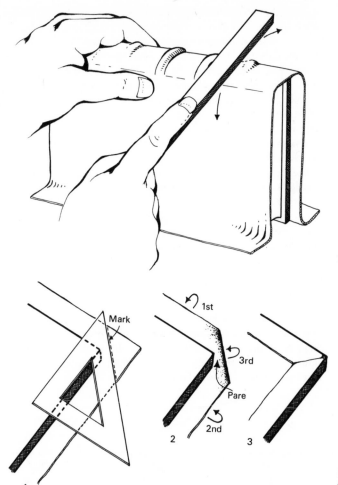

148 Use of the bandstick

149 Bevelling, paring and turning in the corners

Place the book on the pitching marks so that the joints coincide with the pared areas. Wrap the leather round the book, and do not rub it down but wipe it over with a damp sponge to keep the paste active. Stand the book on its foredge and shape the middle band into prominence with thumb pressure. Tilt the bandstick slightly inwards against the band and rock it to and fro to firm the leather against the edge of the band; then firm the other side. Working first upwards and then downwards, ease the leather with the thumbs towards each band, setting each with the stick and firming both sides before continuing to the next. If the leather on one side of a band lifts while you are working on the next band, the leather has not been pulled down enough to mould to the shape and adhere to the spine. Firm down the spaces between the bands with thumb pressure, stretching the leather down towards the sides. Lay the book down, lift off the leather from the side until it is free of the joint and pull all excess leather away from the spine; smooth it down again on the side. Repeat on the other side and work the bandstick on the sides of the bands again. Sponge over the leather with a little water.

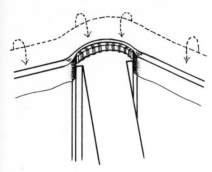

150 Turn-in at the headcap

Mark the corners, using a 45° set square, and with a paring knife scoop out a bevel about twice the thickness of the board away from the corner. (At this stage do not turn in the corners.) Fold back the turn-in at the tail, stand the book up and open the boards. Pull the leather back from the head almost down to the first band. At the spine, paste the turn-in on the outside and fold it over on itself, unrolling it upwards to remove creases until it is level with the top of the headband. (If it is above it, creases will form in the headcap turn-in.) Tuck the turn-in between the joint and the board and, without creasing, model the leather tightly to the board along to the corners. Repeat at the tail and work on the bands again.

Peel back the leather at the corners and paste again. Paste the foredge, turn it in and mould it down, pulling and stretching away the creases until the leather is firm and tight on the boards. Merge the bevels of the corners together to form a line at 45° from the corner; the leather protruding at the corners is modelled over with the thumb, forming a minute rounded pleat.

Setting the joint

An important operation in the covering of a flush-jointed book is to set the joint. If the board is thrown back at this stage it will be seen that it has moved out of position either backwards or at an angle from the joint; if it is allowed to dry in this position the squares will be uneven, the opening of the boards poor and the endpapers will split down the joint.

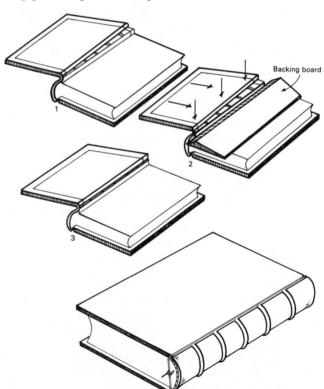

151 Setting the joint

152 Tied up prior to forming the headcaps

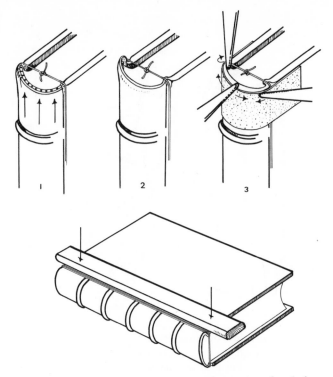

153 Forming the headcaps

154 Shaping the leather along the joint

Push the board down into position with its spine edge flush on top of the joint, closing the gap at the hinge to form a right angle. It will help if a backing board is placed into the joint and the board pushed flush with this. Set both joints. Firm the leather against the bands and tie up with thin sewing thread hooked in the back corner recesses. Pull the thread tightly and knot it between the boards.

Without disturbing the leather at the bands, stretch the leather at the head and tail with the fingers and thumb to gain enough to cap over the thickness of the headbands. Damp the headcaps and wrap a strip of vellum round the spine, lining it up to the edges of the boards. Turn over the capping leather with a folder, sharpening the folded edge against the edge of the vellum and modelling it to a precise, neat cap level with the top of the boards. Hook out the leather on either side of the headband against the thread with a pointed folder making an S shape so that the line of the spine is straight and not pulled in at head and tail.

Look along the profiles of the boards and tap out any unevenness. Run the bone folder along the bevel of the boards to shape the leather; line a slat of hardwood to the thread and press it down to firm the leather along the joint. To emphasize the bands, use either the stick, the grooved bandstick or band nippers. The latter are not used in the same way as a pair of pincers as this bruises the leather; instead, the jaws are set and held to the thickness of the band and pushed along on either side of it. Wash over the leather to remove paste and finger marks, and place it between paper-lined boards with a medium weight on top to dry out. Books newly covered in leather must never be put in the press.

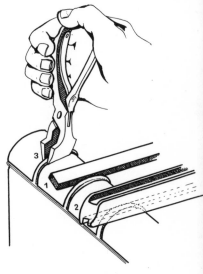

155 Bringing up the bands: three methods

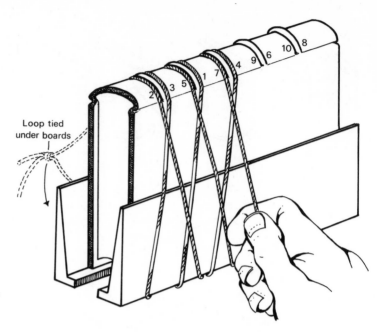

Loop tied
under boards

156 Book in tie-up boards

Use the hands for covering; excessive force with a folder will crush the grain and mark the leather. Do not over-wet the leather, as on drying it will contract and warp the boards more than necessary. Protect the work from gritty working surfaces, dirty tools and fingernail marks. If the book is large, and the leather hard and resistant, it is difficult to mould the leather over the bands. Such a book should be placed between tie-up boards, and soft string tied in a loop under the boards and neatly criss-crossed alongside the bands in the order illustrated. Keep a tight, even tension and when all bands are tied, bind the string round the ends of the boards twice before taking it under the boards to the beginning and tying it again. Allow the leather to dry before removing the string.

When the book is dry, cut off the retaining thread and open the book as described on p. 111. Trim out the leather turn-in, leaving it as wide as possible. The covers will have warped outwards because of the pull of the dried out leather, and no attempt is made to put down filler and endpapers until the boards are flat. Counteracting the warp of the boards is, of course, essential, and takes time. Cut a bond paper to fit into the trimmed-out area, reducing it by trimming a little off the spine edge so that, when pasted and rubbed down, it will stretch to fit exactly. Leave the book overnight under a heavy weight with wax papers inside the boards. Remove the weight and leave the book out for one hour; observe the shape of the boards and if they are still warped outwards, paste in another bond. Continue until the boards are flat, when the remaining recess is filled with glued pulp card. Sandpaper this – and the leather if necessary – so that the endpapers may be pasted down evenly. Expose the board paper by tearing away the waste sheet from the joint. The board paper will provide the extra pull to shape the board snugly to the book.

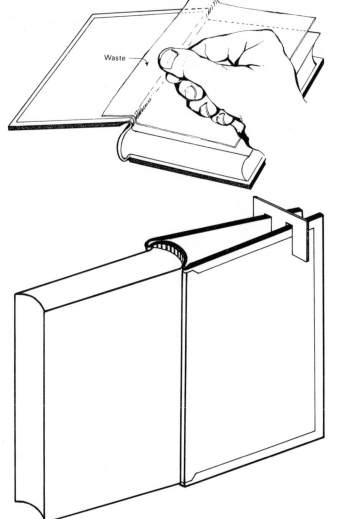

Waste

157 Modelling the paper into the joint

158 Method of holding back drying boards

Endpapers

Endpapers are trimmed to size as described on p. 112, and the conditions of size, paper and paste are the same, but the method of sticking them down differs. Endpapers of all flush-jointed books are put down 'open' and the paper modelled by hand into the joint. Throw back the board to rest on the bench, place a piece of waste under the board paper and paste thinly and evenly to stretch the paper. Push the paper into the joint, modelling it with finger and thumb to the edge of the board. Once it is firmly in the joint, rub the paper down on to the rest of the board. Use white paper as a shield and firm down with a bone folder. Rub the joint again under white paper, leave it for five minutes, and rub it down again. Leave it for twenty minutes more before shutting the book. The other side can be done immediately provided the drying board is not disturbed and both boards can be held back to dry with the aid of a specially shaped card.

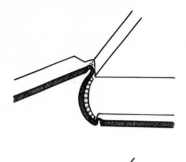

An alternative method of ensuring perfect margins without the problem of size and stretch is to put down the ends without trimming. Immediately they are in place mark the board paper with dividers set to the desired margin and trim out the wet paper with a scalpel and straight edge. This needs a light stroke and a very sharp blade. The finish of the board paper at the joint is a matter of choice.

As usual, the last step in the process is to press the book.

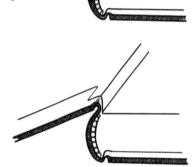

Operations for the flexible style

1 Collate
2 Pull
3 Knock out the old groove
4 Repair
5 Press
6 Make the endpapers
7 Mark up for sewing and saw in the cerf
8 Set up the sewing frame
9 Sew
10 Tip endpapers into position
11 Mark up the depth of the joint
12 Glue up
13 Knock up square
14 Round
15 Back
16 Cut boards to size in the plough
17 Prepare boards for lacing
18 Prepare and lace in the slips
19 Press, set and clean off the spine, straighten bands
20 Loosen boards
21 Cut the foredge using trindles
22 Drop boards to cut head and tail
23 Gild the foredge if necessary using trindles
24 Gild head and tail if necessary
25 Sew headbands
26 Set the boards back into position
27 Line the outside and the inside of the boards
28 Back corner the boards
29 Cover the sections with a protective envelope
30 Apply first lining of mull
31 Apply second lining of kraft paper and/or leather
32 Sandpaper the spine and the sides smooth and bevel boards
33 Make a template for the leather cover
34 Cut out and pare the leather
35 Prepare the book for covering
36 Cover and set the joint
37 Tie up and form the headcap
38 Leave to dry and 'open' the book
39 Trim out the inside of the boards
40 Line the boards inside to counteract the pull of the leather
41 Fill in
42 Trim and paste down the endpapers
43 Title and decorate
44 Press

159 Three styles of endpaper margins

THE SUNK CORD STYLE

Sawing channels in which to sink cords into the backs of sections seems a crude method, and as many do not consider it to be sound binding practice it has raised more controversial issues than any other style. Its prevalence dates roughly from the introduction of machine-made papers and coincides with the rise in the demand for

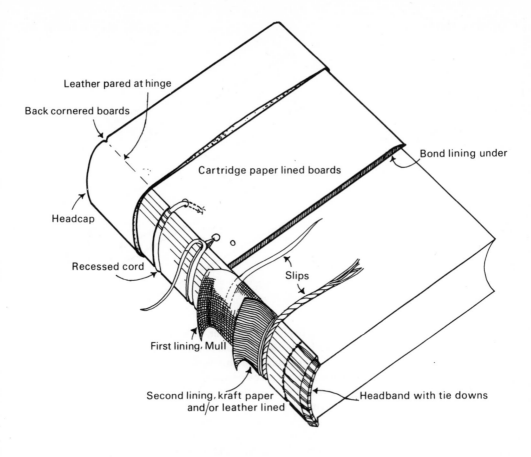

Leather pared at hinge

Back cornered boards

Cartridge paper lined boards

Bond lining under

Headcap

Recessed cord

Slips

First lining, Mull

Second lining, kraft paper
and/or leather lined

Headband with tie downs

books. More binderies entered into competition and, in order to reduce prices, unskilled labour was employed and inferior materials were used. Inevitably the result was a lowering of standards. Previously, apart from some books covered in vellum, bindings were in the genuine flexible style and binders sought to imitate this in an economical way. Thus the mock-flexible or sunk cord style was introduced as the 'extra letterpress' style – a convenient and non-committal description of a false flexible binding.

160 Sunk cord style: principal parts

The binder realized that sewing on sunk cords was not only better for the weaker machine-made papers but could be sewn in one-fifth of the time. Following tradition, the books were sewn on five cords and five false bands were attached. Each of these cords was laced into the boards but in a later period, to save time, two were cut away and only three laced in. Soon it occurred to the binder, harassed by price-cutting, to sew on fewer cords, yet still retain five or more false ones. Books were then sewn on thinner and fewer cords, and weak marbled paper needed lining to give endpapers substance. Calf leather was treated with acids to remove natural grease, in order to produce leather cheaply by rapid tanning. The binder weakened it further by excessive paring.

In consequence, bindings became extremely elegant with thin boards, neat bands, and covers opening as if on silken hinges. Spines and covers were decorated richly with gold impressions

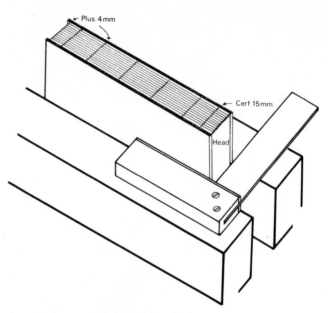

Plus 4mm

Cerf 15mm

Head

161 Marking up for sewing

from finely cut tools but, although the books were ornate, the weak construction could not withstand ordinary use. The result of inferior binding in that period is evident today for there is an unceasing flow of rebinding and restoration.

Paradoxically, the sunk cord style is still used by binders for their fine work as the tight, smooth back lends itself to contemporary design; but these books are sewn on thicker cord, acid-free leather is used, backs are reinforced, the joints are strengthened with cloth or leather, and books are given additional protection in boxes. The sunk cord method is now accepted as a satisfactory style for fine binding.

The following describes the method for a full extra binding in the sunk cord style with leather joints and 'illuminated' doublures. The sections are forwarded to the stage of marking up for sewing and the Middleton leather-jointed endpapers are made. Knock the sections square at head and spine and place them, without the endpapers, between two thick millboards tightly in a finishing press. Decide on the number and thickness of the cords relative to the size and weight of the book. In craft work, no book should be sewn on fewer than four cords and although the cords may vary in thickness they must be strong. Measure the length of the spine and subtract 4 mm. Mark, equidistant within this length from the head, the position of the required number of cords. The extra 4 mm will always increase the length between the lowest cord and the tail for optical centring. Draw lines across the spine at these marks, and cut cerfs 15 mm from each end with a fine saw. Grooves sufficient to take the thickness of the cord are cut into the backs of the sections with a tenon saw – or a circular file may be preferred as it will make a cleaner channel. Do not cut too deeply, or the cord will show on the inside of the section; it is better to make a shallow channel and beat the cord flat when backing;

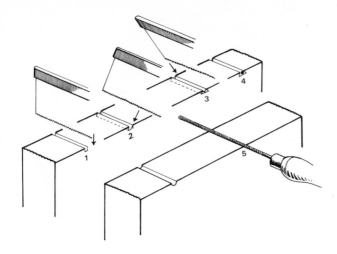

162 Sawing in the backs of the sections

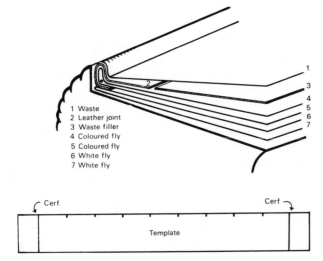

1 Waste
2 Leather joint
3 Waste filler
4 Coloured fly
5 Coloured fly
6 White fly
7 White fly

Cerf   Cerf

Template

163 Endpapers sewn through the joint; the paper template is shown

subsequent spine linings will disguise the raised lines. Set up a sewing frame as for flexible sewing and select thread for the correct swell, as described on p. 62. During sewing beat down each group of sections with a loaded stick. At this stage endpapers, other than the leather-jointed ones, are sewn as in the flexible style and not sawn in.

Remove the sections from the frame and tip on the first and last sections. Trim the heads of leather-jointed endpapers square, using the folds as the lay edges, and cut them to the length of the book. Tip these on flush with the spine edge and leave them under a weight to dry. Mark up the depth of the joint, which is the same as the thickness of the boards, and mark up the head, foredge and tail for cutting. Glue up; knock up; cut the foredge; round, back, and cut the head and tail.

The endpapers are sewn through the joint as follows. Mark the length of the book on a strip of paper, mark off the positions of the

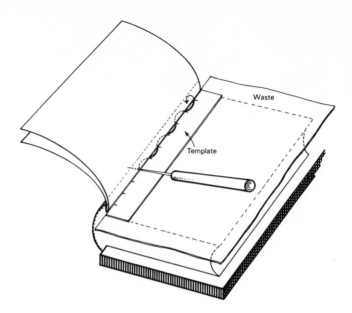

164 Piercing the holes for sewing

cerfs and divide the distance between into an odd number of spaces approximately 18 mm (¾ in.) apart. Line this template up to the head between the first and second coloured fly leaves and, with a needle or fine piercer held almost horizontally, make a hole through from the bottom of the joint at each mark on the template to emerge two or three sections down from the top of the joint. Pierce the holes on both sides, beginning just below each cerf, to avoid breaking the thread at the kettle stitch. Thread a fine needle with coloured silk or dyed linen thread toning with the coloured fly leaves. Beginning from the outside, push in and out and return through the same holes to make a continuous line of stitches. Pull the thread tightly and tie the ends firmly with a reef knot at the back.

Gild the edges if gilding is required. Cut millboards of the correct thickness, larger than the book, and trim them to size in the plough. Prepare the boards for lacing and attach them as in the flexible style (p. 122). Clean off the spine and set the back, back corner the boards, sew headbands and envelop the sections in a protective covering. The spine is lined first with mull, and if it is wide, with one or two layers of kraft paper. A fine binding usually has a tight back and the spine is lined with a piece of morocco cut exactly to the width of the spine and slightly longer than the book. This will strengthen the sections and support the headband, as well as ensuring free opening and increasing the durability of the book. Paste the leather twice and glue the spine. Position the leather, dampen it, rub and beat down firmly; when it is dry, smooth it down with coarse sandpaper. If paste is applied to the roughened leather, it may be smoothed by rubbing with a bone folder.

Boards are lined on the outside with thick cartridge paper, which is glued on; any unevenness showing from the laced-in slips can be removed by sandpapering. This method is a recent

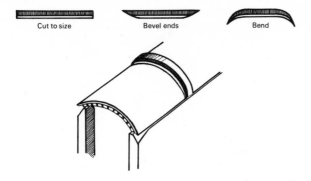

Cut to size   Bevel ends   Bend

165 False bands

innovation in bookbinding, for previously boards were lined before lacing in, and the slips were left unpasted for 12 mm ($\frac{1}{4}$ in.) to allow the boards freedom of movement. When covering, these slips were pasted down. With the newer method of lining afterwards, the boards are held firmly to their squares, thicker cord can be used, and the unevenness of thick slips is hidden under the sandpapered board linings. As the book is not cut in boards it is unnecessary to have movable boards, nor are they required for headbanding as this is carried out after back cornering. To compensate for the outside board lining, the inner side is lined with well pasted and stretched bond paper.

Bevel the boards with a knife and sandpaper. Make a template for full leather, and pare and cover as for the flexible style; covering, however, is simpler than in the flexible style as the back has no bands.

In the treatment of the spine the sunk cord style can be adapted in four ways:

1 Tight smooth back as described above
2 Tight back with false bands
3 Hollow back without bands
4 Hollow back with false bands

Tight back with false bands

Known as the 'mock flexible' style, this is difficult to distinguish from the genuine flexible. The difference lies in the sharp appearance of the bands, which do not always coincide with the laced-in slips. The false bands are strips cut from leather and glued to vellum. The use of thick wide bands is a common fault, which gives the spine a clumsy appearance. The positions of the bands are planned as for flexible work, and the bands are cut to the width of the spine and glued on.

Hollow back without bands

The hollow back, described in the section on library buckram work (p. 115), is used for any book that must open freely, particularly for address books, visitors' books, registers, music books and lectern bibles. Hard covering materials such as buckram and

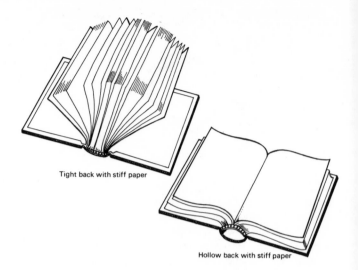

Tight back with stiff paper

166 Tight and hollow backs

Hollow back with stiff paper

vellum must be given a hollow back. In order that they may be opened flat, small books of stiff paper also require a hollow back, but larger books with paper of the same substance may be bound with a tight back as the paper will fall open by its own weight. The hollow retains the shape of the spine, while the sections open to lie flat. Although the hollow overcomes a number of binding problems connected with free opening, it is a weaker construction because there is strain on the sewing and linings.

Hollow back with false bands

This is a combination of the two preceding methods. The bands are decorative and used to imitate bindings of earlier periods where the qualities of the hollow back without bands are required.

Details of covering a hollow-backed book are described in other styles, but two points must be emphasized: the hollow is slit down on either side at head and tail to allow the leather to be turned into it; and the joint is set as in flush-jointed work.

After covering and drying out, the boards are warped round with bond paper. Any unevenness on the inside of the boards made by the lacing in is removed by sandpapering the bond paper. The leather joints are put down as follows. Make a pencil line on the board at 45° from the inside corner and pare away the turn-in almost up to this line in a long bevel. Remove the endpaper filler and waste sheet to expose the leather strip. Pull the leather hinge tightly against the joint and on to the board, mark the leather a little beyond the 45° line and cut it off with a pair of scissors. Return the joint flat, put a piece of millboard under it and pare off a bevel parallel to the cut so that it fits back to the angle line. Carefully pare away the excess leather (shown shaded) until the joint 'feels' even and level with the turn-in. Should the leather joint be too thin, a strip of cartridge paper is glued along the board to bring the leather up to the same level as the turn-in. Paste up the

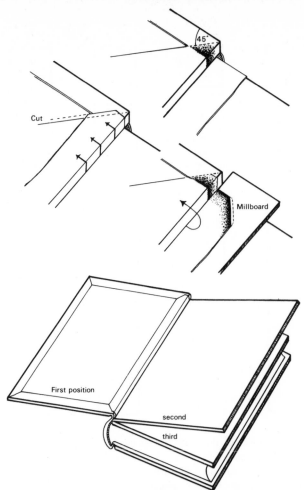

167 Making the leather joints

168 Pasting down a leather joint

leather and model it into the joint and to a mitre at the inner corners. After fifteen minutes the board should be half shut, and supported with a ball of screwed-up paper. After a further ten minutes, close the board down. This procedure will prevent the board from sinking and the leather from becoming too 'set' in the open position while drying. Examine the hinge for flutes of unstuck leather and if, through inefficient craftsmanship, they occur, use a hypodermic syringe to inject them with thin paste. Trim out the leather joint to the same measurement as the turn-in. Keep a check on the shape of the boards: if they are straight, fill them in with glued pulp card; if not, line them with bond paper again.

A hundred years ago it was fashionable to have doublures of silk but this is now considered pretentious and out of keeping with contemporary ideas. Pleasing effects are, however, obtained in three ways with doublures of paper or leather. A sheet, to match the coloured fly, is cut square and 6 mm ($\frac{1}{4}$ in.) larger than the exposed board, but one edge is trimmed smaller in the grain direction to allow for stretch. With the dividers, mark off pitch lines on the turn-in, paste the doublure sheet and position it so that it covers the leather edges by 3 mm all round. Protect it with a piece of white waste paper and rub it down firmly.

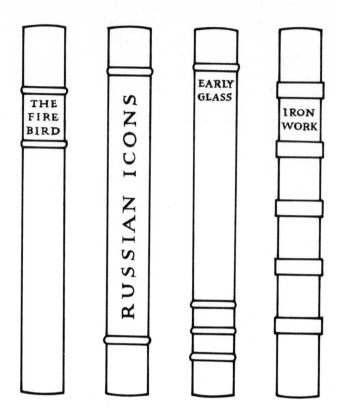

169 False bands on titled spines

An 'illuminated' doublure (for want of a better term) gives distinction to the inside cover. The coloured sheet is cut the same size as the exposed board and trimmed to allow for stretch. Glue this on to a piece of paper, which is identical with the white fly leaves, 12 mm ($\frac{1}{2}$ in.) larger all round. Nip this in the press and dry it under pressure. Cut the white sheet down with a 2-mm border all round the coloured piece and glue this to pitch marks on the leather, leaving an even border all round.

The entire area of the inside of the board can be covered in leather, left plain so that the beauty of the skin may be appreciated or decorated with tooling. Cut a piece of leather from the centre of the skin, a little larger than the board, and pare it down very thinly and evenly all over with the spokeshave. Cut it square and the same size as the boards, and bevel it to a fine edge. Cut a piece of medium-thick cartridge paper a little shorter than the boards, smooth the edges away with sandpaper and glue the sheet firmly to the inside of the board. When it is dry, sandpaper the whole surface until it is perfectly smooth. Paste the leather once only and place it in position, pushing and modelling the leather almost up to the edge of the board; allow it to dry before covering the other side. It is important to consider the pull of both cartridge paper and doublure, so the bond linings are limited to prevent the boards from excess warping. It is advisable to include an unattached piece of pulp card on top of the endpapers just before lacing on the boards, to compensate for the extra thickness of the leather doublures, otherwise the boards may gape a little.

Press the binding with thin pieces of tin or two sheets of blotting paper inside the boards.

For design purposes, in this style, the sewing may be a mixture of sunk cord and raised cord; a decorative effect may be achieved by containing the title between two raised cords (or false bands) and sewing the rest of the book on three sunk cords. False bands are also decorative if they are cut thin and wide and the spine leather is modelled over them. With all decorative features attached to the spine there should be no restriction on the freedom of movement in the back.

Operations for the sunk cord style in full leather with leather-jointed endpapers

1 Collate
2 Pull
3 Knock out the old groove
4 Repair
5 Press
6 Make the leather-jointed endpapers
7 Mark up for sewing and saw in the cerf and the channels
8 Set up the sewing frame
9 Sew
10 Tip the endpapers into position
11 Mark up the depth of the joint and guide lines for cutting the head, tail and foredge
12 Glue up
13 Knock up square
14 Cut foredge
15 Gild the foredge if necessary
16 Round
17 Back
18 Cut the head and the tail
19 Sew the endpapers on through the joint
20 Gild head and tail if necessary
21 Cut the boards to size in the plough
22 Prepare boards for lacing
23 Prepare and lace in the slips
24 Press, set and clean off the spine
25 Line the outside and the inside of the boards
26 Back corner the boards
27 Sew the headbands
28 Cover the sections with a protective envelope
29 Apply the first lining of mull
30 Apply the second lining of kraft paper and/or leather
31 Sandpaper the spine and the sides smooth and bevel the boards
32 Make the template for the leather cover
33 Cut out and pare the leather
34 Prepare the book for covering
35 Cover and set the joint
36 Tie up and form the headcaps
37 Leave to dry and 'open' the book
38 Trim out the inside of the boards
39 Line the boards inside to counteract the pull of the leather
40 Trim and pare the leather joint
41 Put down the leather joint
42 Fill in
43 Paste down the doublures
44 Title and decorate
45 Press

Vellum is a beautiful material of apparently unlimited durability which, for hundreds of years, has been used for the leaves and covering of books. The lighter, thinner skins of calf are used for writing, fine printing, limp work and small books, and goat vellum for large heavy bindings.

When selecting a skin, look for distinctive patch markings, veining, 'colour' and texture that will give life and quality rather than a pallid plastic-like surface to the binding. Transparent vellum provides opportunities for design and can be lined with coloured, textured or painted paper. Vellum, however, is difficult to handle and reacts drastically to changes in humidity unless controlled by the method of binding. Its chief limitations are that it is translucent, horny and inflexible.

The most satisfactory construction for vellum books is the library style, with the vellum attached solidly to the boards or 'drummed' on. The forwarding of a library style in vellum is continued to the attachment of the boards, sewing the headbands and lining the back. The modifications are a stiffened hollow, made with white cartridge paper consisting of 'one on' and 'three off' and boards made a little thicker than usual to withstand the pull of vellum. The boards are lined with cartridge paper on the outside and a well pasted bond on the inside; their edges are whitened with an emulsion paint. These modifications are necessary as the board and any dark-toned paper will show as a grey tone under the vellum.

The hollow back is essential when using vellum as its inflexibility is impractical on a tight-backed book; however, the French groove will allow the vellum to fold back on itself when the boards are thrown open.

Method of working

Envelop the text in waxed paper. Slit the hollow down for 25 mm (1 in.) at head and tail and gently round the back corners of the boards. Using a template, cut the vellum to size, allowing 18 mm (¾ in.) turn-in all round, and cut a sheet of thin opaque handmade paper 5 mm larger all round. The area of vellum to be turned into the hollow at head and tail is sandpapered to a fine edge. Lay both out and paste with thin paste, brushing away the excess. Keep pasting at intervals until the paper is fully stretched and the vellum limp. Softening of the vellum can be accelerated by sponging the outer surface with water.

Position the vellum on the paper with the 5-mm overlap and nip it in the press between clean, smooth boards. Check that there is no air between vellum and paper. Paste the lining papers, the spine of the book and the sides near the spine. Pitch the book on the lined vellum and fold the cover over. Gently push the vellum into the French groove with a folder, to establish its position. Rods ready joined with elastic bands are clipped into the groove and with the pressing boards in place the book is nipped in the press.

170 Vellum binding: slitting the hollow

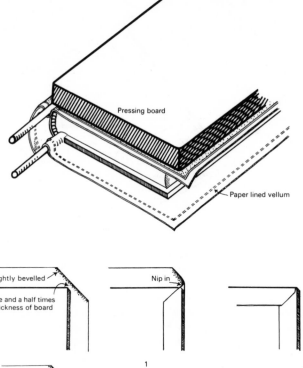

171 Vellum held in French grooves

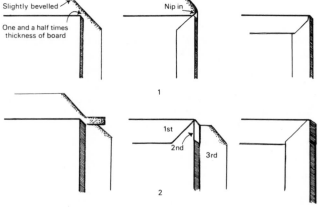

172 Corners: *1* normal method, *2* for thicker boards

Remove the rods and sponge over the vellum to keep it soft and the paste active. Pare off the corners but do not turn them in. (If the board is thick, however, the corners should be cut, pared and turned in.)

Stand the book up and open the boards. Hold the paper-lined vellum against the hollow back, pull it back and turn it inside the hollow and between the joints and the boards. Cord can be inserted inside the fold of vellum or, if headbands have been sewn, bring the vellum a little above the headband. Pull and mould the turn-in at head and tail and turn in at the foredges and corners. If the corners do not go down easily, repaste them, and tap them with a light hammer.

Replace the rods and nip the book in the press again. Take it out, tie it up in the groove with cotton string and model the headcaps. Wash it over, remove the string, place the book between sheets of blotting paper with the rods in position and put it between boards with a heavy weight on top. The book may be left to dry in the press with the rods in the grooves. (To avoid the risk of rust stains, the rods should be of plastic or non-ferrous metal.)

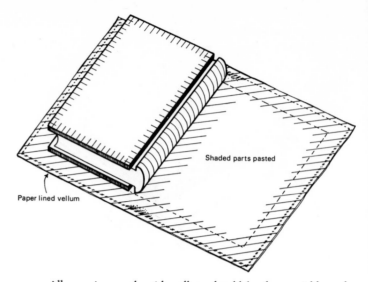

Shaded parts pasted

Paper lined vellum

173 Drumming on

All covering work with vellum should be done quickly and efficiently; frequent dampening will keep it pliable. The vellum must be soft enough to model headcaps and corners; thick and horny parts can be sandpapered to reduce the thickness. The method of 'drumming on' vellum is necessary if the boards are likely to warp excessively by the pull of the cover. The preparation of the vellum is continued, but after lining with paper, only the turn-in, the spine of the book, the French groove and the spine edges are pasted. The covering is carried out as described above. The vellum contracts on drying and pulls tightly to the boards. As it is drummed on, there is little pull on the boards and the warping is controlled more readily.

Another method

The vellum is lined and when it is almost dry PVA is used as the adhesive; as this contains less water, warping is controlled and there is quick adhesion. When it is dry, trim out the excess vellum and lining on the inside of the boards. Observe the warp of the boards and counteract this by lining them with pasted thin hand-made paper or a strong bond. Each lining is allowed to dry for twenty-four hours and its effect noted before the decision is taken to line again. No attempt is made to fill in or put down endpapers until the board has been pulled straight by linings. The endpapers are put down in the same way as in the library style (p. 105).

Some early books, bound economically in vellum without boards, were a form of case binding. William Morris used this style for standard issues from the Kelmscott Press. These vellum styles are attractive and acceptable today; here are two.

Sew the book stoutly on to strips of vellum 4 mm wide and at least 75 mm (3 in.) longer on either side of the spine. The number of strips and their positions depend on the size of the book, but a minimum of four is required. Strong endpapers of handmade or mould-made paper are sewn on. Cut the vellum cover, allowing slightly larger squares and a generous turn-over of 25 mm (1 in.). Glue up the spine of the book, round it slightly and allow it to dry.

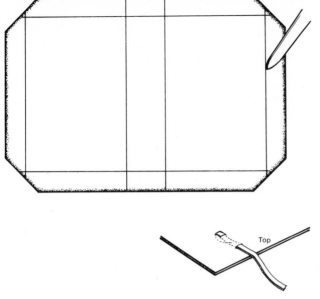

174 Vellum cover cut, shaped, pared and scored

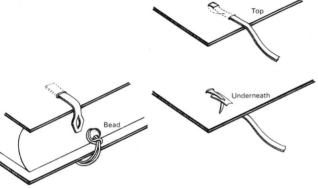

175 Vellum ties or thong catches

With a scrap of paper, measure the width of the spine at its widest part and add 2 mm. Mark the measurement on the underside in the middle of the vellum and indicate the amount of the turn-in. Score the vellum on these lines with a straight-edge and a pointed heavy folder. Pare off the corners and sandpaper the edges away all round.

Glue the turn-ins and fold over on the scored lines, rubbing down until they are firmly held. If the corners are difficult to work, tap them with a hammer and nip the cover in the press between boards. Bend the two centre creases, place the book inside, set the squares and mark off the position of the vellum strips in relation to the cover. With a 4-mm chisel, cut slots on these marks 1 mm away from the creases; corresponding slots are cut 5 mm away so that the strips can be laced through the first slot and returned to the inside by the second.

Trim the slips down evenly 25 mm (1 in.) from the return slot. Endpapers are put down with thin glue; to avoid impressions of the slips, shield the text with thin metal plates while it is in the press. Though the inside appears uneven, the book will not open completely flat, and there is strain on the endpapers, the text is well protected and the binding has charm. If the covers have a tendency to gape, two vellum ties or thong catches can be inserted before putting down the endpapers.

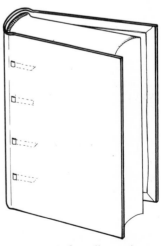

176 Slots cut for vellum strips

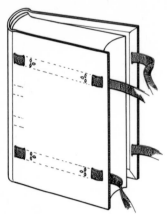

177 Ribbon ties threaded through vellum

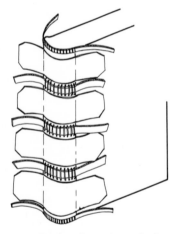

178 Leather thongs instead of tapes

179 Template for vellum binding with yapp edges

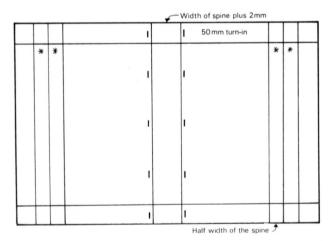

180 Folded and creased yapp binding

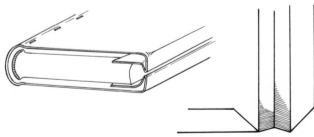

The book can be sewn on brightly coloured petersham ribbon instead of vellum strips; the forwarding is the same. The ribbon is laced through the cover at the spine edge and foredge and the extra is used as ties. Shaped holes can be punched through the vellum to show the ribbon in a decorative way.

Medieval bindings in vellum were sometimes sewn on leather thongs, a method once regarded as commonplace but now considered decorative. Sew the sections as for tape, sewing on thongs of white pigskin or thick fair calf 6 mm (¼ in.) wide and extending 50 mm (2 in.) on either side of the spine. Instead of endpapers, sew on an extra eight- or twelve-page section of handmade paper. Glue up, knock up, cut the foredge, round only and cut the head and tail or leave the edges uncut if you prefer. Sew plain headbands, using ordinary sewing thread on a similar thong the same length as the others but only 3 mm wide. Line up with strips of thin vellum, glued to the spine only, between the thongs but extending 50 mm (2 in.) on either side. Make a template for the vellum, allowing 6-mm squares plus a turn-in of 50 mm at both head and tail, and at the foredge allow 6-mm squares plus the thickness of the book and the 50 mm turn-in. Measure the width of the round of the spine and add 2 mm, marking this measurement down the middle of the vellum. Score these marks, as well as the 50-mm turn-in and the yapp folds. Fold, crease and treat the corners as shown in the figure.

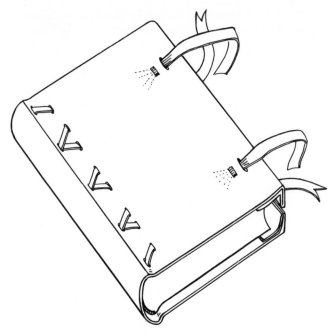

181 Cutting and threading of the thongs

Place the book accurately into the cover, mark off the positions of the thongs at the joint, and cut slots 6 mm wide just outside the fold. Mark off positions 12 mm away from these slots and 45° above and below, and cut slots 3 mm wide. At head and tail make cuts at the joint 6 mm from the edge of the cover, and another 12 mm away and at an angle of 45°. Divide each thong up to the sewing thread and lace these into the slots, pulling the thongs tightly back until the book is pulled into its case. Endpapers are not put down and no attempt is made to stick the thongs to the cover. The vellum linings are left exposed. The book can be secured at the foredge by lacing in silk or petersham ribbon ties. No glue is necessary if the slits are narrow and the ties forced in.

LIMP BINDINGS

Some early books were bound – economically, for those times – in vellum wrappers without hard covers, the vellum extending beyond the normal squares and enclosing the foredge completely. The method continued (leather taking the place of vellum), and in 1850 the extended squares became known as the Yapp edge, after a bookseller of that name. Many devotional books are still bound with extended squares; a bible carried to church is held with the fingers round the foredge, thus the cover receives the wear and the text is protected.

Method of working

These books are sewn quite firmly in the French style without tapes, but should extra strength be required three or more narrow

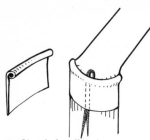

182 Simple headband, not sewn (with marker)

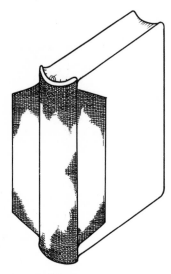

183 Mull lining glued and trimmed

tapes can be incorporated. Four-page endpapers can be tipped on or the common made endpaper is sewn and tipped into position Swelling can be emphasized as the book is rounded only, and it will retain its shape better. The edges are cut, for easy reference, and the corners rounded with a chisel to prevent them from becoming dog-eared. Edges may be coloured or gilded.

Glue up the spine with flexible glue or PVA and round it by hand or shape it with a cutting board (a hammer may damage the flimsy paper). Make the round of the spine a little more than the usual one-third of a circle.

Hold the book in shape, place it between two pieces of scrap board in a finishing press, and allow it to dry. A regular headband can be sewn but a simple variant is traditionally accepted, made from a strip of leather contrasting in colour, pasted and rolled round a core of string. Stick a marker ribbon or two to the back at the head and on top of this, at each end, glue the headbands, cut to the width of the spine. Tuck the remainder of the ribbon inside the book.

Line up with good-quality mull, extending it to support the headbands and overlapping the joint by 30 mm ($1\frac{3}{8}$ in.). Trim as shown in Fig. 183. If the book is heavy an added lining of kraft paper is an advantage, but do not line up excessively as the spine must be flexible.

Boards, of thin manilla, may be cut in two ways. The first method is to cut them larger on all three sides by half the thickness of the book less 1 mm. In this case the leather yapp edge is stiffened by the manilla. The second method is to cut the manilla 2 mm larger on all three sides of the book so that the yapp edge will be the turned-in leather only. In both methods the manilla is cut 2 mm less from the spine; this distance is called a pinhead joint. Round the outside corners.

To make a template for the leather in the first method, place the book with the manilla in position on waste paper so that the distance from the edge of the waste is equal to the overlapping

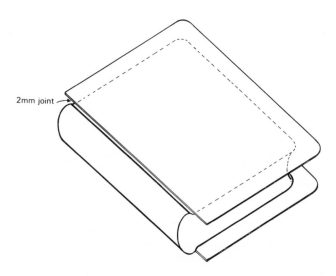

2mm joint

184 Manilla boards, showing pinhead joint

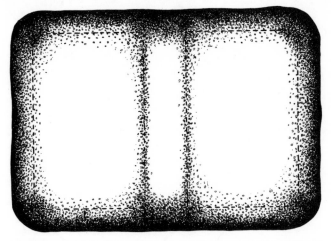

185 Leather cut, shaped and pared

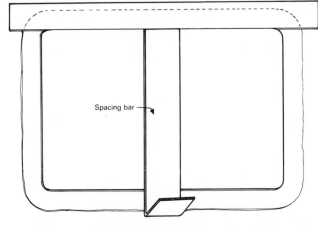

Spacing bar

186 Manilla boards glued in position

boards plus 8 mm. The template for the second method is made by adding to the 2 mm squares the distance of the thickness of the book plus 5 mm. Wrap the waste round the book, mark off the width and length and cut out the leather from the template.

A morocco leather with a well-defined grain looks handsome, and although black is popular, bright colours are equally acceptable. Pare the leather all round, beginning about 50 mm (2 in.) from the edges and thinning to a very gradual bevel, until the edge is mere 'colour'. The corners should be well pared and the spine may be thinned a little, depending on the hardness and thickness of the leather.

Carefully measure the width of the spine of the book at its widest point by wrapping a strip of paper round. Add to this 4 mm, which is extra for the pinhead joints. Cut a spacing bar from waste board to this width. Glue one of the manilla boards and place it on the leather so that the three turn-ins are equal. Lay a ruler against the top edge of this board, place the spacing bar in position and glue and line up the second manilla. Remove the spacing bar and rub the manilla down firmly before leaving it to dry under a weight. Pare off the thin leather at the corners, or leave it unpared as the alternative in Fig. 187. Paste the turn-in, pushing and

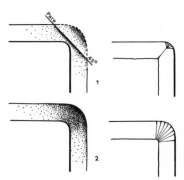

187 Treatment of the corners

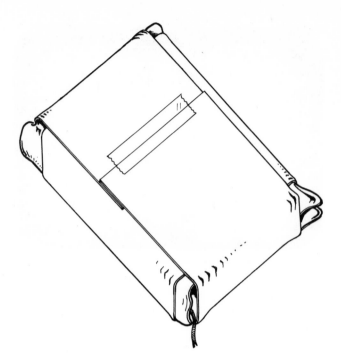

188 Limp binding wrapped to form yapp edges

stretching the leather firmly over the edges of the manilla or folding the leather back on itself to form the yapp edge. The corners are modelled into a neat fan shape by gathering minute folds of leather with the edge of a small folder and manipulating them into pleats, gradually working round the corners. When it is dry, pare away any bumps and creases at the edge of the turn-in, provided that these pared areas will be covered by the end-papers. Trim out the inside neatly but avoid cutting through the manilla.

It is convenient to work on the cover when it is flat, so titling and decoration on the spine and sides can be carried out at this stage.

It is important that the leather be stuck firmly to the spine before the endpapers are put down. Paste the leather, glue the spine and position the book, allowing even overlaps and the 2-mm joints. Wrap the leather over and rub the spine vigorously with a folder, using a scrap piece of soft leather as a shield. Allow it to dry between boards under a weight. Endpapers are put down with glue as the covering leather does not, in this method, exert a great pull on the manilla. Put a waste sheet under the board paper and glue both mull and paper, remove the waste and close the cover down. Rub firmly, using a protecting shield, and repeat on the other side. Lift the cover a little and check that all is well. Insert protective wax paper of the same size as the leaves inside the cover.

If necessary, further decoration of the sides can be carried out at this stage with a metal plate under the cover to give a firm surface.

Cut two pieces of kraft paper, one the same width as the text paper and over twice the length of the book, the other as wide as the length of the text paper and over twice its width. Wrap these very tightly round both ways to pull the yapp edges into shape and hold them in position with adhesive tape. Allow it to set overnight.

LOOSE-LEAF AND GUARD BOOKS

Loose-leaf work is a minor branch of craft bookbinding; it is a cheap, quick method of holding sheets together in a protective cover with some degree of security. There are some advantages. Sheets can be removed and others inserted without difficulty. Stiff paper, card, plastic and even metal sheets can be included and will open flat. Usually they are not sewn but are held together with the cover by cords, rings, posts or gripping bars of spring metal or plastic. The disadvantages are the movement of the sheets within the covers and the weakening of spine edges by punched holes or slots. There are office files and binders in which manufactured metal grips, wire or plastic spirals and locking mechanisms hold the sheets together, but these are not within the scope of the hand binder. However, a loose-leaf binding can be both economical and presentable.

Method of working

To make a simple loose-leaf book, cut two pieces of strawboard 6 mm ($\frac{1}{4}$ in.) larger at head, tail and foredge than the text paper. The thickness of the board is estimated according to the thickness and weight of the text paper, but should be heavy enough to keep the contents down when closed. From one of the boards cut 25 mm (1 in.) off the spine edge, then cut off another 8 mm ($\frac{5}{16}$ in.). Bevel the boards with sandpaper on all outside edges. Cut two pieces of book cloth, one larger than the larger board by 20 mm ($\frac{3}{4}$ in.) all round, and the other by 20 mm at head, tail and foredge but with 60 mm ($2\frac{3}{8}$ in.) extra at the spine edge.

Glue up the smaller piece of cloth and pitch on it the larger board. Cut off the corners and turn in the edges. Nip it in the press if necessary. Glue up the larger piece of cloth and pitch on it the other board, 20 mm from the head, tail and foredge. Using the 8-mm strip as a spacing bar, place it flush with the board and then position the 25-mm piece. Remove the spacing bar, and the gap between the boards will be the width of the hinge. Trim the cloth and turn in the edges, modelling the cloth to the profile of the boards. The extra cloth at the spine edge reinforces the hinge and both boards will be the same size. The turn-in is trimmed out evenly and the board filled in as for the library style. Line both boards within 3 mm of all edges with pasted coloured paper to counteract warping, but do not carry the linings across the hinge. Cut a strip of waste paper 25 mm wide and as long as the text from head to tail. Mark two centres 50 mm from head and tail. This measurement is judged according to the length of the text. Centre a 6-mm punch on these marks and make holes. Using the strip as a template, line it up against the spine edge of the text paper and

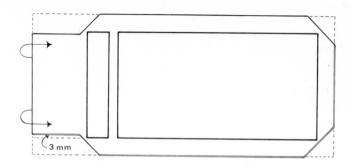

189 Loose-leaf book: cutting
of boards and cloth

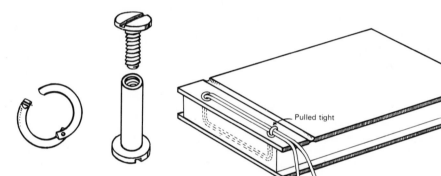

190 Broken ring and screw
post

191 Threaded cord method

punch holes. (When punching the covers, line the template against
the spine but allow the 6-mm squares at head and tail.)

Sheets are held to the covers by 'broken' rings or posts, and
these limit the number of sheets that can be inserted. Cord can be
threaded through and will take any number of leaves; the covers
usually have eyelets inserted. Ring binding allows the sheets to
open flat but posts and cords unless removed or loosened will
restrict the opening by the width of the back strip.

An amplification of the loose-leaf method is the guard book.
When photographs, cuttings or other material are added after the
book is made up, the spine must be increased by strips of paper to
compensate for the extra thickness. These strips (called 'guards')
are of the same paper as the text and are inserted between each
sheet at the spine. An album-bound loose-leaf has one guard fewer
than the number of sheets, and if the sheets are stiff they are scored
to make opening easier. In Fig. 192, *1* shows this; *2* and *3* show
alternative methods. If the sheets are strengthened and hinged
with linen, the linen takes the place of the guard (*4*).

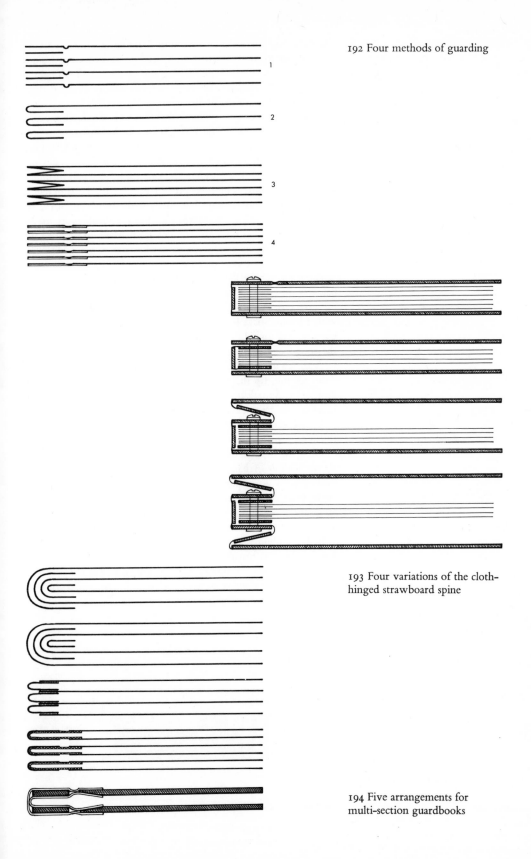

192 Four methods of guarding

193 Four variations of the cloth-hinged strawboard spine

194 Five arrangements for multi-section guardbooks

Covers can be made as above but the binding will look better if the sheets and guards are tied with cord or held by posts inside cloth-hinged strawboard spines. Posts can be obtained in different sizes. Four variations are illustrated but the number of sheets that can be inserted is limited by the width of the spine board.

Work of a higher quality, more durable and better-looking, can be made up as multi-section guard books, but as the sections are secured it is no longer classed as loose-leaf. Sections can be arranged in any of the methods in Fig. 194; the last is for thick plates or photo mounts guarded with linen on either side, each pair forming a section. Sections cannot be pressed because of the difference between spine and foredge but each, with guards in place, is nipped hard in the press to sharpen the folds. Endpapers are made with the hidden cloth hinge. Sections are marked up for cord or tape sewing but an extra tape or cord is put in for additional strength.

The spine can be flat, backed or only rounded. If the spine is flat, sew on tapes and choose a sewing thread that will be strong but give little swell. While sewing, beat the thread into the paper with a loaded stick. If it is to be rounded only, sew on tapes and use a thicker thread to give a slight excess swell which will retain the round of the spine in spite of strain and wear. If it is to be backed, sewing can be on tapes or cord depending on the style. After sewing, tip the endpapers and the first and last sections in position, and mark up for cutting and the depth of the joint. The latter equals the thickness of the board if forwarded in the library style and sunk cord style but one and a half times the board thickness for a case binding.

The spine is twice the thickness of the foredge and to overcome the difficulties of handling, cutting and pressing, the sheets are packed with waste paper. Interleave the book up to the guards with waste cut to the same size, until, apart from the necessary swell at the sewing, it is the same thickness throughout. Glue up, knock up, and allow it to dry.

If the binding is to have a flat or rounded only back, cut the foredge first. When cutting the head and tail, the swell of the sewing is evened by fanning some sheets of paper out and positioning them on the book, otherwise the cutting press would crush or distort the spine.

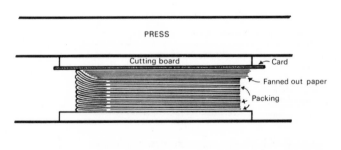

195 Packing a guardbook: the spine is twice as thick as the foredge

The procedure for the backed book is to cut the foredge, soften
the glued spine with paste, round, back and cut head and tail. The
flat or rounded only spine is forwarded as for a case binding.
Boards are selected, slightly thicker than is usual, cut with generous squares and set 9 mm ($\frac{3}{8}$ in.) from the spine. If the book is tape-
sewn and to be covered in leather, the backed book is forwarded
as in the library style; if in vellum or buckram, it must be given a
hollow back and a French groove. If it is cord-sewn, follow the
operations for the sunk cord style.

Guard books in general use are made up with thick paper and in
consequence have bulky sections. The foredge of the centre fold of
each section will project beyond the others, so precise cutting to
the smallest page is essential. Allow bigger squares and a fuller
round than normal as the landscape format causes more movement
at the foredge. To weigh down the bulk of inserted matter the
boards should be thicker than usual and bevelled to appear thinner.
Packing paper is removed only at the end of finishing. If a book is
bound 'solid' without guards it is easier to forward, but uncon-
omical because the extra sheets are cut away on completion or as
the book is filled.

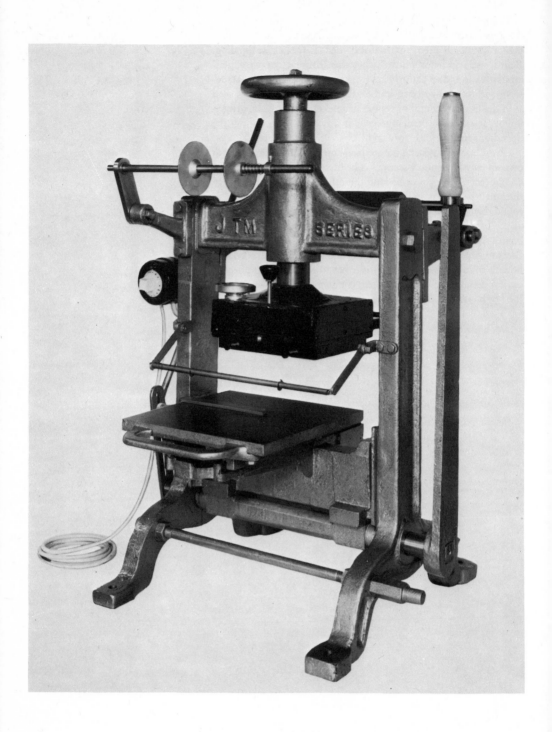

7 Finishing

Finishing – lettering, decorating and polishing the completed binding – is undoubtedly the most skilled and satisfying work in the craft. Yet it is very difficult and the student will benefit from a study of lettering and a course on basic design. It is not suggested that forwarding is of secondary importance, for no matter how well the book is titled or how lavish is the decoration and polish, it is the skill of the forwarder which preserves the book and makes light the finisher's work. All books must be titled and all need some decoration to please the eye.

Since gold tooling was introduced into England in the sixteenth century it has been popular for its appeal, durability and the legibility of its titles. Regrettably, the art of gold tooling is passing; skilled finishers are rare and the tools are no longer available. The situation is not unhappy, however, though fashion and the tyranny of the ready-cut tool have stifled book design for centuries; there is a welcome and long overdue change to other forms of decoration. It is the book restorer who requires a wide range of decorative hand tools, letters, rolls, pallets, gouges and fillets to match the period of the book he repairs or copies; but contemporary binders can be successful using elementary gold-finishing equipment. Few apprentices receive training as finishers because of the economics of the binding trade and the introduction of blocking presses and foils. In the smaller binderies fine work is being accomplished with hand tools but the intricate designs cut by the tool-cutter are being relegated rapidly to the past where they belong. Present-day book decoration involves many exciting and experimental techniques. This chapter does, however, explain the principles of gold finishing.

TOOLS, EQUIPMENT AND MATERIALS

Blocking powder – powdered shellac – is used as the sticking medium for tooling nap surfaces such as suede or velvet.

Blocking press: the Marshall blocker is capable of a wide range of work. Heated by electricity, it occupies a bench space of 650 × 550 mm (25 × 21 in.). The sliding table measures 250 × 250 mm (10 × 10 in.) and the blocking surface is 187 × 143 mm (7 × 5½ in.). The maximum thickness of work is 81 mm (3 in.).

Brass type, set up in a hand type holder, is a popular method of titling when separate letters are not available and speed is essential.

196 (*Opposite*) The Marshall blocking press

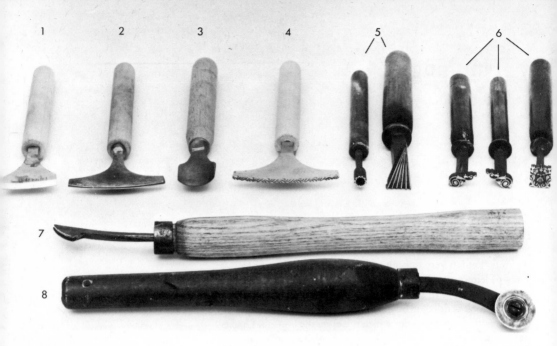

197 Finishing tools: *1* single-line pallet, *2* double-line pallet, *3* gouge, *4* decorative pallet, *5* modern and (*6*) traditional decorative hand tools, *7* creaser, *8* farthing wheel.

Founder's lead type can be used but the shoulder is shallow and there is a possibility of the lead melting or becoming distorted with heat and pressure. Point sizes should be the same as for hand letters.

Cooling pad: a wad of wet cotton wool in a shallow bowl or saucer is used for cooling down tools and for assessing the correct heat for tooling.

Creasers, shaped iron hand tools, are used hot to blind and burnish straight and curved lines in leather.

Decorating tools have the decorative elements cut in cameo on the face of a brass shaft to leave an impression in intaglio. There are countless designs covering a whole range of motifs, and some are cut in matching pairs.

A *fillet* is a disc of brass in an iron shaft with a wooden handle. It is used hot for impressing lines in gold or blind, usually on leather, and may give single, double or triple lines in thick or thin variations. Some are mitred, with a portion of the disc cut away so that the end of the line can be well defined. Continuous fillets have matching *pallets* to complete the lines. A similar tool, called a 'farthing wheel', is used for gently curved lines. Lines can also be broken or dotted.

The *finishing press* is a hand-operated bench-top press made of beech, which holds the book firm while it is being tooled. It is used, as we have seen, for many forwarding operations.

Finishing stoves vary in quality and power. Gas-heated stoves can be more easily controlled, but are inconvenient in a modern workshop. The thermostatically controlled electric type in common use should be fitted with a warning light.

Glaire is the medium applied to leather and other covering materials to make the gold stick. When the glaire is dry, the gold is laid on the area, and heat and pressure are applied to set it. Organic glaire is made by shaking together one part of white of egg, two parts of distilled water and a half part of vinegar; this is

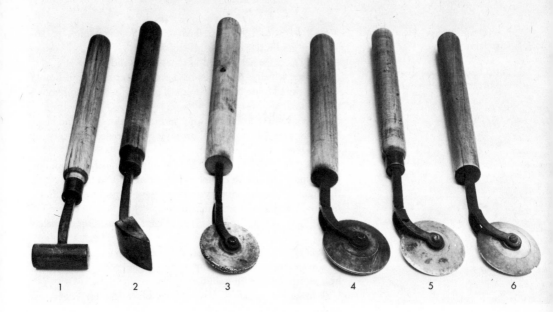

left overnight and then strained. Alternatively, combine one part of egg albumen in crystal form with four parts of water and allow it to stand until dissolved, when it is strained. It should be a deep yellow colour and slightly viscous. Synthetic glaire, which has a shellac base, has some distinct advantages over natural glaire. Although this has not yet been proved, there seems to be no deterioration in storage. No preparation of the material is needed, and one coat is sufficient; it is very successful with porous leathers, and tools can be used at a lower temperature. Tooling can take place months after the application of synthetic glaire, with satisfactory results.

Glaire brushes, small sable watercolour brushes, are used to paint in the areas to be tooled. They should not be used for anything else.

The gold cushion, a wooden board 250 × 125 mm (10 × 5 in.) padded with cotton wool or cellulose wadding and covered with leather with a fine nap surface, is used for laying out and cutting the gold leaf. The surface is kept free from grease by periodic treatment with bath brick powder, sprinkled on to the surface and beaten out. As it is a common practice to polish the faces of finishing tools, a strip of coarse leather is attached to one end of the cushion for this purpose.

Gold foil is metal deposited on the surface of cellophane, plastic or paper by vaporization in a vacuum, and backed by a sticking medium. The deposit is released by hot-press stamping. Invented in 1932, it revolutionized the titling of mass-produced books. It is ideal for lettering on bookcloth, paper, plastic and other difficult surfaces as no preparation is needed; however, it is not used for good work. Other brilliant colours are achieved using an aluminium substitute. Some gold foil is available which works with pressure only; this is ideal for designing.

Gold knife, a long, blunt, straight-bladed knife, is used to handle and cut gold leaf.

198 Finishing tools: *1* side or barrel polishing iron, *2* polishing iron, *3* decorative roll, *4* double-line fillet, *5* continuous single-line fillet, *6* mitred single-line fillet.

200 (*Opposite above*) Hand-lettering tools

201 (*Opposite below*) Type cabinet and type holder

Gold leaf was fully described under 'Edge gilding', p. 80. Transfer gold is not used in this craft.

Gold rag, a flannel steeped in almond oil and 'dried' out, and *gold rubber*, which is pure latex rendered down to a soft, malleable state by the addition of a few drops of paraffin, are used to remove surplus gold after tooling.

Gouges, hand tools of brass for impressing curved gold and blind lines, are available in sets. A large range is needed to satisfy all curved lines.

Pallets are brass hand tools used for impressing straight gold or blind lines. The length of line ranges from 1 to 80 mm in many thicknesses. There is much variation: one-, two-, three- or four-line, thick and thin or a combination of both. Some are mitred for panelling on a spine and others have engraved patterns to match rolls.

Pigment foil is coloured pigment coated on to a plastic or paper ribbon and backed by a sticking medium. The colour is released by heat stamping, as with gold foil.

Platinum or *palladium leaf* replaces silver leaf for edges and tooling because it does not tarnish. It is sold in books similar to gold leaf and is used in the same way.

Polishing iron: a heavy iron or chrome-plated tool set in a wooden handle, it is used to polish and crush the grain on leather books. It is losing favour now, since a reaction against modern plastic materials has resulted in a renewed appreciation of natural surfaces.

Petroleum spirit such as benzine has been restricted or banned in many educational establishments as it is a danger to health and a fire hazard. The substitute is *Robinol*, a non-toxic, non-flammable liquid. Cotton wool soaked with this and rubbed over the area after tooling removes surplus gold.

Rolls – discs of brass with raised patterns cut in the faces – are used to make impressions in gold or blind on leather and some cloth. A great number were cut through the centuries, some exceedingly beautiful, but they are a form of decoration that belongs to the past. They are available new but are very costly.

199 Equipment for gold-leaf work: *1* gold cushion or pad, *2* book of gold, *3* gold rubber, *4* gold knife, *5* finishing press, *6* cooling pad, *7* finishing stove

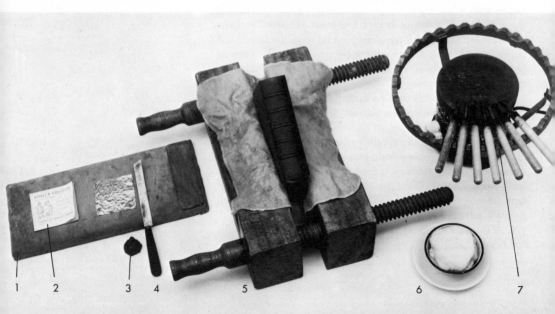

1 2 3 4 5 6 7

Serif hand lettering tools carry classical and legible styles of letters cut on the face of a shank of brass or phosphor bronze with wooden or asbestos handles. Most books are printed in serifed type and should be titled in the same style. They come in sets of 40 characters comprising the alphabet, numbers, Æ, Œ and &, dot and comma in printers' point sizes, of which 8, 12, 16, 18, 22 and 30 point cover most work. They also come in sans-serif faces: these modern-style letters are mistakenly called 'block'. They are used for books with contemporary typography and modern designs.

A *type holder* is a metal frame with a wooden handle in which brass type is set up. Heated on the stove, it impresses one line of type at a time. Handle letters are difficult to obtain, therefore type holders are used increasingly. Self-centring holders are efficient but may be too heavy.

Blind impressions prepared for gilding are given a very fine coat of *vaseline* to hold the gold in position prior to tooling. *Coconut oil* serves the same purpose but evaporates quickly.

The workshop

The ideal finishing workshop is an enclosed, draughtproof area with excellent lighting. Benches should be 900 mm (3 ft.) high as it is often necessary to lean over the work. Each working area has its own stove, finishing press and bench light. All tools are kept in glass-fronted cupboards, with rolls, fillets, farthing wheels and polishing irons clipped in brackets – each with an identification mark and with its head protected in a draw-string bag. Pallets, gouges and decorating tools are stored in racks, each position identified with a black impression. Handle letters are kept in boxes with the point size and style indicated. Type is in labelled type cabinets beside the blocking press, labelled on the outside with point size and impressions. (The size and design of type and handle letters should be the same.)

Cupboards under the bench provide space for cushions, gold knives, foils and type holders, also quoins, lead furniture, carbon paper and chases for the blocking press.

The blocking press is a most efficient machine, used extensively in the trade for titling and decorating books in gold, blind and in colour. Brass type and relief printing blocks may be impressed on all flat surfaces using foil activated by pressure and heat. This is ideal for repetitious work on cased bindings, but although the result is satisfactory, the effect is mechanical and characterless.

Type is set up in the middle of an iron frame called a 'chase', which is then filled with lead shapes called 'furniture' and all held in position with expanding devices called 'quoins'. When the type is in place and the chase complete it is known as a 'forme'.

The forme is locked into the press and heated, the pressure is adjusted and the work is raised by a lever to impress the title.

To establish the position of the title on the bed, place a sheet of carbon paper on a piece of strawboard covering the bed of the machine and make a 'blind' impression. Draw lines vertically and horizontally from this impression to give the lay positions of the

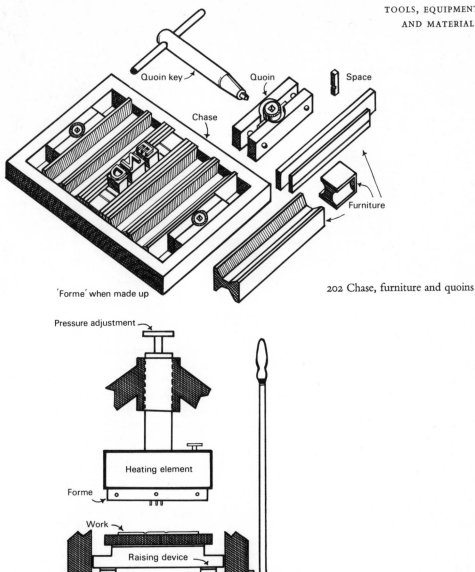

Quoin key

Quoin

Space

Chase

Furniture

'Forme' when made up

202 Chase, furniture and quoins

Pressure adjustment

Heating element

Forme

Work

Raising device

203 Blocking press

foil and of the work to be blocked. Strips of strawboard may be glued to the card on the bed to make it easier to place the work.

The temperature needed to fix the gold or pigment foil varies according to the foil used but for most work the temperature is between 79° and 93°C (174°–200°F). A light pressure and instant dwell (the time the type and foil are in contact with the work) are best for clean, sharp impressions although some adjustments must be made for different materials. Heavy pressure will cause the type to cut into the material and over-heated type or longer dwell will make blurred impressions.

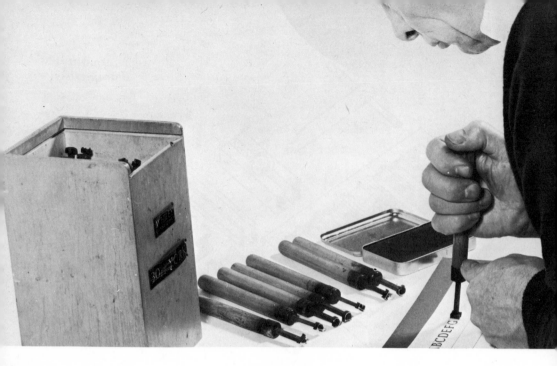

204 Using hand-lettering tool

THEATRE

THEATRE

205 Spacing of letters

WORKING METHODS

Practice in finishing should begin with exercises in handling and positioning hand lettering tools. With dividers, mark a straight line on bond paper with strawboard underneath and arrange a 30-point alphabet. Hold the first tool, with the nick in the shaft away from you, firmly in the fist with the thumb on top; dab the tool on an ink pad to check the evenness of the imprint, as this is essential for solid gold tooling. Hesitating above the paper, position the tool below but touching the line. Making certain that the shaft is vertical, strike the impression with a quick, small, round movement of the hand. Practise those letters that are sloping or uneven and in the same way practise with smaller point sizes. The second exercise is the arrangement of words; here the aim is to achieve an even balance in the spacing, and this can only be done by eye as mechanical spacing is unsatisfactory. Give words dignity by generous spacing between letters, particularly those with adjoining vertical lines.

A cloth case should be lettered flat before the book is cased in. Small point-size letters are unsatisfactory as the weave of the cloth distorts the shapes, but larger letters can be used on the front board or placed to read up or down the spine. Letters should not be placed underneath each other as unfamiliar patterns will not help legibility. To be certain of the spelling, write the title from the title page of the book and reduce it if possible. For instance, *A Book of Deep Sea Fishing* can become *Deep Sea Fishing*; the other words are unnecessary. Letter the title out on bank paper and with adhesive tape fix the paper impression on the book to either front or spine. Slip gold foil underneath the paper with the gold side uppermost. Heat the stove and arrange the tools in order with only the face of the tool on the hotplate. Pick up the tool and, if it is very hot, lay the shaft on the soaked cooling pad. The working

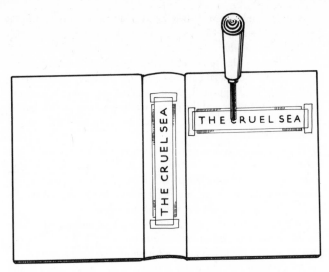

206 Tooling through paper

temperature is fairly critical and the professional will listen to the hiss of the cooling tool. At the correct heat, a spot of water touched on to the shaft will disappear slowly. Gold foil works with heat, pressure and dwell; a hot tool requires only slight and instantaneous pressure but a cooler one needs longer dwell and harder pressure. Experience is the only guide. When the heat is right, use the template for positioning the letters and strike through the paper.

Gold filling the negative parts of the letter and the sides of the impression is a common fault, which indicates that the tool may be too hot, the dwell too long or the impression too hard; or too much movement was given at the top of the tool. If the gold shows as a 'ghost' of a letter, this results from a cool tool and light pressure. If only a portion of the letter is impressed the heat and dwell were correct but the tool was not held at right angles to the surface nor was it impressed evenly.

With practice, tooling can be done directly through the foil. A paper template of the layout of the letters can be made and positions marked, with a sharp pencil, on a line drawn on the foil. After foil tooling it is possible that the letters or motifs are incomplete, or show as a 'ghost' of the character. This can be due to uneven or weak pressure, insufficient heat, incorrect dwell or damaged foil. The character can be completed by heating the tool and placing it in the impression. Tilt the tool away from the missing part and quickly slip foil under the tool before bringing it down with extra pressure on the missing part. If necessary, the other part is completed by tilting the tool the other way and repeating the process.

With further experience, tooling can be carried out without guides, but the template is recommended for beginners. Decorating tools, fillets and rolls can be put down following guide lines on the foil, which must be firmly taped to the work. Use of these tools is described below.

A note should be made here concerning the information to be tooled on the spine. Libraries catalogue and identify their books with the title, author, volume, date, press mark and library name by tooling on the spine, but these details are unnecessary on personal and individual bindings and only the title and sometimes the author need appear. Lettering on the spine depends on the whim of the owner and the design of the binding, and should be decided before work begins. Few fine bindings have the author's name on the cover.

Contemporary layout of titles across the spine may follow one of four set shapes. Small words such as 'to', 'on', 'off', 'of', 'a', 'an', 'by' should be included with other words, not on lines on their own. Arrangement and point size of letters depend on the width of the spine. Make a word arrangement and choose a size which will allow the longest line to be placed within the readable width of the spine: this is about 3 mm on each side short of the full width, so that the letters are not foreshortened by the curve.

As a general rule, the distance between the lines is equal to the height of the letters. Measure this height with dividers and, on bank paper, prick a series of spaces and join up every other one with a divider mark. Letter off the longest line, which must fit within the spine. If necessary, use closer spacing, or a smaller size of type, and if possible use the ampersand. Count the letters and mark a centre line, taking account of the relative sizes of the letters. Count the letters in the next line, each space being counted as one letter, and arrange, using the positions of the letters in the first line as a guide. Complete the title. Spacing can be adjusted by eye to suit the different 'weights' of the letters, but the spaces should be visually the same in each line. Traditionally the spine was divided into a series of six panels by gold or blind lines or bands, the title appearing on the second panel down and the author on the third. This placing of the title is valid for general work but today, as most books have a smooth spine, letters may be placed elsewhere. A simple arrangement can make an attractive spine.

Should the title be long and the spine narrow, the lettering can be larger, and placed to read up or down the spine. The direction is a matter of personal preference, but for a visitors' book, address book, register or any book that is usually laid flat, the title should read down. Any title reading up or down is positioned with more space at the tail than the head. This question of optical centring is important as the true centre will appear lower. Set the book with the leather spine in the finishing press and plan the layout with dividers. In order to mark the lines across the spine, wrap a strip of vellum from point to point, and use its edge as a guide to mark the leather with a fine-pointed finishing folder.

Move the press so that the book is parallel to the body, warm a suitable pallet and hold it as for handle letters (p. 166). Keeping the elbow high in the air, so that the wrist has free movement, steady the tool handle with the other thumb and follow the guide line in a decisive swinging movement to make a straight, clean impression. The vellum strip can be used as a guide edge if necessary. Alter the position of the book in the press to an angle of 45°. Cut out the title (previously lettered on bank paper) and tape it in position.

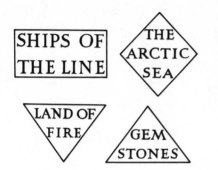

SHIPS OF THE LINE

THE ARCTIC SEA

LAND OF FIRE

GEM STONES

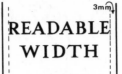

READABLE WIDTH

3mm

3rd. THE
1st. SOLDIER OF
2nd. FORTUNE

207 (*Above left*) Four layout shapes

208 (*Above*) Width and separation of lines

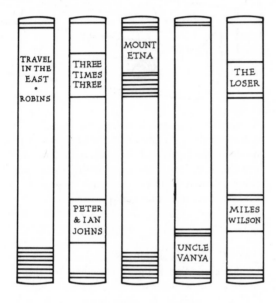

TRAVEL IN THE EAST
·
ROBINS

THREE TIMES THREE

PETER & IAN JOHNS

MOUNT ETNA

THE LOSER

UNCLE VANYA

MILES WILSON

209 Various spine layouts

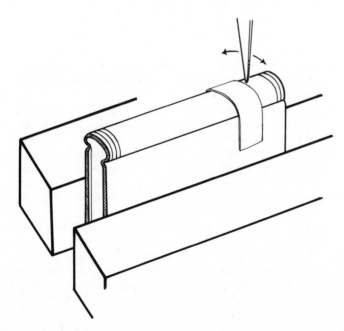

210 Marking the spine

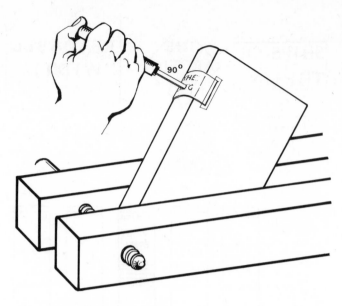

211 Tooling the spine

If it is to lie within panels, arrange the containing lines so that the space from the line to the top of the letters is a little more than the height of the letter, and the space at the bottom is fractionally more than the top space. Impress the warm tools through the paper to make shallow impressions, keeping the tools at right angles to the plane of the curve.

Tooling

After 'blind' impressions have been made, the leather is prepared for tooling. Most leathers (depending on their porosity) are sponged over with a paste wash of a thin, milky consistency. Calf will need a thick wash, while sheepskin may need a 3 per cent solution of warm gelatine size; both act as a filler to retain the glaire on the surface. The wash will also clean the leather and put some moisture into the skin to help the quality of the tooling. When the wash is dry, paint in or sponge over the area to be gilded, twice, with the glaire, allowing the first layer to dry before the second is applied. Do not froth the glaire in the impressions. Put it aside to dry.

Gold should be handled only with the gold knife, which is frequently polished on the gold cushion to keep the blade free from grease. Place the book of gold on the left of the cushion and bend the book in half. Control the dropping of each page of the backing paper with the gold knife until a sheet of gold lies on the surface. Gently tap the knife close to the edge of the leaf until it folds over. Slip the knife underneath, gently blow and lift so that the leaf is draped over the knife. Convey it to the centre of the cushion, turning the knife blade over and over until the gold is free. A gentle breath on the centre will flatten it.

Assess the height of the letters, allow a little more and cut the gold, with a sawing action of the knife, first into strips and then, at right angles, to small lengths. Cover the gold on the cushion with

a box lid to protect it from currents of air. With a small pad of
cotton wool, pick up a little vaseline and rub this on the back of
the hand to distribute it evenly. Rub very little over the area to be
tooled. Shape a second pad to the size of the cut gold, and touch
the side of the nose with it before pressing it on the leaf with a
light touch. The gold will adhere to the pad but will be relin-
quished on to the vaselined area, where it is pressed gently downwards. Overlap each piece of gold. One layer is enough for cheap
work but usually two layers are needed, the second being placed
without vaseline. Shadow the placed gold with one hand, and if
cracks are apparent fill them with extra small pieces.

Tool immediately, using tools as hot as for gold foil. Hesitate
above the impression and, once certain, strike deliberately and
firmly. It is possible to sense the tool slipping into the previous
blind impression but if this cannot be seen beneath the gold change
the light direction until the shadows throw up the impressions
clearly. A second impression with a warm tool will burnish the
the gold and subsequent layers, laid without glaire and tooled, will
make the gold more solid. Surplus gold can be removed by rubbing with a gold rubber or gold rag or by swabbing it with cotton
wool steeped in Robinol. If the gold has not taken in places apply
more vaseline, lay on more gold and tool again. If the results are
still not good, apply glaire once again, and vaseline, lay on more
gold and tool.

If the letters are incomplete the fault could be due to (a) insufficient paste wash (b) glaire not strong enough (c) tool not hot
enough (d) insufficient or uneven pressure (e) tool face not clean,
or perhaps (f) the use of unsuitable leather with a cellulose-dressed
surface.

Over-heated tools will burn the gold, char the leather and
destroy its affinity to gold. On removing tools from the stove it is
necessary to polish their faces on a piece of coarse leather before
checking the heat.

Pallet lines are tooled in the same way; the book is laid straight
in the press, parallel to the body. Pallets are sighted on the guide

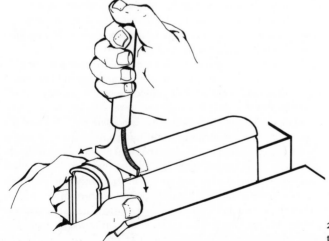

212 Impressing pallet lines
through gold leaf

line with the flat side nearer the eye. Firm, direct pressure at right angles to the plane is necessary. A strip of vellum may be used as a guide but care must be taken not to wipe off the laid gold.

Traditional designs, using decorative hand tools and rolls, can be worked out on blotting paper but a master template of the selected arrangement is made on bank paper, which is then taped to the cover and used as a guide for blinding in the impressions. Straight lines are marked at either end and lines made with a finishing folder and a straight-edge. In casual work, lines parallel and close to the edge can be marked with dividers, running one leg of the dividers against the edge of the book. The lines are tooled in blind and, if required, gilded afterwards.

The fillet is held with the straight side of the wheel nearer the eye. Stand with the feet apart so that the body is balanced. Hold the tool low down by the wooden handle in the right hand and pull the top into the shoulder, keeping the right elbow well into the side of the body. Guide the wheel into position with the thumbnail, press down and push the wheel deliberately with a forward movement of the body without moving the right arm. The shoulder leaning down and the left hand placed just above the right will steady the wheel and keep it at right angles to the surface. If the wheel binds, put a little vaseline on the spindle. Mitred fillet lines are begun at the break in the wheel and by adjustment during the run the line is ended sharply also on the break. Continuous fillets are run into the leather just beyond the beginning of the line and are lifted off just before the end, the line being completed at each end with a matching pallet.

Straight fillet and curved farthing wheel lines that have been blinded in are paste-washed, glaired, vaselined, and the gold laid and tooled as already described. The working temperature is the same but, as the tool is larger, considerable heat can be retained, and care must be taken to cool down the tool sufficiently for work.

If there is a risk of wet preparations and vaseline staining the paper or cloth the work is tooled in a different way. All preparations are painted in carefully with a fine brush and the gold is cut in 3-mm strips to the full width of the leaf. The edge of the hot fillet is patted with the vaseline pad and run gently on the gold strips, overlapping them as they adhere. Blow on the edge to flatten the gold to the tool, sight it, and tool as usual. This method can be used with decorating tools and letters.

Rolls are not blinded in first but are put down direct on the gold as it is difficult to coincide with a blind impression. However, a guide line can be put in with a folder to run on the edge of the pattern; this will serve as a guide for the preparations and it can be seen under the laid gold. Considerable pressure is needed, and the action and heat are the same as for using a fillet. If the pattern is wide and intricate the tool is rocked from side to side as it slowly proceeds, or it can be advanced a little, run back a little, then forward again and this is repeated to the end of the line. Few rolls have matching mitred pallets to complete corners with an even return pattern and indeed part of their charm is in this discrepancy. Mitre by removing gold at 45° from the corner and on approaching with the tool bear more heavily on one side of the wheel so

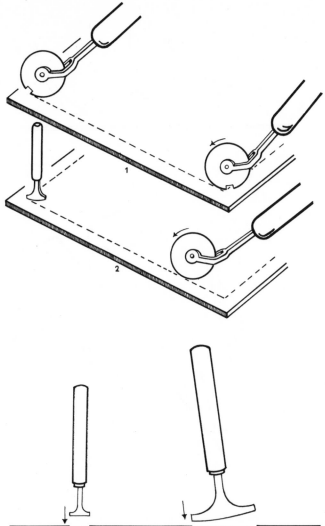

213 Fillet lines

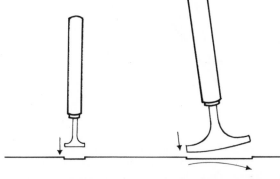

214 Methods of using small and large pallets

that the pattern tails off. Beginning at the corner at right angles to the previous impression, exert more pressure on one side of the tool to mitre the corner neatly. Another method is to run the tool on to a positioned razor blade or strip of thick paper so that no heat or impression sets the gold. Any blank spots at the corners can be completed with dots or similar hand tools.

The methods of using pallets and gouges differ according to their size. Small ones can be put straight down but larger ones have a slight curve to the edge, and these are 'rocked' so that only a small area of the tool is in contact at one time, thus increasing the pressure necessary.

Finely engraved decorating tools were cut specifically for use on smooth calf, and their quality is lost on the heavier-grained leathers. Before using small letters and fine tools, the grain of leather may be crushed with a hot polishing iron.

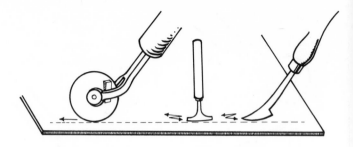

215 Darkening and burnishing
blind fillet lines

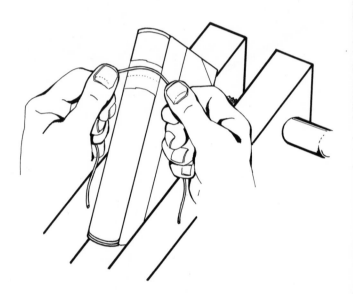

216 Making guide lines through
gold

Blind tooling can be as attractive as gold; it is satisfying on light-coloured leathers and beautiful on calf, but may need different working methods to achieve the best results. After blinding, dampen the leather evenly and let all traces of moisture disappear from the surface. Heat the tool to the usual working temperature and with a quick, confident movement make an instant impression. Make another with the tool a little cooler, and keep it in place a fraction longer, twisting it with a minute movement to burnish and darken the leather. Continue in this way, combining the cooling tool with longer dwell and firmer pressure. Alternatively, without dampening the leather, cautiously and instantaneously impress a very hot tool into the impression. As this cools, the dwell can be increased until a depth of tone is reached. Blind fillet lines can be darkened and burnished by fixing the wheel with a wedge and skidding it along the impression; similar results are obtained by burnishing with a hot small pallet or creaser. The creaser is an ideal tool for the blind lines as it can be guided along the edge of a ruler and the tip can be used to finish lines at a point. However, it cannot be used for gold work.

Given confidence and experience, it is quick and economical to tool gold directly on to leather without first making blind impressions, but for work of quality and value this is not recommended. The use of paper patterns is a comparatively modern innovation to ensure correct position and prevent errors. Fine tooling on old books was executed by master finishers who used only folder marks on the leather and relied on their supreme judgement. Perhaps the best gold work is achieved by the first direct impression – certainly on smooth leathers. After the paste wash, glaire the whole area of the leather as the exact position of the tooling is uncertain. Apply vaseline and lay gold to cover the glaired area. The technique for the layout of the title has already been described, but guide lines are pricked on the gold with dividers and made by drawing a fine thread across the gold just above the positions of the letters. Mark the centre of the spine and, under this, tool the middle letter of the longest line. Complete the line by positioning the letters left and right of centre. The remaining lines are tooled using these letters as a guide.

The type holder

Brass type in a type holder is replacing individual handle letters except on fine bindings. The charm of separate letters lies in the play of light on the different facets of the impressions, whereas the type letters are flat and mechanical. If, when using handle letters, one letter is slightly out of place, the others can be put in straight; but with a type holder the whole line is out of true. Nevertheless, both are efficient if well placed.

The type is set up as follows. Hold the type holder in the left hand with the parallel screw to the right. Put a thin space in close to the screw, and arrange the type, with the nick towards you, in order from right to left. Fill the remainder of the holder with spaces or other lines, placing wide spaces between each line. (This is so that the end or beginning of another line will not register on the gold.) Push the type down firmly on to the bed of the holder and tighten both screws. Check the letters and spacing by making an impression on blotting paper. It is well to remember that

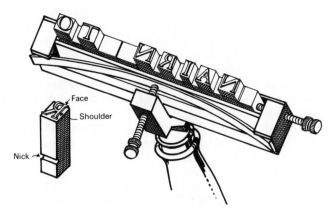

217 Brass type and typeholder

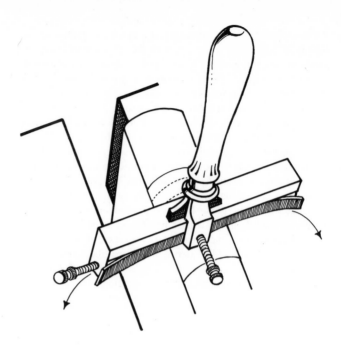

218 Use of the typeholder in tooling the spine

pressure must be varied according to the type of leather, and that the weight of the holder helps to make the impression. Hard-grain morocco, for instance, needs more pressure than soft-surfaced leather, while calf needs hardly any at all. If room allows, the letters should be well spaced as those without spacing look irregular.

Attach foil to the spine with tape, and with the point of a pencil mark lines, using a strip of vellum as a guide for the tops of the letters. If leaf is used, the leather is prepared as before and gold laid on. Guide lines are marked with thin sewing thread and the centre of the spine pricked off with dividers just above the lines. Methods of tooling vary and all should be attempted to find the most suitable.

Mark the centre of each line on the type. Heat the tool and test for working temperature with a little moisture on the type. To reduce heat it is important to place the type holder, and not the type, on the cooling pad because otherwise the metal frame will hold the heat and transfer it to the type, which would remain too hot. Coincide the centre of the line of type with the marked centre of the spine. Work gently to the left to the extent of the line and press over to the right, biting each letter into the leather as it comes into contact. The action is similar to using the pallet, and in the same way the shank of the type must be at right angles to the plane of the surface.

Alternatively, impress the letters on to blotting paper to find the width of the line and place marks representing this measurement on the gold. Begin tooling from these marks.

Another method is to mark a strip of vellum and hold this round the spine with the mark in the centre. The edge can be used as a guide for the type. When using gold leaf a blind impression can be made with the type before preparations are applied, but the nature and efficiency of the tool demands working direct on the gold.

The type holder is ideal for buckram work as it will take both leaf and foil. If leaf is used, no paste wash is necessary as buckrams usually have a starch dressing. Glazed buckrams are rubbed over with a damp sponge to remove surface polish. Glaire once only and use very little vaseline. Lay gold over the area and tool with the usual heat.

Aluminium and coloured pigment foils can give an added interest to the title, especially on cloth covers, but use discrimination in their application on leather to avoid vulgarity. The working temperature is the same, but foils from different manufacturers may vary in this to some extent.

Other methods and materials

Although vellum and parchment are hard, and inclined to be greasy, the technique of tooling is the same. Blind impressions can be made if necessary but hot tools on vellum may skid on the slippery surface. The preparation differs; after a thin paste wash has been used to clean over the cover the area to be tooled is washed over with vinegar to remove grease. Glaire the blind impressions – or the area to be tooled – by painting twice with a fine brush and proceed with tooling as before after using vaseline and applying gold. The tools should be used a little cooler than usual.

Two other ways of lettering on vellum are attractive. First, make blind impressions. Printers' ink of any colour is then smeared on paper and dabbed with one finger evenly to make an ink pad. Touch the face of the cold tool on the inky finger and transfer the ink to the vellum. Allow it to dry without smudging, and then the letters can be made permanent either with an aerosol fixative or by painting them carefully with varnish. Alternatively, letters can be designed to suit the character of the book and these painted on with waterproof ink and fixed in the same way.

Covering books in velvet, suede, silk or any material with a soft or nap surface is no longer fashionable, but there may still be occasions when such books require titling without any staining or matting of the surface. A blind impression is made with cool tools to crush the texture; blocking powder is then lightly sprinkled over the area. The warm face of the tool is smeared lightly with vaseline and touched on two layers of gold. The leaf will adhere and, when it is tooled, the heat will dissolve the blocking powder and fix the gold.

Polishing and crushing the grain of leather is no longer the common practice it was twenty years ago, as natural grains, particularly morocco, are now appreciated. However, leather may be polished in various ways.

A polishing iron, heated a little above the temperature used for gold tooling, is gripped near the base of the wooden handle. First it is cleaned by rubbing on a piece of coarse leather. The tool is then worked in small circular movements, gradually increasing the area covered and allowing the weight of the tool to polish the leather, though pressure may be increased by bearing down heavily on the handle and leaning the body forward over the work. The iron must be squarely on the leather, otherwise scoring will result. The tip is used to polish between the bands of raised cord work and the barrel-shaped iron is used for the sides of the book. This 'side' iron is used in an up-and-down movement, traversing the length of the book each time. Uneven paring shows up badly after polishing as the iron blackens the bumps. An iron that is too hot will darken some leathers; and on calf, which bruises easily, polishing should be minimal and done with only a warm iron.

Setting a book in the press with the thin tin plates inside, and chrome-plated metal sheets outside, each cover and putting it under considerable pressure is known as 'plating'; this glazes the leather and crushes its surface beyond recognition as a natural substance.

A good polish can be effected by dampening the leather with water and a sponge, leaving it until no moisture is seen on the surface, and working vigorously in all directions over the surface with a clean natural-bristle brush. Tooling is unaffected if it has been done correctly. Alternatively, the dry leather may be burnished by pressure with a bone folder. An effective protection as well as a polish is British Museum leather dressing, rubbed over the surface and left overnight, after which the cover is rubbed with a cloth. Very little is used, and to avoid possible stains none should be applied to fair calf or light coloured leathers. However, it is safe and satisfactory to use one of the micro-crystalline wax polishes.

The practice of using varnish to achieve an artificial gloss is not recommended.

8 Boxes

It is unnecessary to bind all books to last for hundreds of years; nevertheless, some should be preserved by all possible means. First editions, fine bindings, prints, drawings, documents and rare objects need protection against the depredation of time and careless handling. They can be stored safely and conveniently in boxes, made light- and dust-proof, and boxmaking is a considerable part of the bookbinder's craft, requiring accuracy in cutting boards and skill in covering them in all materials.

Slip cases

The slip case is a common means of protection but unsatisfactory as the spine of the book is exposed to damage and the bleaching effect of light. For most boxes, 2·3-mm millboard is suitable, built up as shown. Place the book on a piece of squared-off millboard, mark off the distance from the joint to the foredge plus 1 mm, also mark the height of the book plus 1·5 mm. Two boards are cut to

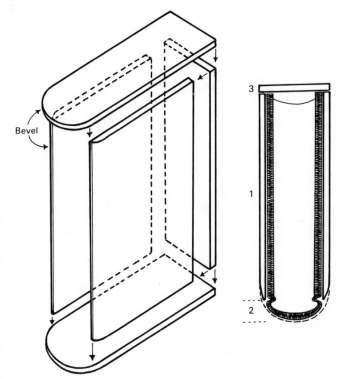

Bevel

3

1

2

219 Slip case: stage 1

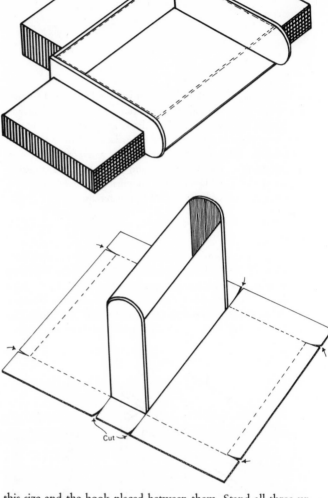

220 Slip case: stage 2

221 Slip case: stage 3

this size and the book placed between them. Stand all three up-right, holding them in the middle, and without exerting any pressure mark their total width on a piece of paper. This measurement is the width of the top, bottom and back strips. The back strip is the same length as the sides and the length of the head and tail strips is the total measurement of the cut boards (*1* in diagram), the distance from the joint to the spine (*2*) and the thickness of the back strip (*3*).

The outline of the spine is drawn on the top and bottom strips and shaped with a knife and sandpaper. At the same time all outer edges are bevelled. All pieces are long grain and each is lined with a pasted good-quality toned paper in harmony with the covering material. The last 12 mm may be left unattached so that it can be put down after the covering material is turned in but usually the boards are lined again afterwards to a depth of 50 mm to make a tighter fit. Make up a block of scrap board equal to the book size

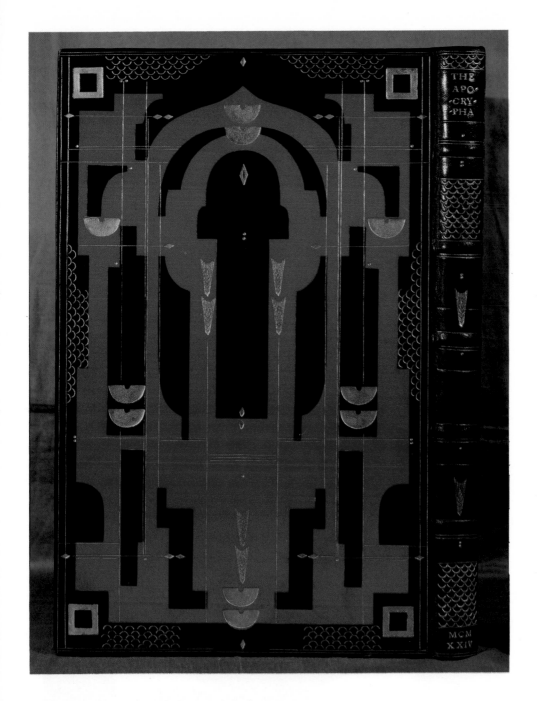

The Apocrypha (313 × 202 mm). Victoria and Albert Museum,
London. Designed and bound by Sybil Pye in 1934. The book is
covered in black morocco and decorated with orange inlays and
gold tooling.

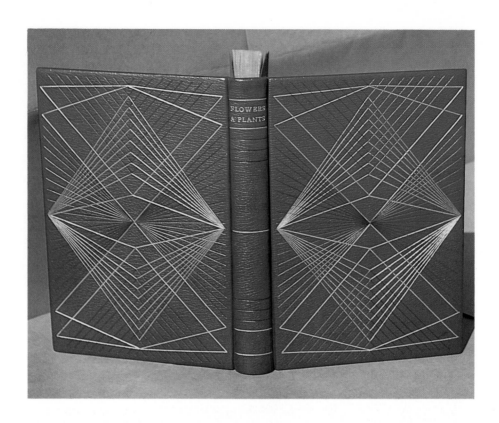

and glue the pieces of the slip case together round the block with an instant glue. Support the glued pieces with metal weights until dry, when any unevenness at the joins may be sandpapered smooth.

Slip cases for large books are reinforced on the outside with strips of jaconette or bookcloth and then lined with thick paper on the outside and sandpapered smooth. The width of the covering cloth is twice the width of the case plus the width of the back and 25 mm for each turn-in. The length is the height of the case plus a little more than half its thickness at each end. Glue the back of the case, centre it in the middle of the cloth and rub down. Make preliminary cuts as shown in Fig. 221. Glue the sides of the box, bring up the cloth and rub it down. Glue the turn-ins and model them over the edges. Glue the overlapping cloth at each end, turning in the smaller flaps first, followed by the others. Without delay cut off the excess cloth at the curves, run a knife cut at 45° from each corner and another up the middle, lift the cloth and peel away the excess so that the ends are covered in one layer only. Glue again if necessary and rub down.

Cover the top and bottom with a strip of cloth as wide as the ends but with an overlap of 12 mm on the inside edge. Round the overlap with scissors and make a series of wedge-shaped cuts. Glue them up and, starting from the outside pieces and working towards the middle, turn each on the other until they cover the edge of the card. Tap and smooth off neatly with the folder and pare off any unevenness with a scalpel. Use pieces of the original lining paper to line the inside for a depth of 50 mm but short of the edges by 2 mm.

A refinement to the slip case is to line the open edges with four strips of thinly pared leather, stopping the covering cloth at the border of the leather, 8 mm from the edge. Thumb holes cut in the sides of the case are unsatisfactory: there is difficulty in covering them and unsightly marks will appear on the binding at the cutouts. It is unnecessary to rely on these to remove the book; if the

Opposite:

Flowers and Plants (full title, *Flowers and Plants for Designers and Schools*) by Edward F. Strange, 1907. Example of geometrical and blind tooling executed with a mitred fillet and a pallet. See p. 206.

Goya by Enrique Lafuente Ferrari, 1955. Example of inlay work and gold applied in large areas. See p. 206.

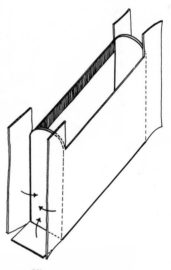

222 Slip case: stage 4

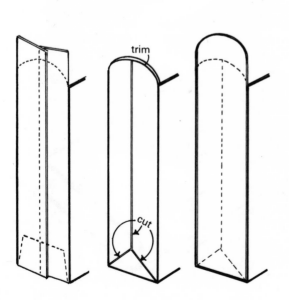

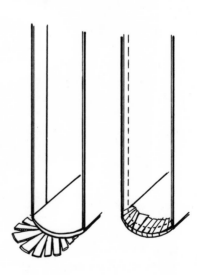

223 Slip case: stage 5

183

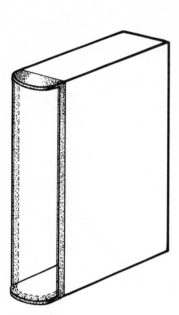

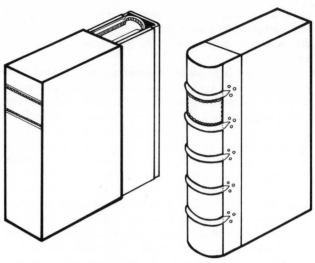

case is properly made, when it is turned over the book will slide out by its own weight. If the fit is loose, line the inside with more paper. To give further protection the book may be enclosed in a board and cloth wrapper before being placed in a slip case. The 'back' may be shaped from board like the spine of a book, with false bands applied and quarter-bound in leather. It will be un-obtrusive in a library of old books.

224 Slip case with leather strips

225 Additional protection in a slip case *(above, right)*

Drop-back boxes

A felt-lined full buckram drop-back box is made as follows. Square up a piece of millboard, place the book on this and mark on the board the length of the book plus twice the thickness of board, plus twice the thickness of felt and buckram, plus 2 mm. The width of the board is measured to the width of the book plus two thicknesses of felt, one of buckram, one of board and 1 mm. Cut the board accurately. Measure the thickness of the book at the centre, or widest point, allow extra for two thicknesses of felt and

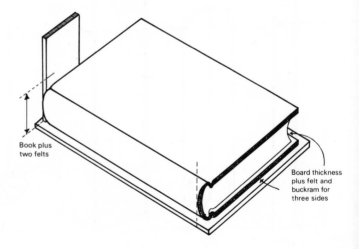

Book plus two felts

Board thickness plus felt and buckram for three sides

226 Measuring up for a drop-back box

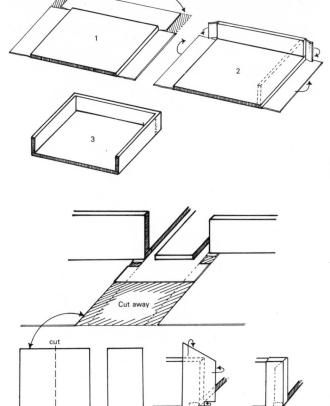

227 Building the tray from board and jaconette

228 Turn-in at the back strip; covering the inner corners of the trays

cut three side pieces, one as long as the base board and two as wide as the board less one thickness of board. Cut jaconette (or book-cloth if the box is large) to cover the board and the sides, glue the board, place it centrally on the jaconette, line up to one edge and rub down. Cut the jaconette as indicated, glue the edges of the card and the cloth and build up the trays, stretching the flaps of jaconette on to the sides to hold them rigid. Remove excess cloth with sandpaper.

Make a second tray, 2 mm larger at the top, bottom and outside edge than the first, and cut an extra back strip. Line the inner base of each tray with well pasted and stretched bond paper. Place the back strip between the two trays with 5-mm gaps for the hinges. The covering cloth measures the length of the larger tray plus enough to cover the two sides and 12 mm extra at each end. The width is the combined measurement of both trays and the back strip, plus sufficient to cover both sides and 12 mm extra at each end.

Mark up the positions of both trays and the back strip on the cloth. Glue the bases of both trays and pitch them in position. Turn them over on to a pile of pressing boards and rub down. Glue the back strip, position it between the trays and rub down well. Each corner is cut as shown above. The turn-in at the back

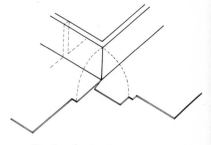

229 Cutting the corners

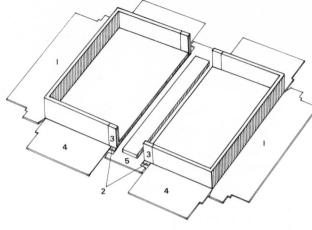

230 Gluing down the cloth

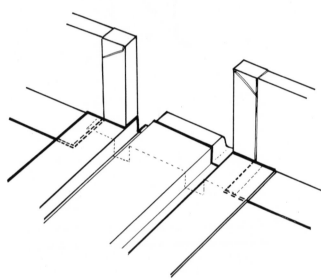

231 Reinforcement of the hinges

strip is cut as in Fig. 228; the shaded portion is not discarded but is used later to cover the inner corners of the trays. Each piece is cut in half and shaped as shown in the sequence 1–4. Number the corners for convenience. The cloth is glued down in the order indicated in Fig. 230 above.

The hinges are reinforced with a strip of the covering cloth extending 25 mm (1 in.) on to each tray, and as long as the length of the larger tray. Cut a strip off the cloth equal to the thickness of the card 25 mm long from the ends of one side so that it butts against the smaller tray. Glue the strip and stick it to the smaller tray first. Work it into the hinge, across the back into the second hinge and finally on to the larger tray.

Fill in the exposed board with pulp card and line both bases with pasted strong paper. This second lining is to counteract the pull of the covering cloth, while the first was against the pull of the jaconette. The base of the smaller tray is lined with felt and the sides lined within 3 mm of the edges and may be put down in

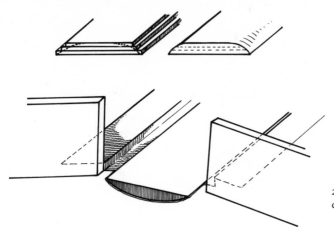

232 Leather drop-back box: construction of 3-ply spine

three pieces. The larger tray is lined with felt, leaving a border of 9 mm all round; the felt should cover the second lining. The back strip is covered with a piece of felt the same length as that for the larger tray but 6 mm less on either side.

Felt may be cut accurately unlined, if it is placed between thin strawboards but is cut and placed more easily if it has been glued previously to bond paper. The bond should be cut shorter than the actual measurement, so that it does not show as a white edge with coloured felt. The bases, sides and back strip of the box are pasted and the felt eased and smoothed into position. The box must, of course, be dried out before the book is put inside.

A leather drop-back box is made in a similar way; the two trays are constructed as above but the spine is made from two or three layers of card cut progressively narrower by 3 mm, glued together and shaped into a curve with knife and sandpaper. Attach the spine by gluing jaconette to the outside and sticking the flanges on to the inside of the trays, leaving hinges of 3 mm. Before it is finally rubbed down make sure that the smaller tray fits neatly into the larger.

233 Covering and turning in

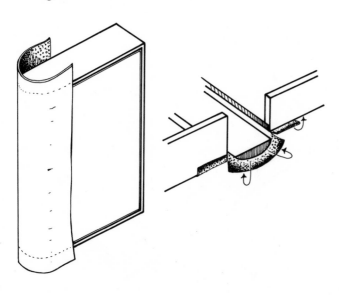

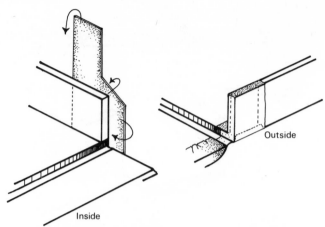

234 Covering the inner corners
with leather

False bands may be attached to the spine. The leather is cut as for a quarter-binding, with a turn-in of 12 mm ($\frac{1}{2}$ in.) and is pared quite thinly so that the hinge will function easily. Cover the spine first but do not stick down the overlap. When it is dry, cut and pare the turn-in. Paste it and model it over the spine and on to the sides. Make paper templates for covering the inner corners with leather, numbering them for identification. Pare thinly a piece of leather, larger than required; from this cut out the pieces to cover the corners, edge-pare them again, and cover. Trim the leather out evenly all round and cover the sides with buckram or cloth. The corners are cut and turned over as already described. The spine is reinforced on the inside with leather or matching cloth. Fill in with pulp card, line the inside of both trays with pasted bond paper and line with felt as required.

Solander boxes

Large, strong, dust-proof boxes of the Solander type are constructed from seven-ply wood and 6-mm hardboard, and covered

235 Solander box

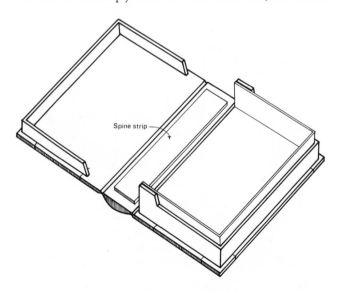

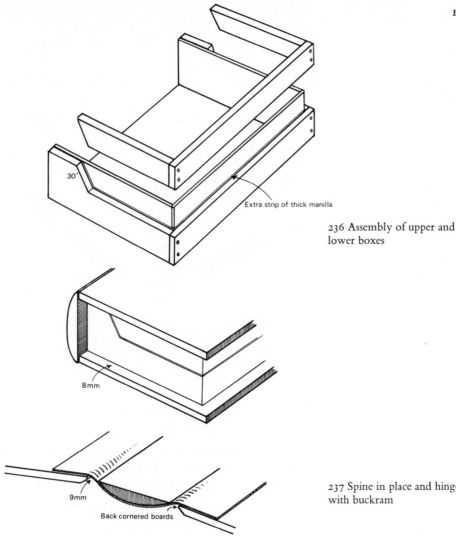

236 Assembly of upper and lower boxes

237 Spine in place and hinged with buckram

in good leather and thick buckram. Measure the book or the bulk of the material to be boxed, add 2 mm each way for free movement and make allowance for the extra spine strip and the thickness of the buckram and felt, as in previous instructions. Having determined the size, cut two frames from seven-ply wood and assemble them firmly and squarely with brass screws, nails or glued dovetail joints. Line the lower tray first with a thick manilla or 500-gsm strawboard to allow play for the fitting of the top tray, and then with 3-mm hardboard. Punch or sink the nails or screws into the board, fill in with Polyfilla or plastic wood and sandpaper smooth.

Cut two covers of 6-mm hardboard, bigger than the frame by 8 mm on the three outside edges, and construct a curved spine from wood or board as long as, and 3 mm wider than, the combined depth of frame and covers. Join the spine to the covers with buckram, giving a 9-mm hinge between each.

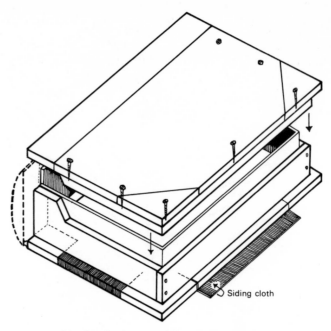

Siding cloth

238 Securing the frames to the covers

Put on false bands if required, bevel the outside edges of the boards and back-corner them. Cover the spine in leather, paring a little down the joint and the turn-in. Trim out the sides when they are dry and pare off the leather where the trays are to be fixed. Glue and screw the frames on to the covers, leaving an 8-mm square on three sides. Countersink the screws and fill in the depressions as before. Cover the corners, bringing the leather to the edges of the screwed-down trays.

As an alternative, the trays may be glued and screwed down to the covers before the leather is attached. A slot is cut with a tenon saw in the bases of the trays at the positions of the leather at the sides and corners. In covering, the leather is taken over the edges and forced through the slots on to the inside. Side the covers with a matching buckram, taking it only to the edges of the frames. Cut the extra spine strip from thick millboard as deep as the frame so that it fits between the sides to make the spine dust-proof. It is tapered very slightly 18 mm from each end before being glued into place, to make allowance for the thickness of the turn-in at the head and tail. Cover this strip, taking the matching book cloth on to the sides to reinforce the hinge. Cover the lower half of the bottom frame first (shaded in Fig. 240) and cut the buckram as shown. (It is wise to shape and cut a paper template first, for accuracy.)

Cover the top half of the bottom frame as in Fig. 241, taking the buckram inside and on to the base. Cover the upper frame and take the buckram on to the inside cover. Fill in with pulp card, line the inside of the trays with a layer or two of strong paper to counteract any warping, and line with felt as required. Fastening clips or locks are screwed to the two halves of the foredge.

The same type of box can be of lighter construction using millboard, when the pieces are assembled using an instant glue and the frames covered with bookcloth or paper.

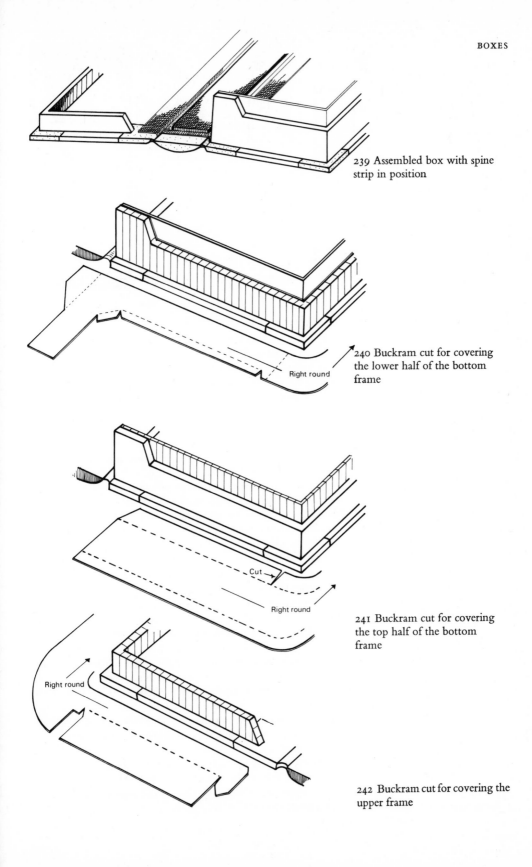

239 Assembled box with spine strip in position

240 Buckram cut for covering the lower half of the bottom frame

Right round

241 Buckram cut for covering the top half of the bottom frame

Cut

Right round

242 Buckram cut for covering the upper frame

Right round

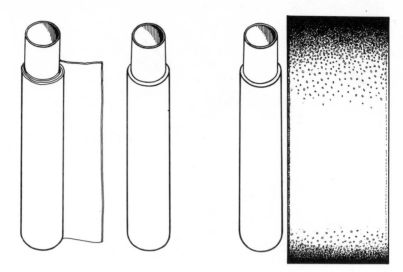

243 Making a scroll cylinder

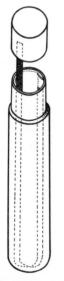

244 Scroll case complete with pull-out ribbon

Scroll cases

Scroll cases are made from a cardboard cylinder of the required diameter and length. Sandpaper the cylinder smoothly all over. Wet one side of a length of kraft paper and paste the other. Beginning 75 mm (3 in.) from the top wrap the paper round the roll, smoothing and boning it down until the roll has increased in thickness by 4 mm. When this is dry, trim off the excess at the bottom and trim the shoulder to a right-angled ledge parallel to the top.

For the cap, five layers of wax paper are wrapped round another cylinder of the same diameter and the edge is taped to hold it in place. Wrap dampened and pasted brown paper round until it is of the same thickness as the other one. When it is dry slide it off the roll, remove the wax paper and trim it down to fit the neck of the other. The fit should be loose to allow for the covering leather. Should the top cylinder be too flimsy, extra linings of kraft paper must be given to both.

Line some thick millboard with a suitably coloured paper and cut circles from this to fit the base and the top of the cylinders. Line the insides of both cylinders with the same paper, using paste. Glue on the top and bottom circles of board, and sandpaper both cylinders evenly. The neck is very gently tapered with sandpaper towards the top. The unpared leather is wrapped round the cylinders to measure the width; 12 mm ($\frac{1}{2}$ in.) should be added to the length at each end. The leather is pared thinly at the base and very thinly at the neck, while the edges are bevelled at 45°, one on the right and the other on the reverse side so that they overlap and marry up perfectly when pasted on. One pasting should be sufficient but the leather should be dampened on the surface so that it may be modelled easily.

Draw a pitching line vertically down the cylinder and smooth the leather round the cylinder, modelling it sharply at the shoulder and neck, easing out any creases, meeting at the bevels and pleating the overlap on to the base and inside the neck.

The cap is covered in the same way. Pare off any unevenness at the top and bottom, fill in with pulp card and sandpaper it smooth. Cover it with a circle of leather which has been pared thinly with long bevelled edges. Trim out the leather on the inside of both cylinders and face with the lining paper 3 mm from the edge and 50 mm (2 in.) on the inside. The cap should fit fairly tightly and come off with a 'plop'; if it is loose, extra linings can be given or, if too tight, the grain of the leather at the neck may be crushed with a hot polishing iron. The join in the leather can be concealed with a blind or gold fillet line worked as part of the decoration.

Some scrolls require a pull-out ribbon to be attached to both cylinder and cap. After covering and trimming out, make two slits in the inner walls of both cylinders – but not through them – the top one level with the trimmed-out leather and the other 25 mm (1 in.) below. Open up the space between and thread the ribbon through. Work in some glue and rub down. Line up so that the paper covers the slits and is on the same level as the ribbon.

9 Changes in bookbinding construction

Changes in book construction in the past cannot be attributed to any particular craftsman. New methods have not necessarily improved the standard, as construction has often been sacrificed for the appearance of the binding. Some binders lay claim to inventiveness but it is usual to find that the claimed innovation has already been used by some unknown craftsman. The sunk cord had its origin in the economics of the trade, the library style evolved from a need for a strong binding, and the case-bound book from the limitations of binding machinery for mass demand. Trade binders have been too busy and too concerned with profit and loss to contemplate radical changes but it is this century, more than any other time, that has seen alterations in design and construction.

Today's technique is superior, and this can be attributed to the influence of amateurs, teachers and chemists who have experimented with the craft and approached it on a scientific basis.

THE HARRISON GROOVE

The preservation of archives and book restoration owe their present high level of achievement to the co-operation between scientist and bookbinder. The technical ability of the trade binder at his best is undisputed and it is to Thomas Harrison M.B.E. that the craft is indebted for his ideas, including an improvement to the library style.

The flush joint is an ideal way of supporting the standing book as the backed sections lean against the upright board (see p. 75), but in the library style the board is set away from the joint and the sections lean against a cushion of leather. This may be sufficient for a small book but it is a weakness in large and heavy volumes. Harrison's suggestion was to increase the thickness and quality of the thinner board of the split and place it flush with the joint, decreasing the thickness of the outer board. Unpared leather can be used in the groove as it is shallow, the board opening has more freedom and the thicker inner board will support the sections. The only other additions to the forwarding are to set the joint after covering and to put down the endpapers by the open method. This is named the semi-French or supported French groove but many binders would prefer to call it the Harrison groove.

245 The Harrison groove

STUB BINDING

Sometimes one has the problem of binding a rare book, or sections of unequal length, or a manuscript in which writing fills the entire page. In two of these cases, backing would harm the book or make the words in the fold unreadable. In the third the spine would be incomplete. The following solution is known as the 'compensating section' or 'stub binding'. Cut paper 100 mm (4 in.) wide and fold it in half, making sections equal in length to, and slightly thicker than, the sections to be bound. (For sections of unequal length measure from the longest section.) Fold round and sew section and folds together with five-hole thread stitching. Fold the stubs back and glue each outside blank to the next with the sections in the correct order. Draw a line 8 mm from the fold and mark this up at 9-mm intervals and approximately 15 mm from each end (Fig. 248). Hold the work in G-clamps between scrap card and make holes through with a needle, bodkin or fine drill (depending on the thickness). Saddle-stitch through the folds with a medium thread, glue the visible stitches and rub them flat with a folder. Glue strips of thick cartridge paper on top and when they are dry sandpaper smooth. Add extra fly leaves if required.

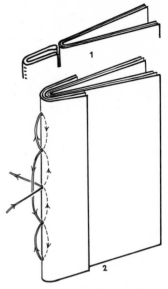

246 Stub binding: folded and stitched

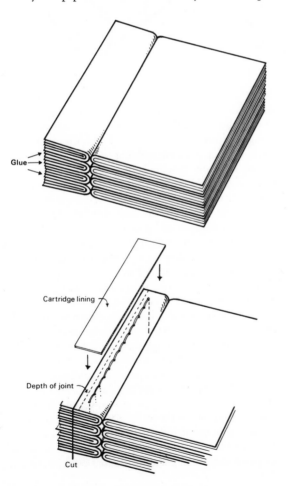

247 Stubs collated and glued together

248 Saddle stitching through the folds

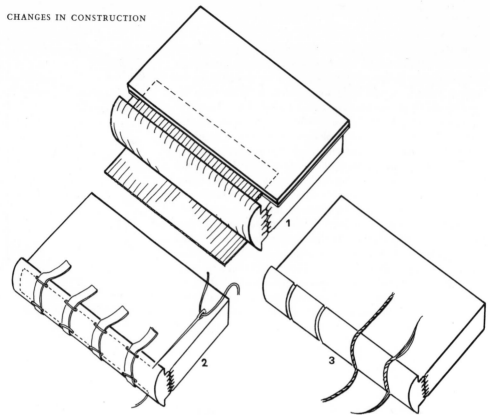

249 Stub binding: completing the spine

Trim the stub in the plough or guillotine, making the cut a little more than the depth of the joint away from the stitches. Tip on four-page endpapers up to the cut and mark the depth of the joint on these. Glue up the spine with hot thin glue or thick paste. Do not round the spine but only back it, using the hammer to form the joint and mould the spine into a solid shape. (In method *1*, above, the compensating folds are backed as ordinary sections.) While it is still moist, line the back with kraft paper and rub it down well. Sandpaper the spine when it is dry, and line with bookcloth or buckram, overlapping the spine on either side for 40 mm (1½ in.); this will be used as a hinge or flange. If the spine is irregular, line it with kraft paper and sandpaper it smooth. Add as many layers as necessary; the solidity of the spine is unimportant as it is not functional. The cloth flange can be inserted into split boards and forwarding continued as in the library style.

There are other variations. Tapes and mull may be glued on the spine and either sewn through the joint before the endpapers are attached or sewn with hidden cloth-jointed endpapers in the same way (*2*). The book can be case bound or bound in the library style. Saw grooves in the false spine and glue in cord: if the saddle-stitching is not cut and the spine is lined heavily, forwarding can continue as for sunk cord work (*3*). Or false bands may be added; the book will open flat as the sections hinge on the compensating folds. Should it be necessary to remove the sections later without damage, cut the stitching and the sections can be lifted away.

FLUSH JOINT SEWN ON TAPES

Sewing on tapes is stronger than on cords and is usually associated with the case or library styles, but a book can be given the benefit of a flush joint sewn on tapes. Sew the book on tapes and proceed with the forwarding until the boards are ready to be attached. Put the boards in place with the squares set accurately and mark off the exact position and width of the tapes where they touch the boards. Remove the boards and draw a line parallel to the spine edge 10 mm in and a similar line 16 mm on the inside. From the tape positions already marked draw lines at right angles to pass through the 10-mm line. Make a slot with a chisel, and a return slot from the inside, and cut away a shallow channel to the thickness of the tape up to the first line, so that when the tapes are laced in they will lie level with the board surface. The tapes are well pasted, threaded through the first slot and returned through the second, pulled tight and cut off flush with the surface. Any unevenness can be hammered down on the knocking-down iron and the book is then put in the press to dry with sheets of tin on both sides of the boards. When the book is dry, line the outside of the board with thick cartridge paper, using glue; any unevenness can be sand-papered away. (If the outside of any board is lined, outward pull is inevitable; to counteract this, line the inside of the board with pasted bond paper.) The book is forwarded as in the sunk cord style.

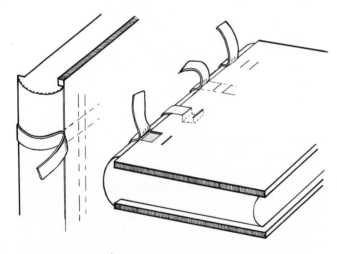

250 Flush joint sewn on tapes

LARGE BINDINGS

To cover large books in leather, two skins may be required or a condition of decoration may require a different colour on the spine. These problems are overcome as follows. Sew on tapes and forward the book until the backing is completed and the edges cut. Four boards are cut square and to size in the plough, each half the depth of the joint. One board is placed flush with each joint and the cut down waste and tapes are glued to this. Line the boards to the

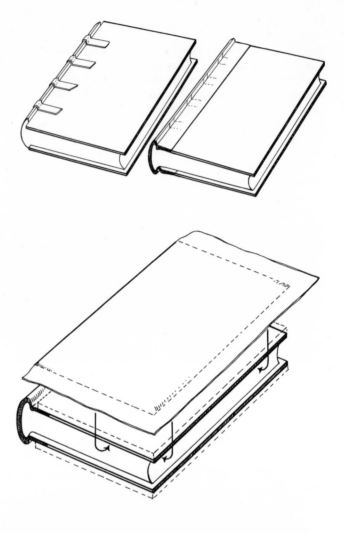

251 Covering large books in leather: first stage

252 Covering the sides

joints with glued pulp card and sandpaper away the unevenness of tapes and waste. Sew headbands and line the spine with first and second linings. If the book is a fine binding, line with leather also and sandpaper the spine smooth. Cover it in quarter leather and allow it to dry. Trim out excess leather and pare the leather on the edges of the boards, the turn-in and the sides. Line the remainder of the board with glued pulp card and sandpaper the join smooth. Compensate the outward warp by lining the inside with pasted bond paper.

The other two boards have their three outside edges sandpapered to a long bevel, finishing to a fine edge. The spine edges are shortened by 5 mm. Cut separate pieces of leather for each board, allowing 25 mm turn-in at head, tail and foredge but only 8 mm on the spine edge. Pare the leather as for normal covering but pare the spine edge to a depth of 12 mm in a long bevel. Paste the leather once and pitch the boards in position. Cut and pare away the leather at a right angle at the corners of the spine edge and turn

The History of Warfare by Viscount Montgomery of Alamein,
1968. Example of onlay work. See p. 207.

King Lear by William Shakespeare. Combination of etched
blocks, stamped into the cover, with onlays. See p. 208.

Extinct Birds by Hon. Walter Rothschild, 1907. Example of onlay work. See p. 209.

Picasso's Erotic Gravures, edited by Ralph Ginzburg. Covered by means of separate pieces of leather fitted together. See p. 209.

in this edge only. Let each board dry under a weight. Glue the inside of the top boards and place them squarely on top of the attached boards, line them up to the foredge and nip in the press, leaving a type of French groove at the spine edge. Paste the overlapping leather and mould the turn-in over the two boards.

Forwarding proceeds as normal although it is often necessary to line the inside of the boards well with pasted bond paper to counteract the warp.

ADHESIVE BINDING

Around 1850, a number of books were produced in single sheets held together by a type of rubber cement – the first experiment in adhesive binding. Few have survived as complete bindings because the adhesive quickly deteriorated. Modern books in single sheets are held together by synthetic glue; they too break up after little use and little can be done to bind them soundly: they can be oversewn, resulting in loss of the inner margins, or made up into sections by guarding, which causes an excess of swell in the spine.

If the sheets are entirely separated, knock them up to the head and spine between thin strawboards and hold them by the foredge in a finishing press. Bend the spine over so that the leaves are fanned out and glue with PVA. Bend them the other way and glue again; all that is necessary is a fine line of glue on the edges. Take the book out of the press, ease off the strawboard and leave the book to dry in good shape.

Should the book be broken in pieces, tip each part to the next by a fine line of glue on the spine edge. With a circular file, saw channels obliquely across the spine, deep enough to take thin

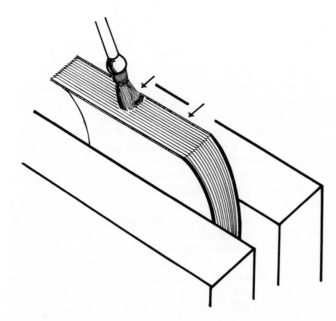

253 Adhesive binding

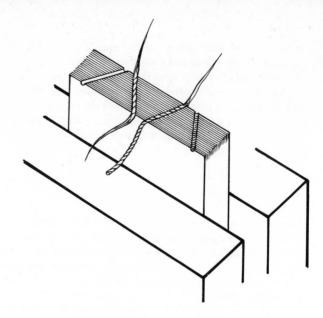

254 Filed channels across the spine edge

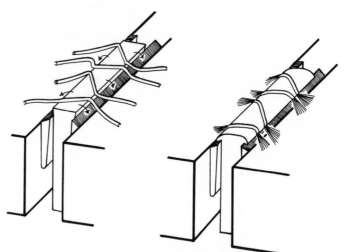

255 Preparations for casing

sewing cord. Tip on four-page endpapers as for a case binding. Glue the channels, and lay lengths of sewing cord in them and immediately back the book. It will not be possible to round first, so try to soften the spine with paste. A shallow but substantial round shape to the spine can be made by jointing and moulding the paper together with a hammer.

An inexpensive book may be given a case binding. The back is given first and second linings, the cord is frayed out and cut down to 25 mm, and operations are continued as for cased work.

A valued book may be bound in the sunk cord style. Use cloth-jointed endpapers and sew these through the joint (as for leather-jointed ends); the cords are left long and thinned out to be laced into the boards. It is preferable to bind with a jointed spine and tight back. Although there is an absence of swell the joint will help to hold the pages in place. There will be no freedom in the back folds and mishandling will break the book down the spine.

An innovation in a case binding is called the 'American groove'. The thickness of the board used is equal to the depth of the joint, and the boards are cut with the usual 3-mm squares but are short of the spine by 4 mm. When they are being covered in cloth, the boards are set away from the joint by 4 mm and held in position until the glued cloth is wrapped round. Narrow rods are set in this groove and the whole is nipped in the press between pressing boards. The book is then removed and the case made in the usual way. When casing in, allowance is made for the groove and the rods are replaced when the book goes in the press for nipping down the endpapers.

Although the depth of the joint is equal to the board thickness the book will open easily even if buckram is used; this method has many advantages compared with the ordinary flush-jointed case.

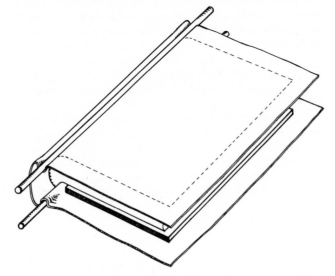

256 Covering, with the American groove

10 Design

A book that is well designed is one in which the binding style and materials have been chosen to fulfil a definite function. The craftsman meets problems in constructional design at every operation; for example, overparing will weaken the leather, but some paring is necessary in certain styles to allow the cover to open freely.

Initially, students are advised to concentrate on construction, to make bindings strong and serviceable and to limit decoration to legible titles, a minimum of gold lines, clean, well-proportioned work and pleasant colour schemes. Cloths should be chosen for their textures, and leathers, sides, endpapers, edges and headbands should be in harmonious colours. Unusual colour combinations make an immediate impact, but may be rejected as unpleasant later.

Colours chosen for the binding may convey something of the subject or character of the book and can be selected from either the warm or the cool range of colours. Colours or tones in proximity to each other are restrained and harmonious but colours opposite each other, such as blue and orange, give a strong contrast and, if used together, could have a disquieting effect on the binding.

Sides and endpapers

With experience, the student may decorate paper for sides and endpapers: to produce one's own gives great satisfaction. Simple methods are best, and these include stencilling, stick, leaf and lino prints, woodcuts, wax resist, paste graining, broad pen patterns and simple marbling with oil colour on water size. Marbled paper, in the past, has often disguised cheap and faulty work, and some modern ones are vivid in colour and restless in design. With all due respect for five hundred years of marbling, the use of these papers could with advantage disappear from contemporary bindings. Marbled papers that are pleasing and unobtrusive are only satisfactory for sides and endpapers when used with discrimination.

Decoration in gold

Cloth cases can be decorated with lines made by fillets, pallets and gouges impressed through gold or pigment foils. These should be simple shapes in accord with the type of book, although gold lines cannot be impressed solidly on coarse cloth without using considerable pressure. Decoration of half-leather books with corners

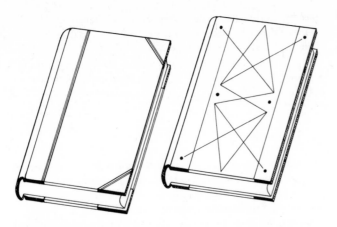

257 Decoration of half-leather bindings

is limited by the shape of the sides and confined to gold or blind lines on the leather against the siding material. Half-bindings with foredge strips have more possibilities, and effective decoration can be achieved by linking the leather with lines across the sides. Decoration is very limited on economy bindings, but a few lines well placed can enhance the book and have value as an exercise in decoration.

For twelve centuries hand tools have been used to decorate leather bindings. A single pattern cut into the face of the tool, or a series of patterns engraved on a wheel, were impressed on the cover leaving a blind (black) or gold decoration. Some old tools may have been made by the binder, but mainly they were cut by the professional engraver who used lines, scrolls and natural forms as motifs for his work. The binder would purchase those that he considered attractive and use them indiscriminately on bindings without reference to the subject of the book. Occasionally an individual would arrange the tools in an imaginative way, but it is regrettable that, today, too many craftsmen copy the efforts of earlier binders. There is a great attraction in leather bindings richly tooled with glowing gold borders, leaves and flowers, and these were beautiful in their period, and still are, but there is not necessarily any merit in their reproduction on modern bindings.

Generally, a modern designer would not use early forms of decoration from tools designed by the tool cutter. The binder must be creative in decoration to capture the character of the book, influenced in his design by the contents, illustrations, layout, typography and the printing process. Knowledge of basic design and the theory of colour is essential, and the only way to produce an original design for a particular book is to read and understand it.

Decoration on a book should originate from its constructional design, therefore ornament on books with raised bands would originate, or be linked, with the parallel lines across the spine. The smooth, rounded spine on a flush-jointed book is preferable as it gives more freedom for decoration. Decoration need not be confined within the rectangle of the cover, like a picture contained in a frame. The design can extend from front to back across the spine and even run off the edges. The intention and form of decoration must be clearly stated in the specifications for a fine binding, with coloured drawings made and instructions written so that tools and materials are known in advance. When the book is bound and the exact measurement of spine and covers ascertained, a master working drawing should be made on bond paper with a sharp pencil.

EXAMPLES

Decoration is a matter of personal choice and an individual approach, whether it be abstract or factual, geometric or free, even serious or comic. Therefore its form cannot be suggested but some methods and applications can be recommended.

Flowers and Plants (p. 182) is an example of geometric gold and blind tooling executed with mitred fillets and a pallet. The design was drawn carefully on to bond paper and the main construction lines were traced on to a separate sheet; this was attached firmly to the cover with adhesive tape. Each of these lines was impressed through the paper with a warm fillet as a guide for subsequent tooling. When the sheet was removed the subsidiary lines of the design were marked on the cover from the master drawing, using dividers and straight-edge. These were tooled with a fillet and gold lines across the spine, linking the design on each side, were made with a pallet. The impressions were paste-washed, glaired and tooled with the usual gold finishing procedure, while the blind lines were burnished by fixing the fillet and skidding the hot tool in the impressions. Gold line tooling is appealing for its brilliance, and the effect as light catches the facets of the impression; blind lines have a subtle, pleasing attraction, especially on light-coloured leathers.

The binding of *Goya* (p. 182) is an example of inlay work. The design is an endeavour to capture, in abstract, the creative zeal of the artist and the conflicts of his time. The violent shapes in crimson and scarlet represent the horrors of war, recorded by Goya, while the white and gold symbolize the artist's hopeful vision of the splendour of Spain at peace.

Parts of the cover are removed and replaced with other leathers. The boards are lined with paper so that the piece of leather can be removed without disturbing the surface. Tracings on bond paper are taken from the master drawing of the shapes to be inlaid. Cut out these templates 2 mm larger all round and tape them to the cover, positioning them by means of the master. Hold a scalpel at an angle of 45°, cut round the guide line through tape, paper and leather and remove the piece. The replacement leather should be the same thickness as the piece that has been removed; if it is thinner, fill the base of the cut-out with glued cartridge paper; if thicker, pare the difference off the leather before the inlay is cut.

Tape the cut template on to the new leather, hold the scalpel at the same angle, and cut on the outside of the line so that the replacement is fractionally larger. The edge of the cover cut-out may be blind-tooled with thin pallets, gouges or fillets, and a small ledge formed.

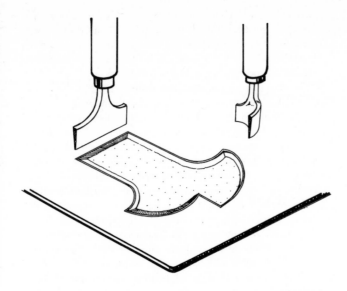

258 Blind tooling round cut-out work

Paste both the inlay and the cut-out, rubbing the adhesive well into the leather. Push it into position exactly, and as it contracts on drying it should fit perfectly. Wipe off excess paste with a damp sponge and leave it to dry. Tool round the inlay, following the ledge left by the first tooling. Some inlay work has no need of tooling, and a good pressing when dry will level up the leathers.

Only simple, large shapes need to be inlaid as detailed work is better onlaid. The title of this binding is an integral part of the design and has been carried out by onlaid leather letters as the traditional serif hand letters would be incongruous on the spine. Also the gold work is unconventional. An area of the inlay is damped, modelled with the point of a folder and flooded with glaire. Gold leaf is floated on and when dry the excess gold is brushed away and the leaf burnished with a dog-toothed burnisher. The irregular surface reflects the light in an unusual way.

The History of Warfare, by Field Marshal Montgomery (p. 199), is entirely onlay work, which is the most direct method of apply-ing other leathers to the cover. Note that in this decoration there has been deliberate use of discordant colours and violent shapes, to capture the subject of the book. The leather to be onlaid is either pared to paper thinness or left fairly substantial, depending on the effect required. (In another method of paring leather very thinly, known as 'wet paring', the leather is soaked in water before it is pared.) Thin leather adds colour to the cover, while thick onlays give the cover a sculptured quality. The shapes of the onlay pieces are carefully traced on to bond paper from the master drawing and these templates trimmed down 2 mm larger all round. Tape them firmly on to the pared leather and cut, without a bevel, through paper, tape and leather with a scalpel. No matter how thin the leather an edge will show, therefore the edge is bevelled with a scalpel; the thicker the leather, the wider the bevel is made. Care is taken not to trim away or distort the shape, so leather is used from the centre of the skin as it does not stretch so much. An alternative method of controlling the shape when cutting and bevelling is to paste the bond paper templates to the leather. They are subsequently soaked off, but it is unsatisfactory as the grain of the pared leather disappears and the colour darkens; these disadvantages also occur when leather is pared wet.

If the onlays are numerous, and similar in shape, they are numbered on the underside to correspond to the numbered master drawing. When applying the pieces, cut out a principal shape from the master and attach the master to the cover with tape at the spine and head. Rub paste into the principal onlay and when it is soaked remove any excess paste and position it, using the cut-away master as a guide. Rub down under paper and, with a small chisel-ended bone folder (illustrated on p. 25), push the edges down to give the onlay a cushioned effect on the cover, build up the decoration, fitting each piece to the principal shape. If the design is complicated, continue to cut out the corresponding shapes from the master. Wash off excess paste carefully and when dry the outline of the onlay and base leather is tooled with hot thin pallets and gouges to bind the edges down and prevent lifting.

Small and intricate curved work can be tooled successfully with pallets only 1 mm, 2 mm or 3 mm wide. An advantage of onlay work is that very thin leather can be continued across the hinge on to the spine and round the edges of the board without the onlay lifting or restricting the opening of the book.

The binding of *King Lear* (p. 199) has been decorated by blocking and onlay work. The blocks are made by etching a design in relief on to 6-mm-thick mild steel plate with nitric acid. Extreme care must be taken when using this corrosive acid, and it should be kept in a coloured poison bottle, clearly labelled and firmly stoppered. The proportion used is one part of acid to two of water, and for safety's sake the acid must be added to the water, never water to acid.

Experiment with a small block first. The design is painted on to the steel plate with stopping-out varnish in three layers, each being allowed to dry before the next is applied. The back of the plate and its edges are also liberally coated. As the fumes given off by the acid are toxic and may destroy man-made fibres, the work is best done in the open air.

Pour the diluted acid into a glass, porcelain or rubber dish and slide the plate into the liquid, handling it only with a pair of tongs. Watch the process continually and, as bubbles form on the exposed metal, brush them away with a feather. After a short period the acid will begin to undercut the painted areas, and it will be necessary to remove the plate from the bath. It is then washed in water, dried, and the edges of the design repainted with the stopping-out varnish. Irregularities in the line caused by the formation of bubbles, by patches of the varnish lifting, and by undercutting can be an advantage in the appearance of the ultimate impression. Etching is continued until the surface has been reduced in depth to 3 mm.*

* Further information on the etching of blocks may be found in Walter Chamberlain's *Manual of Etching and Engraving* in this series.

The cover is prepared by dampening the leather; while the moisture is evaporating from the surface, make the plate fairly hot. Put a tin plate inside the cover of the book, quickly position the block with a thick strawboard on top, place it between pressing boards directly under the centre of the press and nip hard for five seconds. The leather must not be too damp; nor should the block be too hot or the cover will be charred. The impression may be intensified by painting with black ink.

In *Extinct Birds* (p. 200) a decorative use has been made of an unusual leather, a Spanish sheepskin dyed in various colours by twisting the leather in the dyebath. As the book is large the spine has been covered in green levant morocco for strength, while the weaker sheepskin covers the boards, using the technique explained in Chapter 9 (p. 197). The lettering is original, cut from pink pared leather and applied as onlay. The bird shape is onlay work and aluminium coloured foil has been used for decoration. The tool for gilding the eye was shaped from a piece of gas piping.

Picasso's Erotic Gravures (p. 200) is covered with separate pieces of leather carefully fitted together. This is economical, as offcuts may be used instead of onlaying or inlaying a cover of one piece of leather.

From a master drawing accurate tracings were made for each piece. The spine and parts of the sides of this book were covered in red leather larger than required and left to dry. The paper pattern of that part of the red leather which was to remain was attached by adhesive tape and the excess red leather cut away with a scalpel, leaving a bevel of 30°. The green piece adjacent to the red was cut larger, and its paper pattern was reversed and attached to the underside. The edge to be fitted to the red leather was bevelled at 30°; the paper pattern was then removed, and the leather pasted and modelled into position, the two bevels meeting in an uninterrupted line. When it was dry the outer edge of the second piece was bevelled to remove unwanted leather, using the pattern as a guide. Piece after piece was cut larger, bevelled, attached, dried and the excess trimmed away until the boards were covered completely.

The reason for allowing each piece to dry before cutting and attaching the next was to control shrinkage and facilitate accurate cutting and fitting. The leathers were the same thickness and paring was critical in the areas of the turn-in. Minor or detailed parts of the design were superimposed as onlays. Joins in the leather were blind-tooled with gouges and a farthing wheel but could have remained untooled. The title was executed with white pigment foil.

Methods of decoration will suggest themselves through actual operations; for instance, natural leather can be stained and painted with aniline dyes or, when the book is being covered, the wet leather can be rucked and modelled into interesting forms. String and cut-outs can be glued to the board before covering, and the leather shaped over them. Leather pared from the surface of rough-grained skins has a feathered texture and can be 'painted' on the cover with an adhesive.

Onlays may be applied to the leather with a water-resistant

synthetic adhesive, after paring the leather but before covering The leather is gently nipped in the press between layers of blotting paper, and when it has dried out the resulting bumps are pared away from the underside with a spokeshave. The onlays will then be perfectly level with the surface.

Transparent vellum has been used in the decoration of books for two centuries, but its possibilities seem to have been neglected in the last decade. The common method is to paint a design on the lining paper with waterproof inks or pigment colour which is further fixed by spraying with an aerosol matt poster varnish. The vellum is lined with this decorated paper, as explained in Chapter 6, in the section on vellum work, and care must be taken not to wet too much, nor brush too vigorously, when preparing for covering. The cover should rather be 'drummed on', and positioned with care. An alternative method is to prepare the book for covering by lining the spine, the French groove, and the inside, outside and edges of the boards with good paper. When the linings are dry the design is painted on the book and fixed with varnish. The book is then covered with unlined transparent vellum. Clear, clean paste is essential.

Other crafts, such as embroidery, batik, lithography and silver work, can be examined for ideas, and non-binding materials such as mother-of-pearl, mirrors and metal foils can be used, if they do not interfere with the function of the book. In fact there are many ingenious ways of decorating books, and students are urged to experiment in an individual way, remembering always that fine craftsmanship and careful planning are essential in placing the decoration when covering a book.

Glossary

A method of joining single sheets together by applying adhesive either to the extreme back margins or to the roughened edges of the knocked-up sheets. ADHESIVE BINDING

Sewing a section along its length with one piece of thread. (See also Two-up.) ALL ALONG

See Coated paper. ART PAPER

Trimming away the corner, either inside or outside, at the spine edges of the boards. It assists the turn-in of the leather, tying up with thread and shaping the headcaps. BACK CORNERING

Impressing finishing tools into leather or cloth as a guide for gold tooling. BLINDING IN

Impressing hot finishing tools into leather to leave a dark or black impression. Alternatively, cold tools may be dabbed on to printer's ink before impressing. BLIND TOOLING

Part of the endpaper; its function when pasted in is to counteract the warp of the board caused by the covering material. BOARD PAPER

Also known as Armenian bole. A pigment of fine red clay used as a filler when gilding the edges of books. BOLE

The folds which occur at head and foredge when a sheet is folded into a section. BOLT

See Kettle stitch. CATCH STITCH

A slit or cutting sawn into the backs of the sections at head and tail, in which the kettle stitch is made. (Can also be spelt 'kerf'.) CERF

Dusting the leaves of books with french chalk before edge gilding, to prevent them from sticking together. Necessary when the paper contains, or is coated with, china clay. CHALKING

Fibres left after the non-fibrous parts of the wood have been dissolved away by caustic soda during paper manufacture. CHEMICAL WOOD PULP

COATED PAPER	Smooth, glossy paper, also known as 'art paper'. The base paper, made from esparto-grass fibre, is coated with china clay and casein glue and glazed with rollers under pressure. Used for fine-screen colour printing.
COLLATE	Check a book thoroughly to ensure that it is complete and in the right order.
COMPENSATING GUARDS	Narrow extra folds or strips of paper in the spine to compensate for the addition of material after the book has been bound. Also added to make up the thickness of folded maps or plates. (See Guard book.)
CUT-IN BOARDS	In some binding styles the edges are cut with the aid of trindles after the boards are attached.
CUTTING WEDGE	When the head and tail of a book with swell at the spine are to be cut by plough or guillotine the difference in the thickness is made up by the addition of a fanned-out piece of paper or a similar block of strawboard; this is called a 'wedge'.
DENTELLE	A toothed or lace-like border of gold or blind tooling made by decorated rolls or separate hand tools.
DOUBLE-PAGE SPREAD	An illustration printed on facing verso and recto pages. This is unsatisfactory as the binding margin interrupts the subject matter, and it is preferable for the illustration to be printed on a separate sheet and thrown out on a guard.
DOUBLURE	The final 'lining' with paper or leather of part or the whole of the inside of the boards, pasted down as a separate piece.
DRUMMING	The vellum covering of a book is 'drummed on' when it is attached only by an adhesive to the spine, the turn-in and the perimeter of the boards; when dry, the vellum contracts firmly without warping the boards too much.
DWELL	The time for which the hot tool is impressed in gold tooling or blocking.
EDGE PARE	Paring away of leather at a bevel for a distance of a few millimetres from the edge.
ENGINE SIZING	The addition of resin to the pulp at the mixer stage before it is made into paper.
EXTRA	The term used to describe a binding for which the best materials have been used and particular care has been taken with forwarding and finishing.
FALSE BANDS	Strips of leather, card or vellum or lengths of cord stuck to the backs of the sections before covering, in imitation of the flexible style or as decoration.

The natural grain of leather. The part of the skin over the backbone of the animal has a pronounced grain when compared with the remainder and is often positioned on the front of the binding to emphasize the beauty of the leather.

FIGURE

The inside and outside of the boards are 'filled in' with pulp card after covering, to level the surfaces and make the siding material or endpapers lie flat.

FILLING IN

A lining of mull stuck directly to the back folds of the sections; used as a reinforcement in all multi-section books.

FIRST LINING

Floriation is a flower-and-foliage decoration in gold or blind tooling, impressed by a number of hand tools applied separately.

FLORIATED

A protective cover made the same size as the text paper (see Squares).

FLUSH BINDING

Part of the endpapers; they may be white or coloured, and their function is to protect the first and last few leaves of the text.

FLY LEAF

The front edge of the book; so-called because originally this edge faced outwards from the shelves and titles were painted, inked or scorched on the edges of the leaves.

FOREDGE

Brown stains, mostly in poor-quality papers, caused by the effects of humidity on impurities in the paper.

FOXING

Sewing together of two or more sections without tapes or cords. Each section is linked to the rest by catching up the loops of thread of the preceding section.

FRENCH SEWING

A full or whole binding is one that is covered entirely in the same material, particularly leather.

FULL BINDING

Collecting the sections or sheets together in the correct sequence to make up a complete book.

GATHERING

Decoration of gilded edges in an elaborate pattern by impressing warm finishing tools into them. Little of this work is done today; it is regarded as pretentious.

GAUFFERING

A preparation of white of egg or shellac used to fix the gold leaf in tooling and edge gilding.

GLAIRE or glair

Orientation of the fibres, in paper and board, determined by the direction in which the wire travelled during the making. The grain in cloth is in the direction of the warp thread. Grain direction in all man-made materials used in bookbinding must run from head to tail of the book.

GRAIN

GROOVE, AMERICAN	If the boards of a case binding are equal in thickness to the depth of the joint and set away from the joint by a few millimetres to allow a free opening with thick buckram, this gap is called an American groove.
GROOVE, FRENCH	In the library style the board is set away from the joint instead of flush to enable thick leather to be used at the hinge; this is known as the French groove.
GROOVE, OLD	The shape of the back edges of the folded sections of a pulled book resulting from the original backing. This must be flattened or 'knocked out' with a hammer before rebinding.
GUARD BOOK	A method of binding in which the folds of the sections at the spine bulk more than at the foredge; the extra paper, in narrow folds or strips, compensates for the later addition of other material. Photograph albums are an example.
GUARDING	Repairing or strengthening the folds of sections or leaves by pasting on strips of paper, tissue or linen.
GUTTER MARGIN	The 'binding margin' or inner margin of a book.
HALF BINDING	An economy covering style in which the spine and corners or foredge are covered by a good material while the remainder is covered by a cheaper one.
HEAD	The top of a binding or page.
HEADBAND	Coloured threads embroidered round a core and sewn through the sections to make up the difference between the top edge of the sections and the edges of the boards.
HEADCAP	A shaped and modelled turn-in over the spine in leather bindings.
HOLLOW or hollow back	A paper tube stuck to the spine of a book, to which the covering material is attached. This allows a freer opening for sections of stiff paper or for books in which entries are made, and overcomes the limitations of vellum and buckram.
INSERT	Additional matter placed within a book or pamphlet without fixing, e.g. a diagram in a pocket at the back of a book.
INSET	To fix additional matter within a book by sewing or sticking; e.g. an illustration plate within the text.
INTERLEAVING	Inserting or insetting sheets of thin tissue paper between leaves for either decorative or protective purposes, for making copies (receipts) or to prevent offsetting of newly printed sheets.
JOINT	The right-angled groove made by backing the sections in which the boards are placed is the inner joint. The hinge of cloth or leather on the outside of the book is the outer joint.

See Cerf.

A catch stitch or knot, made at the end of each section to join it on to the preceding one. (From the German *ketteln*, to pick up stitches.) KETTLE STITCH

The sections or sheets are 'knocked up' even and square by tapping them at the spine and head; this is important in nearly all binding operations, especially before cutting the edges. KNOCK UP

A soft cover, very often with the squares extending to half the thickness of the book to enclose the edges. Bibles are often limp-bound. LIMP BINDING

Kraft, bond or other strong paper pasted to the inside of boards to counteract warping of the boards by the covering material. Can also denote the mull (first lining) and kraft paper (second lining) glued to the backs of sections. LININGS

Addition of kaolin or similar substances to the pulp at the mixer stage before the paper is made, to give a receptive surface for printing. LOADING

Single sheets or other material, with or without holes punched or slots cut in the back margins, held together by thongs, cords, posts, rings, wire spirals, plastic combs, bars or spring mechanisms. LOOSE-LEAF

Paper which has a slightly rough surface as it leaves the paper-making machine; it is used for general bookwork, particularly for non-illustrated books. MACHINE-FINISHED (M/F) PAPER

Two or more pieces of paper or board laminated by an adhesive are termed 'made', as in the common made endpaper. MADE

One or more pieces of narrow ribbon glued to the spine at the head before lining and then placed between the sections, for the convenience of the reader who wishes to mark a particular page. MARKER

Wood, usually spruce, disintegrated by grinding to pulp and sub-sequently made into paper. As it contains many impurities it soon deteriorates and is used only for ephemeral printing. MECHANICAL WOOD PAPER

A binding imitative of the flexible style; the cords on which the book is sewn are let into the backs of the sections instead of remaining on the outside. The back is lined up smoothly, false bands are applied and the covering leather is stuck directly to the spine. MOCK FLEXIBLE

A groove cut in the shanks of decorative finishing tools, handle letters and type to assist in accurate placing and setting. NICK

The transfer of ink from newly printed matter on to the facing page, particularly under pressure. This can be overcome by inter-leaving. OFFSET

OVERCASTING or oversewing	Reinforcing a section or joining a number of single sheets together by sewing through the back margin.
OVERHANG	See Squares.
OVERLAP	In all books, except for some flush bindings, the covering material overlaps the edges of the boards to protect them; the term is synonymous with 'turn-in' or 'turn-over'.
PENCIL CASE	A derisory term for unstuck portions of leather or paper occurring as flutes, usually at the inner joints, through incorrect procedure when putting down endpapers or leather joints.
PITCH MARKS	Guide marks or lines drawn on material to assist in positioning that material quickly and accurately, especially when glue is used.
POCKET	A paper, cloth or board wallet, sometimes gusseted, placed usually at the back of a book to contain inserted sheets.
PRELIMINARY MATTER ('prelims')	Information concerning the book, such as title page, contents etc., forming the first section; usually numbered with roman numerals.
PROTECTION SHEET	A sheet of waxed or plain paper placed during binding to keep the leaves clean or protect them from the effects of moisture.
PULLING	Freeing the sections of a book from the original binding in preparation for rebinding.
PULP CARD	A soft, thick paper made from printers' waste, which does not stretch too much when adhesive is applied; it is used for filling in the outside and inside of boards after covering. It is not recommended for fine binding as it may be highly acidic.
QUARTER BINDING	An economical covering method in which the spine and part of the sides are covered in one material and a cheaper one is used on the remainder. The effect can be quite pleasing if good materials are used.
RECTO	The right-hand pages of a book, usually the odd numbers.
S/C PAPERS	Paper is 'calendered', or smoothed, by passing it between a number of hot polished rollers. Extra smoothness can be gained by adjusting the pressure on the rollers, which is called 'super-calendering'. S/C papers have a surface very receptive to fine screen illustrations.
SECOND LINING	A layer of kraft paper glued to the spine over a lining of mull, to strengthen and consolidate the sections.
SETTING THE BACK	Permanent fixing of the shape of a book's spine. After the book is backed and the boards attached, it is put in the press in good shape and a thick layer of paste applied to the spine. In five minutes the paste is scraped to clean off the old glue and the book left to dry, when the shape of the spine is permanently fixed.

Pushing the board into a right-angled position on the joint – an important operation in covering a flush-jointed book with leather. | SETTING THE JOINT

Covering with cloth or paper the remainder of the exposed boards after attaching the leather or cloth in half and quarter styles. | SIDING

A printed letter or number placed usually at the bottom of the first page of each folded section to assist in the collation of the book. | SIGNATURE

The cords or tapes on which the book is sewn are known as slips when they are laced into, or fixed on, the boards. | SLIPS

A strip of board used, generally, to separate the two boards to a desired measurement when making case bindings to an identical size; it is removed when the covering material is turned in. | SPACING BAR

One of the constructional features of the library style, where the board is made up of a laminated millboard and strawboard with a slit to contain the flange of tapes and waste sheet. | SPLIT BOARD

The difference in measurement between the text leaves and the edge of the board. The protective boards or covers of a book are larger than the text, and the difference (the squares) is dependent on the size, use and binding style of the book. Although the squares protect the leaves they should not be too large for the leaves must support the covers. A less commonly used name is 'overhang'. | SQUARES

A strip of paper or thin card, cut to the width of the spine of a case binding, placed between the boards and glued on to the covering cloth to stiffen or strengthen the cloth spine. | STIFFENER

A piece of paper attached by an adhesive to another to increase its substance and strength. The common made endpaper is an example of this. | STIFF LEAF

Method of binding in which the sections are sewn on to 'stubs', narrow folds of paper; it is these stubs which form the spine. The original section hinges on the stub and is unaffected by the binding operations. Sometimes called a compensation section binding. | STUB BINDING

This is an improvement to the split board of the library style. The inner board is increased in thickness and quality and placed flush with the joint to support the sections while the thinner outer board is positioned away from the joint so that thick leather can be used at the hinge and the boards will open freely. | SUPPORTED or SEMI-FRENCH GROOVE

The additional thickness in the sewn folds of the sections caused by the sewing thread and any repair paper. | SWELL

The bottom of a binding or a page. | TAIL

THROW-OUT	A map, diagram or illustration larger than the book, which is folded and bound in with the sections. On reference it is opened or 'thrown out', usually towards the tail.
TIE DOWN	To loop the thread under the kettle stitches at intervals when embroidering headbands; this secures the headband to the book.
TIGHT BACK	A spine in which the covering material, usually leather, is attached directly to the lined or unlined backs of the sections. This is a much more durable method than the hollow back, with the cover attached to a paper tube.
TIP IN	A narrow strip of adhesive is applied to the back margin of single sheets or plates and insetted into the back fold of the accompanying leaf; as a result this leaf will have a restricted opening.
TIP ON or TIP UP	A narrow strip of adhesive is applied to the back edge of endpapers and these are positioned to line up with the first and last sections.
TRINDLES	Two flat pieces of metal tied together with a short length of string. They are used to flatten the rounded spine of a book so that the foredge may be cut after the boards are attached.
TUB-SIZED	A term applied to paper which, after manufacture, is immersed in a bath of animal gelatine; this tub sizing, or surface sizing, improves the strength and durability of the paper.
TURN-IN or TURN-OVER	See Overlap.
TWO-UP or THREE-UP	Sewing two or three sections with one length of thread to reduce swell. (See also All Along.)
UNSEWN BINDING	See Adhesive Binding.
VERSO	The left-hand pages of a book, usually the even numbers.
WASTE SHEET	A protective sheet of paper usually incorporated in the end papers and either cut down or discarded during binding.
WHOLE BINDING	See Full Binding.
YAPP	A form of binding with squares extended beyond the normal, to overlap the three edges and cover them completely. Yapp bindings are usually limp with rounded corners, and are mainly used for devotional books.

Further reading

BRASSINGTON, W. Salt: *A History of the Art of Bookbinding*. London, 1894.

BURDETT, Eric: *The Craft of Bookbinding*. David & Charles, Newton Abbot, 1975.

CLEMENTS, Jeff: *Bookbinding*. Arco Publications, London, 1963.

COCKERELL, Douglas: *Bookbinding and the Care of Books*. Pitman, London, 1953.

CORDEROY, John: *Bookbinding for Beginners*. Studio Vista, London, and Watson-Guptill, New York, 1967.

DIEHL, Edith: *Bookbinding: its background and technique* (2 vols.). Rinehart, New York, 1946.

LANGWELL, W. H.: The *Conservation of Books and Documents*. Pitman, London, and Greenwood, Westport (CT), 1957.

LUERS, Heinrich: *Das Fachwissen des Buchbinders*. Stuttgart, 1941.

MANSFIELD, Edgar: *Modern Design in Bookbinding*. Peter Owen, London, 1966.

MIDDLETON, Bernard C.: *A History of English Craft Bookbinding Technique*. Hafner, London and New York, 1963.

ROBINSON, Ivor: *Introducing Bookbinding*. Batsford, London and New York, 1968.

VAUGHAN, Alex J.: *Modern Bookbinding*. Skilton, London, 1960.

Gold Tooled Bindings. Bodleian Library, Oxford, 1951.

Paper Making: a general account of its history, processes and application. British Paper and Board Makers' Association, Kenley (Surrey), 1949.

Index

Page numbers in italic refer to illustrations

ACID, 37, 38
  nitric, 208
acidity, 37, 38
address book, 168
adhesive binding, 201–2
adhesives, 38, 41–3, 52, 76, 201
air pollution, 38
alkalinity, 37, 38
aluminium sulphate, 38
American groove, 203
aniline dyes, 209
archivist's repair paper, 54
Armenian bole, 81, 83

BACK CORNERING, 126, *127*, 139
backing, 76–9, 196
  boards, 23, 76, 77, 78
  hammer, 24, *26*, 75
  thin books, 78
back linings, 61
  first lining, 95, 107, 125, 138
  leather, 126, 138
  removal of, 50
  second lining, 95, 107, 125, 138
band nippers, 24, 131
bands:
  double, 68
  false, 139, 140
  raised, 119, 205
  sewing on, 64, 68, 121
  shaping, 129, *131*, 138
  single, 68, 119
  straightening, 121, 124
band stick, 24, 129, 131
bank paper, 33
bar binding, 153
Basil, 41
beeswax, 81, 84, 114
benzine, 162
Berthelet, Thomas, 15
bibles, 46
binding:
  account book, 33
  adhesive, 201–2
  bar, 153
  case, 93 *ff*.
  cord, 103, 118
  extra, 136
  flat back, 75, 94, 156
  flexible, 118 *ff*.
  half, 47
  large, 197, 209
  library style, 103 *ff*.
  limp, 86, 149–53
  machine, 17
  medieval, 148
  music, 60

pamphlet, 101
post, 153
quarter, 47
ring, 153
single-section, 65
single-sheet, 65, 66
spiral, 153
stub, 195–6
sunk cord style, 134 *ff*.
thong, 149
three-quarter, 47
unsewn, 201
vellum, 144–9
whole or full, 47
black lead, 81, 83
bleaching, 55
blind impression, 164, 177
blind stamping, 14, 15, 16
blind tooling, 164, 174
blocking powder 159, 177
blocking press, *158, 159*, 164, *165*
board paper, 57, 132
boards:
  attachment of, 122, 138
  backing, 23
  bevelling, 101, 126, 157
  cutter, 20, *22*
  cutting, 25, 98
  cutting in plough, 121, 138
  decimal measures, 37
  gilding, 81
  lacing in the slips, 122
  limp work, 150
  lining, 138, 141, 142, 144, 197, 198
  preparation for lacing, 121
  pressing, 27
  selection, 95
  tie-up, 28, 132
  warping of, 38
  weight of, 37
  wooden, 13
bolts, 36, 48
bond paper, 33
bone folders, 24, 25, *113*
book cloth, 39, 100
boxes, 179 *ff*.
  book form, 184
  drop-back, 184–8
  scroll case, 192–3
  slip case, 179–84
  Solander type, 188–91
brass type, *159*, 164, *175*
British Museum dressing, 114
Brom Cresol Green, 38
brushes, 25, 161
buckram, 39, 100, 116, 203

burnishers, *24, 25*, 81, 84

CALATON C. B., 52
calcium hypochlorite, 56
carbon tetrachloride, 55
case binding, 66, 93 *ff*.
  depth of joint, 79
  flat back, 62, 75, 94, 156
  full leather, 101
  list of operations, 103
  rounding and backing, 75
  strengthening, 101
casein, 38
casing in, 96, 101
Caxton, William, 14
cedarwood oil, 114
cellulose, 30
cellulose nitrate, 39
chalking, 82
chase, 164
chemicals, 29
china clay, 33
chisels, 25, 197
chloramine-T, 38, 56
citric acid, 55
Cobden Sanderson, T. J., 17
cockle, 32
collating, 45, 49, 56
compensating guards, 46, 51
compensating section, 196
cooling pad, 160, *162*
cord:
  binding (loose-leaf), 153, 154
  hemp, 41
  sewing on, 120
corners:
  cutting, 96
  leather, 103, 108, 130
  mitred, 103
  pleated, 152
  round, 150
  tips, 47
  universal, 117
  vellum, 145
corrosion, 38
cottage roof style, *11*, 16
covering, 108, 129
  buckram, 115, 118
  cloth 96, 98, 100, 203
  large books in leather, 197, 209
  preparation for, 108, 128
  template, 95, 100, 107, 116, 128
  vellum, 144, 145–6, 147, 148, 149
  with leather pieces, 209
creasers, 160, 174

cutting:
  boards, 25, 70
  boards in plough, 72
  boards to size, 72, 94, 106
  edges of books, 70
  in boards, 124, 139
  marking up for, 70, 94
  press *see* laying press
  stick, 75
  wedge, 75
  with boards, 71
  without boards, 72
  with swell, 156
cuttlefish bone, 55
cyclohexylamine carbonate, 38

DE-ACIDIFICATION, 38
deckle, 30
deckle edges, 31, 101
decorating tools, 160, *161*
dentelle, 18
depth of joint, 78, 98, 105
design, 204
Designer Bookbinders, 19
dictionaries, 46
discoloration, 55
dog-eared leaves, 55
double cords, 68
doublure, 60, 103, 141
  illuminated, 136, 142
  leather, 141, 142
  paper, 103
  silk, 141
Doves Bindery and Press, 17
drop-back box, 184–8
drumming on, 146, 210
dwell, 165, 167
dye, 55, 209

EDGES:
  antiquarian books, 48
  beeswaxing, 48
  coloured, 48
  cut, 48, 69
  gilding, 48, 79, 82
  uncut, 48
egg albumen, 161
embroidered covers, 15
endpapers, 45, 57–61, *114, 134*
  adhesive for, 58
  common made, 59, 98
  exposed cloth joint, 60, 66
  four-page, 58
  hidden cloth joint, 60, 112,
  156, 196, 202
  leather-jointed, 60, 61
  paper for, 57
  put down open, 133, 134
  put down shut, 112, 147, 152
  reinforced, 104
  sewing on, 137
  tipped on, 58, 94, *99*
engine sizing, 31, 38
etched blocks, 208

ethanol, 52
extra binding, 136
eyelets, 154
eyelet tools, *25, 26*

FADING, 55
false bands, 139, 140, *142,* 188
farthing wheel, 160, 172
feathered onlays, 209
files, 23, 26
fillet, 160, *161,* 172, *173, 174,* 206
filling in, 103, 108, 112, 132
finishing, 7, 159 *ff.*
  faults, 171
  press, 160, *162*
  stove, 160, *162*
  techniques, 166, 172
  workshop, 164
first-aid box, 29
first editions, 48
Fisher, George, 18
flange, 96, 106, 115, 196
flexible style, 118 *ff.*
  list of operations, 134
flimsy paper, 150
flush joint, 44, 130, 133, 197
flyleaves, 57
foil:
  aluminium, 177, 209
  gold, 161, 162
  pigment, 162, 177
folders, 24, *25*
folding, 35–6
foredge, 45
  cutting, 48, 69–70
  painting, 15
  strips, 205
formaldehyde, 56
forme, 164
forming the back, 101
Fourdrinier, Henry, 31
fox marks, 56
French chalk, 81, 82
French groove, 104, 106, 144,
  145
French knife, 89
French sewing, 66, 149
full binding, 47
fungi, 42
fungicide, 56
furniture, 164

G-CLAMPS, 26. *90*
gelatine size, 56
gilder's tip, 26, 81, 83
gilding, 82–5
glaire, 81, 160, 161
glue, 42
  application, 43
  brushes, 25
  casein, 38
  cold water, 42
  flexible, 42, 76
  manufacture, 42

pots, 21, *22*
polyvinyl acetate emulsion
  (PVA), 43, 52
  Scotch, 42
  synthetic, 43, 201
  use of glue brush, 43
glueing up the spine, 76, 98, 107
gold:
  blocking, 93
  book, *162,* 170
  cushion (pad), 83, 161, *162*
  floated on, 207
  foil, 161, 162
  handling, 170
  knife, 83, 161, *162*
  leaf, 80, 83, 162
  raised, 72
  rag, 162, 171
  rubber, 162, 171
  tooling, 15, 170
Gospel of St John, 13
gouges, *160,* 162, 173, *207*
grain direction, 30–2, *33*
grammage (g.s.m.), 35
grease stains, 55
Gregynog Press, 18
groove, 50
  American 101, 203
  cutting, 136
  French, 104, 106, 144, *145*
  Harrison, 194
  supported French, 194
guard books, 153, 154, *155,*
  156–7
guarding, 50, *51, 62*
guillotine, 23, 73, *74, 75*
gussets, 52

HACKSAW, 90
half binding, 47
  corners, 47
  foredge strip, 47
  leather, 107, *110–11,* 205
hammer, backing, *26,* 75, 77
Harleian bindings, 16
Harrison, Thomas, 194
headbands, 85, 139
  beads, 87
  core, 86, 87
  double, 85, 86, 87, *88*
  false, 86, 93
  leather, 150
  silk, 86
  single, 85, 86
  tie-downs, 87
headcaps, 85, 111, 117, 126, *130,*
  131, 145
  inserted cord, 86, 103, 108,
  109, 116, 117, 145
heat-set tissues, 52
heraldic panel stamps, 14
hexane, 114
hole punch, *25, 26,* 153
holland cloth, 39

hollow back, 101, 115, *116*, 139, 140, 157
    making of 115–16, 144
    slitting the hollow, 116, 140, 144
hook guards, 46, 51
Hughes Stanton, Blair, 18
humidity, 42
hypodermic syringe, 26

IMPOSITION, 35, *36*
in-board cutting, 124, 139
indicator ink, 38
industrial atmosphere, 38
Ingres paper, 34
ink marks, 55
inlaying leather, 206, *207*
insect pests, 42, 114
inserted cord, 103, 108, 109, 116, 145
insetting, 52
interleaving, 57, 156
International Standards Organization (ISO), 35
isinglass, 56

JACONETTE, 39, 105
Japanese tissue, 34, 50, *51*
joint, 79
    case binding, 98, *99*
    depth, 78, 98, 105
    flexible style, 121
    flush, 197
    forming the, 75, 76, 77
    library style, 105
    pinhead, 150
    setting the, 130
    sunk cord style, 137, 140–1

KETTLE STITCH, 64–5
knives:
    cobbler's 25
    French, 89
    guillotine, 73
    paring, 27
    plough, 69
    scalpel, 28
knocking-down iron, 26, 50, 122, 123
knocking out old groove, 50
knocking out swell, 51, 62
knocking up, 70, *76*
knot, weaver's, 64, 87
kraft paper, 33, 152

LACING ON BOARDS, 122
lanolin, 114
large books, 197–8, 209
laying press, 22, 69
lead blocks, 26
lead type, 160
leather, 39–41
    care of, 114
    corners, 103, 108, 151
    marking and grading, 40

onlaid, 207
paring, 89–92, 107, 127, *128*, 151
polishing, 162, 173, 178
stained, 209
tanning, 39–40
thongs, 148
wet, 209
leathers, 29, 39–40, 114, 178
    alum-dressed (tawed), 41
    Basil, 41
    calf, 40, 103
    cellulose-dressed, 40
    cloth, 39
    goat, 39
    hide, 40
    Levant morocco, 40
    morocco, 39, 104
    Niger morocco, 40
    pig, 41
    seal, 40
    sheepskin, 40
    skiver, 41
    tie-dyed Spanish sheepskin, 209
leather joints, 103
    making, 60, 61
    preparing, 140
    putting down, 140–1
lettering, 100, *163*, 164; *see also* tooling
letters, 164
    onlaid, 207, 209
Lewis, Charles, 17
library style, 103 *ff.*
    construction, 104
    covered in buckram, 115–18
    list of operations, 115
light table, 29
limp binding, 86, 149–53
linings, 61, 95, 107, 125, *126*, 138
    boards, 101, 126, 132, 138, 141, 144, 197–8
    with leather, 126, 138
Lissapol, 55
loaded stick, 26, 62, *63*
loose-leaf, 153–7
lying press, 22, 69

MACHINE DIRECTION (grain), 31
machine-made paper, 31
machinery, binding, 17
made endpapers, 59, 98
Maioli, 18
maps, 51, 52
marbled paper, 204
marbling, 34, 204
marker ribbon, 150
marking up:
    boards for lacing in slips, 121
    for cutting, 70
    for depth of joint, 70
    for limp vellum, 147
    for sewing, 119, 136

master drawing, 206, 207, 208, 209
materials, 37 *ff.*
Mearne, Samuel, 16
medieval binding, 148
methoxymethyl nylon, 52
Middleton, Bernard, *60*, 136
millboard, 37, 48
    decimal gauges, 37
missing pages, 52
mock flexible, 135
morocco, 39, 40, 104
Morris, William, 17
mould-made paper, 32, 34
mull, 38, *97*, 150
music binding, 60
mutilated leaves, 54

NAP SURFACES, 159, 177
Nash, Paul, 18
newsprint, 38
Niger morocco, 40
nipping press, *20*, 22
nitric acid, 208
    etched blocks, 208
nylon:
    gossamer fabric, 53
    liquid size, 56

OFFSETTING, 57
oilstone, 27, 29
old groove, 50
onlays, 207, 210
    feathered, 209
opening after covering, 111, 132
optical centre, 168
overcasting, oversewing, 47, 65, 66
    on tapes, 66, *67*
overhang *see* squares

PACKING, 156
palladium, 162
pallets, *160*, 162, 168, 171, *173*, 206
pamphlet binding, 101
panel stamps, 14
    heraldic, 14
    pictorial, 15
paper, 30 *ff.*
    ageing, 42
    antique finish, 33
    archivist's repair, 54
    art, 33, 82
    bank, 33
    bleaching, 55
    blotting, 33
    bond, 33
    cartridge, 34
    chemically pure, 34
    classification, 32
    cleaning, 55
    coated, 33, 38
    deckle in, 30, 31, 101
    decorated, 34, 204

deterioration, 38
Dover, 34
drawing, 33
fabric, 39
flimsy, 150
folding, 35, 36
foxed, 56
glueing, 43
grain, 31
grams per square metre, 35
handmade, 30
hot-pressed, 30
Ingres, 34
Japanese, 34, 50
kraft, 33
laid, 32
ledger, 33
machine-made, 31
marbled, 34, 204
mould-made, 32, 34
newsprint, 38
pasting, 43
patterns, 175
printing, 33
repairing, 34, 52, 53, 54
resizing, 38
Roger Powell, 34
rough, 30
silicone release, 52
sizing, 56
specials, 32
stained, 55, 85
storage of, 29
stretch, 32, 42
substance, 35
surfaces, 30
templates, 95, 107, 172
tissue, 34
washing, 38, 55
weight of, 35
wet strength, 32
wove, 32
wrappings, 33
writings, 33
paper manufacture, 30, *31*
  air-dried, 30
  beating, 30, 31
  calendered, 33
  chemical wood, 31
  coating, 33
  colouring, 31
  coucher, 30
  dandy roller, *31*, 32
  deckle, 30
  engine sizing, 31, 38
  half stuff, 30
  head, 31
  loading, 31
  machine direction (grain), 31, 32
  mechanical wood, 31, 55
  mixer, 31
  pulp, 30
  refining, 31

sheets per ream, 31
sizing, 30, 31, 56
slice, 31
suction boxes, 32
tub sizing, 30, 31, 33, 82
vat man, 30
waterleaf, 30
watermark, 32
wax, 33
wire part, 31
paper sizes 34–5
paranitrophenol, 114
parchment, 41
paring, 89–92, 107–8, *127, 128, 129*, 207
paring knives, 27, 89–90
paring stone, 27, 90
paste, 42
  application, 43
  brushes, 25
  wash, 170, 175
paste pots, 27
Payne, Roger, 16
pencil manuscripts, 56
petroleum ether (hexane), 114
pH, 33, 37
photocopies, 52
photo mounts, 156
pictorial panel stamps, 15
piercer, 27
pigment foil, 162, 177
pigskin, 41
pinhead joint, 150
pitch lines, 96
pitch marks, 112
plastic fabric, 39
plates, 46
  guarding, 51
  hingeing, 51
  inlaying, 54
  mounting, 54
  polishing, 27, 178
  position in book, 46
  pressing, 27, 57, 119
  thick paper, 156
  tipped in, 46
platinum, 162
plating (polishing), 178
plough, 22
  blade, 69
ploughing, 69–72, *73*
  boards, 72, 121, 138
pockets, 52
polishing iron, *161*, 162, 173
polyvinyl acetate emulsion (PVA), 43, 52
post binding, 153
potassium lactate, 114
preliminary matter, 45, 49
preparation for binding, 49 *ff.*
preparation for gold tooling, 170
presses:
  blocking, *158*, 159, 164, *165*
  cutting, 22

finishing, 160, *162*
gilding, 22
laying, lying, 22, 69
nipping, 22
pin, 22
standing, 23
pressing, 56, 103
  boards, 27, *97*
  books, 57, 119
  plates, 27, 57, 119
  sections, 57
press-stud tool, 27
Printing Industry Research Association (PIRA), 40
publishers' edition binding, 49, 93
pulling, 49–50
pull-out ribbon, 193
PVA *see* polyvinyl
Pye, Sybil, 18
Pynson, Richard, 14

QUARTER BINDING, 47
quarter leather, 107
quoins, 164

RAISED BANDS, 119, 205
raised cords, 68, 119, 121
rectangular style, 16
reference books, 48
register, 168
reinforced hinge, 153, 186
repairs, 50 *ff.*, *51, 53, 54*
  heat-set tissue, 52
  replacing paper, 52, 53
  tears in paper, 52
  tissue paper, 34
  with silk fabric, 53
resin, 33
resizing, 38, 56
rexine, 39
Reynes, John, 14
ring binding, 153, 154
Robinol, 162
rods, 27, 116, 144, 203
roll, 14, 162, 172
round corners, 150
rounding, 75–6, 150
rubber, 55
  gold, 162, 171
  powdered, 55
rulers, 28

SADDLE STITCH, 195
saw, 136
  tenon, 28
scalpel, 28, *90*, 206, 209
scissors, 26
scrapers, *24*, 28, 81, 82
screw post, 154
scroll case, 192–3
sections:
  folding of, 36

plates in, 46
pressing, 56
repairing, 50
signatured, 45, 49
set square, 28, 70
setting the back, 107
setting the groove, 109
setting the joint, 130–2
sewing, 61 ff.
  all along, 62, 66
  blanket stitching, 65
  case binding, 66
  cords, 64, 120
  correct swell, 61, 78
  double cords, 68
  flat-backed bindings, 62
  flexible (raised cord), 68, 119
  frame, 22, 63, 98, 99, 120, 121
  French, 66, 149
  keys, 27, 28, 99, 120
  library style, 66
  overcasting, 47, 65, 66, 67
  pamphlet, 65
  raised cord, 68, 119, 121
  side sitching, 65
  single section, 65
  single sheets, 65, 66, 67, 68
  stub, 195
  sunk cord style, 67, 68, 137
  tape, 66, 197
  tension, 62
  thongs, 68
  thread, 41, 61
  three- and five-hole, 65, 101
  two and three up, 62, 66, 67, 121
shaping bands, 129
sheepskin, 40–1
shoulder shape, 61
side iron, 161, 178
siding, 112
signatures, 45, 49
silicone release paper, 52
silk fabric, 53
single-section binding, 65, 101, 102, 103
single-sheet binding, 65, 66
size, 56
sizes of paper, 35
skiver, 41
slip case, 179–84
slips, 122, 123, 124, 126, 138, 147
sodium hypochlorite, 56
Solander-type box, 188–91
spacing bar, 153
specials, 32
specifications, 48
spine, 61, 75–6, 77
  design of, 166, 168, 169, 207
  glueing up, 98, 107
  knocking up, 70, 76
  shape of, 61
split board, 104, 106
spokeshave, 28, 89, 90, 92

square, carpenter's 25, 72, 77
squares (overhang), 62, 86, 94, 95, 96, 98, 106, 124, 146, 147, 148
staining, 85
stains, 55–6, 85
standing press, 23
starts (steps), 62
stiffener, 93, 98, 100, 101
stiff leaf, 59
stopping-out varnish, 208
strawboard, 37, 48, 95
striking, 166
strop, 27, 28, 92
stub binding, 195–6
sunk cord style, 103, 134 ff., 197
  hollow back with false bands, 140
  hollow back without bands, 139
  list of operations, 143
  marking up for sewing, 136
  mock flexible, 135
  tight back with false bands, 139
  tight smooth back, 138
swell, 61–2, 68
  excess, 62, 78
  knocking out, 51, 62, 121
  reducing, 51, 62, 78, 94
  thin books, 62
  too little, 62, 78

TANNING, 39, 40
tape, 41
  sewing, 63, 197
template, 95, 107, 172
terylene, 53
thongs, 147, 148, 149
thread, 41
  choice of thickness, 61–2
three-quarter binding, 47
throw-out maps and sheets, 46, 51, 52
thymol, 56
tie-downs, 87
ties, 147, 148–9
tie-up boards, 27, 28, 132
tight back, 104, 138, 139, 140
tipping on (in), 137
  endpapers, 76, 98, 99, 121
  plates, 46
tissue:
  heat-set, 52
  Japanese, 34, 50
titles, 166–8
tooling, 166 ff.
  blind, 17, 174, 177
  buckram, 177
  gold, 170, 171, 174
  inlays, 207
  nap surfaces, 177
  vellum, 177
trimming out, 96, 112, 132, 146
trindles, 27, 28, 124, 125

tub sizing, 30
two and three up, 66, 67
tying up, 131, 132
type, 164, 175
  brass, 164, 175–7
  lead, 160
type cabinets, 163, 164
type holder, 164, 175–7

UNIVERSAL CORNER, 117
unsewn binding (adhesive), 201

VAPOUR PHASE DE-ACIDIFICATION, 38
varnish, 114, 115, 178–210
vaseline, 164, 171
vellum, 13, 41
  binding, 41, 144–9
  calf, 41, 144
  construction of vellum books, 144
  core for headbands, 86
  drumming on, 144, 146
  goat, 41, 144
  limp, 144, 146
  lining of, 144
  making size from, 56
  softening, 144
  strips, 146, 168, 176
  ties, 148
  tips, 47
  transparent, 17, 41, 144, 210
  wrappers, 149
  writing, 144
velvet binding, 15, 159, 177
vise, 28
visitors' books, 168

WALL CABINETS, 29
wallets, 52
warp in cloth, 32, 39
warping of boards, 38, 103, 146
washing of paper, 38, 55
washing-up liquid, 55
wax, micro-crystalline, 178
wax papers, 33
weaver's knot, 64, 87
webbing, 41
wedge, cutting, 75
weft, 39
wet paring, 207
Whitaker, John, 17
whole binding, 47, 107
window mounting, 54, 55
wooden boards, 13
word arrangement, 168
workshop, 28
  finishing, 164
wrappers, 152

YAPP EDGE, 148, 149, 152

ZAEHNSDORF, 17, 18